File
for
Divorce
in
New York

File
for
Divorce
in
New York

Second Edition

Brette McWhorter Sember

Attorney at Law

SPHINX® PUBLISHING
AN IMPRINT OF SOURCEBOOKS, INC.®
NAPERVILLE, ILLINOIS
www.SphinxLegal.com

Published by: **Sphinx® Publishing, A Division of Sourcebooks, Inc.®**

Naperville Office
P.O. Box 4410
Naperville, Illinois 60567-4410
630-961-3900
Fax: 630-961-2168
www.sourcebooks.com
www.SphinxLegal.com

This publication is designed to provide accurate and authoritative information in regard to the subject matter covered. It is sold with the understanding that the publisher is not engaged in rendering legal, accounting, or other professional service. If legal advice or other expert assistance is required, the services of a competent professional person should be sought.

From a Declaration of Principles Jointly Adopted by a Committee of the
American Bar Association and a Committee of Publishers and Associations

This product is not a substitute for legal advice.

Disclaimer required by Texas statutes.

Library of Congress Cataloging-in-Publication Data
Sember, Brette McWhorter, 1968-
   File for divorce in New York / by Brette McWhorter Sember. -- 2nd ed.
       p. cm.
   Includes index.
   1. Divorce--Law and legislation--New York (State)--Popular works. I.
Title.

KFN5126.Z9S457 2007
346.74701'66--dc22

2007016669

Printed and bound in the United States of America.
RRD — 10 9 8 7 6 5 4 3

Contents

Introduction

If you are considering divorce or are in the process of getting one, you are probably overwhelmed and confused. There are so many choices to make, so many things to deal with, and so many problems with which to cope. This is probably one of the most confusing and frightening times in your life, whether you want the divorce to happen or not. This book is your guide to all the choices you face, and the many problems you might encounter.

Divorce in New York is not a simple process. The options might seem confusing—annulment, uncontested divorce, mediation, arbitration, contested divorce, or separation. The cost of hiring an attorney might be more than you can afford. The things that have to be decided in your divorce—who gets the house, where the children will live, how to survive financially, how to divide up all the stuff, and who will pay all the bills—may seem mind-boggling.

The actual paperwork and court process of the divorce itself might seem imposing or scary to you. How do you get a fair shake, ask for everything you want, and make sure your spouse does not walk off with the whole store? How do you deal with judges, attorneys, and all the forms?

This book will help you understand what your options are, what the law says, how the actual divorce process works, how to use mediation, how to find and work with a lawyer if that is what you want to do, and how to fill out the forms and file them yourself if you want to handle your own divorce. Even if you do not want to handle your own divorce, the forms in this book will save you time and money with your attorney. You will have all the information ready for your attorney and you will not have to spend a lot of time asking basic questions about New York divorce law at a rate of over $100 an hour. You will also find helpful resources and practical advice about managing your emotions, dealing with paperwork, gathering evidence, and planning.

Using this book will help you control your costs. It answers many of your questions, thus reducing the hours you need from an attorney. The book also allows you to do some or all of the divorce paperwork and court appearances on your own. Many people use this book to get a head start on their divorce, then turn to an attorney for assistance if things get complicated or frightening.

Chapter 1 helps you with your decision to divorce. Chapter 2 explains the divorce process in New York. Chapter 3 explains how to work with an attorney. Chapter 4 discusses mediation. Chapter 5 looks at the law about custody and visitation. Chapter 6 discusses child support. Chapter 7 looks at financial information. Chapter 8 discusses court procedures. Chapter 9 explains how to get temporary assistance. Chapter 10 discusses separation. Chapter 11 explains the uncontested divorce procedure. Chapter 12 discusses the contested divorce procedure. Chapter 13 considers certain special situations. Chapter 14 discusses life after divorce.

NOTE: *If you are a victim of domestic violence, you need an attorney to assist you. You can obtain an Order of Protection against your spouse yourself by going to your local Family Court.*

You should also be aware that this book does not discuss situations involving out-of-state spouses. If you or your spouse reside in another state, you need an attorney to assist you.

USING THE FORMS IN THIS BOOK

This book includes all the forms needed to handle a divorce on your own. It is important to note that you should make copies of all the forms before filling in anything. Most judges will not accept forms that have printing on both sides, so make sure that when you complete the forms, you do so on one-sided copies.

Keep a copy of each form you complete in a file. Try to keep the forms organized in the order in which you file them. When you file some forms with the court, you will receive a receipt or a stamped copy. Keep those in your file as well.

Be aware that forms change and some judges have particular requirements. If something you submit is not accepted by a clerk or judge, ask politely how to correct the mistake.

Divorce is not easy for anyone, but with the help of this book, you can approach it in an organized and intelligent way.

You may contact the author at her website:

www.brettesember.com

Deciding to Divorce

Making the decision to get a divorce is probably one of the most difficult and painful choices you have ever faced. You might not be completely sure at this point if divorce is the answer or if your marriage can be saved. When considering divorce, it is important to understand its legal, social, and emotional ramifications. It is also a good idea to consider all of your options before making a final decision.

UNDERSTANDING THE MEANING OF DIVORCE

When most people think about divorce, they think about a piece of paper that comes at the end of a long and expensive legal process, saying the marriage is over. There is a lot more to divorce than the legal process and the divorce decree.

Legal Divorce   A *legal divorce* is a decision by a court that you are no longer legally married. A *divorce decree* is the legal document ending the marriage. It states how you and your spouse must divide your belongings, share your debts, share time with your children, support your children, and possibly, support each other after the divorce. A legal divorce wraps up all of these issues in one neat package.

Physical Divorce

Most experts agree that there is more to a divorce than getting a piece of paper from a judge saying your marriage is over. A divorce is something that really happens in stages. The first and most important stage is usually the decision that you are going to seek a divorce. Most couples physically separate once this decision has been made. This is what is called the *physical divorce*—the point when you stop living together and live in separate residences.

It is possible to physically separate while still living in the same residence. Some couples simply move to separate rooms, while others adjust their schedules so they are not home at the same time. However it happens, the physical divorce is the point where you decide to be physically apart in a calculated and decided way.

Emotional Divorce

The *emotional divorce* is the most difficult part of the divorce and can take a long time to fully resolve itself. It involves the feelings, thoughts, and emotions you cope with as you adjust to, accept, and heal from a divorce. The emotional divorce starts long before the physical divorce, and continues long after the legal divorce has been resolved.

CONSIDERING YOUR OPTIONS

If you are considering divorce, but are not completely certain, you should look to other options first. A *nonlegal separation* is an option that helps many people clear their heads and make important decisions about their marriages. You and your spouse can physically separate, and do not need to use the legal system to do so. You can also choose to obtain a *legal separation* (see Chapter 10) that decides issues of custody, visitation, child support, maintenance (spousal support), and finances while you are living separately.

Some couples choose to physically and emotionally divorce, but remain legally married. There is no requirement that you make your divorce legal.

Other couples considering divorce choose to see a therapist, counselor, or other mental health professional—either to help them resolve their differences and find a way to make their marriage work, or to find a way to end their marriage with as little conflict as possible.

GETTING HELP

When making a decision about whether to divorce or choose another option, many people find they need help and support. Family and friends are an excellent source of support. They often make good sounding boards. Be wary of friends and family who have agendas, though—some might be very opposed to the idea of divorce, while others might dislike your spouse and try to steer you toward divorce. Remember that, in the end, this is your decision.

Clergy members are another place to turn if you need someone to talk to. Clergy are trained in dealing with family conflicts and in helping people make life-changing decisions. In addition, many religious organizations have special marriage-related counseling sessions, retreats, and services.

You might choose to seek out a mental health professional for couples counseling or for individual counseling. There are many choices when considering mental health care. Social workers, psychologists, nurse practitioners, trained therapists, trained counselors, and many others are available. Consider asking your family doctor for a referral to find a mental health professional who is right for you. If you have already retained an attorney for your divorce, he or she can probably refer you to a counselor.

For assistance in locating a mental health professional, contact:

New York State Counseling Association
P.O. Box 12636
Albany, NY 12212
877-692-2462
www.nycounseling.org

New York State Psychological Association
6 Executive Park Drive
Albany, NY 12203
800-732-3933
www.nyspa.org

WEIGHING THE CHOICES

It is important to know that, while a divorce does not sound like a walk in the park, it can be a tremendously positive thing if you are in a bad marriage. Ending a relationship that was not a positive one can bring you new life, create a better home environment for your children, make you happier, and give you more freedom.

In the end, you are the only one who can decide if a divorce is the solution to the problems you face. Any time you need some time to process what is happening, consider your options, or just slow things down, do so.

As you go through this book, you will find that there are a lot of choices to make, even after you decide that you want a divorce. At each step of the way you will need to make choices about what you want, how you want to approach the situation, and how you want things to turn out.

Once they have decided that divorce is the answer, many people approach the situation with the attitude that their spouse is the enemy. Most of the time this approach will hurt everyone involved. Particularly if you have children, it is important to find an approach to divorce that is moderate. Generally speaking, it is important to be open to compromise, willing to give an inch once in a while, and sensitive to how your decisions affect others. Divorce does not have to be complete war in every case.

chapter 2

New York's Divorce Process

The process of getting a divorce in New York can seem like a lengthy one. Actually, completing the paperwork can be done in a day, but waiting for the court to move through the necessary process takes much longer. The paperwork you need to file for divorce in New York is included in this book and is discussed in detail in later chapters. There is a specific order to the papers that must be filed, and certain papers must be filed before deadlines. The process is designed to make sure both spouses have enough time to respond to and file papers, and also to allow both sides time to prepare for hearings in court. The system may seem foreign to you, but it does follow a logical order.

DIVORCE TERMS

Throughout this book you will come across various legal terms, most of which will be explained as they arise. However, there are three basic words you need to know up front.

- The *plaintiff* is the person who files for divorce, asking the court to grant a divorce.

- The *defendant* is the other spouse, who did not file papers first.

- The word *parties* refers to both spouses in the divorce.

COSTS

A divorce can be very expensive, but it does not have to be. The biggest cost involved in a divorce case is attorney's fees. If you hire an attorney (and most people do), your total bill could run into tens of thousands of dollars. If everything involved in the case is contested and involves a thorough trial, the cost could possibly top $100,000. Most people usually spend between $5,000 and $15,000 on a divorce case (less if it is uncontested).

When calculating how much your divorce is going to cost, start with how much your attorney charges per hour. This is probably between $100 and $300. Ask your attorney for an estimate of how many hours the case will take. Then take into account the court costs, which run several hundred dollars.

Your costs can be significantly reduced if you choose to use mediation or collaborative lawyers. Mediation usually costs between $1,000 and $4,000, and hardly ever exceeds that amount. (See Chapter 4 for more information about the benefits of mediation.)

DIVORCE VS. ANNULMENT

A *divorce* is a legal decree by a court that your marriage is legally over. An *annulment* is a decree by a court that your marriage was not legal at the time it happened, and thus was never a legal marriage. Most people opt to seek a divorce, but there are some situations in which an annulment is the best choice. New York's Domestic Relations Law (DRL), Section 140, details the six situations in which you can get an annulment in New York.

1. *Married to someone else.* If you or your spouse were still legally married to another living person at the time of the marriage, the marriage was not legal.

2. *Underage.* The marriage was not legal if one of the spouses:

    ✪ was married with the consent of a judge, but was under age 14;

✪ was married with the consent of a parent, but was under age 16; or,

✪ was married under any other circumstance, but was under age 18.

Only the person who was underage at the time of the marriage can seek an annulment for this reason. Then, the annulment is only possible if the parties did not cohabit after the person reached the age of consent.

3. *Failure to understand.* One of the parties was mentally retarded or mentally ill at the time of the marriage and did not fully understand he or she was getting married. If mental retardation is the reason, a family member of the afflicted person can bring the annulment case on his or her behalf.

4. *Physical incapacity.* One of the parties was physically unable to consummate the marriage because of an ongoing and incurable condition. This reason for annulment can only be used within the first five years of marriage.

5. *Fraud, force, or duress.* If one of the spouses was threatened or under pressure to enter the marriage, or entered the marriage for a fraudulent reason (for instance, so he or she could inherit from the other person without having any intention of cohabiting), the marriage is null. If the parties cohabited willingly after force or duress or after the fraud was revealed, then the marriage can no longer be annulled.

6. *Incurable mental illness.* If one of the parties has an incurable mental illness that has lasted at least five years, and the illness was present at the time of marriage, the marriage is not valid.

   NOTE: *With this reason for annulment, the court can order the healthy spouse to pay spousal support to the mentally ill spouse. (DRL Sec. 141.)*

Because there are many fewer annulments in New York than divorces, this area of law is not as well defined. If you decide you want an annulment, it is a good idea to consult with a matrimonial attorney.

Religious Annulments

A *religious annulment* is a completely different thing from a legal annulment. Some religions allow you to have your marriage annulled in the eyes of the church or religion, even though you have obtained a traditional legal divorce. See Appendix A for links to organizations that can assist you with religious annulments.

LEGAL SEPARATION VS. DIVORCE

A *legal separation* is almost the same as a divorce except the marriage remains legally intact. However, everything else—money, debts, children, possessions, and so on—will be divided by the court.

The most common reason for a separation is that once you have obtained a legal separation, you can then get a divorce one year later through a simplified process. Separations are covered in DRL Sec. 200–203. There are two ways to obtain a legal separation in New York: a separation agreement and a judgment of separation.

Separation Agreement

Most people seeking a legal separation do so via a legal separation agreement. A *separation agreement* is a document signed by both spouses and submitted to the court. Separation agreements are usually created by attorneys or mediators, and are a result of negotiation and compromise. The terms of a separation agreement are basically written by the spouses themselves. They choose how they are going to divide assets and debts, how they will share time with their children, how they will support their children, and so on. All of these decisions are then incorporated into the separation agreement and submitted to the court. The court must approve it, but once it does, the terms of the separation agreement will eventually become the terms of the divorce decree issued by the court. Appendix A contains a sample **SEPARATION AND PROPERTY SETTLEMENT AGREEMENT**. (see form 27, p.224.)

Judgment of Separation

Another way to get a separation is to go through a court process almost identical to the one needed to get a divorce. To do this, you simply substitute the word "separation" for the word "divorce" in the papers that are filed with the court. The court proceedings are the same as those for divorce.

Grounds for Separation

There are five reasons, or *grounds*, for a legal separation in New York. These are similar to the grounds for divorce discussed in detail on page 14.

1. ***Cruel and inhuman treatment.*** For a full discussion of what cruel and inhuman treatment means, see page 14, where it is discussed in detail. This is the most common and all-encompassing reason for separation.

2. ***Abandonment.*** Abandonment occurs when one spouse leaves the other without provocation, and does not return for one year.

3. ***Failure to support.*** Failure to support occurs when one spouse fails or refuses to support the other financially.

4. ***Adultery.*** Adultery occurs when one spouse has sex with someone else during the marriage.

5. ***Imprisonment.*** Imprisonment occurs when one spouse is imprisoned for at least three years during the marriage.

COURT SYSTEM

To understand how a divorce case is handled by the court system, it is first important to understand the court system in New York. There is a *Supreme Court* in every county of New York where divorce or matrimonial cases are handled. However, New York's Supreme Court is not the highest court like it is in the federal system. There are two courts that are above the Supreme Court in New York. If a Supreme Court case is appealed, the appeal goes to the *Appellate Division*. If an Appellate Division case is appealed, it goes to the *Court of Appeals*—the highest court in New York. To find your local Supreme Court, check the government section of your phone book, or go to **www.courts.state.ny.us/courts**.

New York also has *Family Courts* in every county. These courts do not handle divorce cases. Instead, they deal with custody, visitation, child support, spousal support, and family offenses (domestic violence) when they are not part of a divorce case. Unmarried couples can go to Family Court for help with custody or support problems. Family Courts can provide similar help to married couples who wish to divorce, but have not yet filed the papers. However, once divorce papers are filed, the Supreme Court will handle all these issues and the Family Court will refuse to hear the case.

DIVORCE LAWS IN NEW YORK

There are two kinds of laws that deal with divorce in New York. When most people think of laws, they think of *statutes*. These are called the *Consolidated Laws of New York State*. The laws about divorce are found in Chapter 14 of the Consolidated Laws of New York—the Domestic Relations Law. References will be made to specific sections of this law throughout this book.

The other kind of law that deals with divorce in New York is called *case law*. This comes from decisions judges have made in cases in the past. Case law is an important part of the divorce law of New York because judges have explained and described the ways in which the statutes should be applied. Cases are listed with the name of the case and then a citation. The citation is a series of numbers and letters telling you in which book to find the specific case.

Following is a list of what abbreviations in case law citations stand for.

N.Y.: New York Reports. This series of books includes cases decided by the Court of Appeals.

N.Y.S.: New York Supplement. This series includes decisions from the Court of Appeals and Appellate Division.

A.D.: Appellate Division Reports. This reports Appellate Division cases.

Misc.: New York Miscellaneous Reports. This includes Supreme Court and Family Court decisions.

If you want to read statutes or case law, you will need to do some legal research. Statutes are easy to find online. Type "laws of New York" into a search engine and several sources will come up. You can search online for case law as well. You can also go to **www.findlaw.com** to search various New York laws.

All of these books have newer and older versions. The newer versions have a "2d" after the book abbreviation, indicating it is the second series.

When you read a case citation, the first number you see is a volume number. Then you will see the abbreviation for the book name, then the page number. In parenthesis, you may also see the year the case was decided. For example, 66 N.Y.2d 382 (1985) refers you to volume 66 of New York Reports, second series, page 382. The case was decided in 1985.

You can find both statutes and case law at law libraries. There is a law library located at the Supreme Court in each county, as well as in law schools. (See Appendix A for a listing.) If you need assistance, you can ask a law librarian to help you. See **www.courts.state.ny.us/ pubacc.html** for a list of law libraries.

ISSUES RESOLVED BY DIVORCE

A divorce is designed to be a complete solution to your marital problems. A divorce ends your marriage and completely dissolves your financial partnership. The court decides how your money, belongings, real estate, and debts will be divided. The court decides how you will spend time with your children, where they will live, who will pay for their expenses, how much child support will be paid, and whether there will be any spousal support.

Also, a divorce is about people and the people involved are always changing. A court order that works for members of a family one year might be completely incompatible with their lives the next. For this reason, it is not uncommon for families to have to return to court to have decisions modified later. (Read more about this in Chapter 14.)

DIVORCE PREREQUISITES IN NEW YORK

In order to get a divorce in New York, you must meet one of the following residency requirements listed in DRL Sec. 230:

- ✪ you were married in the state, and one or both of you is a resident and has been a continuous resident for at least one year immediately prior to the time the divorce papers are filed;

- ✪ you both lived in New York while married, and at least one of you has been a resident for the year immediately preceding filing;

- ✪ the reason for the divorce took place in New York, and at least one of you has been a resident for the year immediately preceding the filing;

- ✪ the reason for divorce took place in New York and both of you are current residents at the time of filing; or,

- ✪ one or both of you has been a New York resident for the two years immediately preceding the time of filing.

If you do not meet one of these qualifications, you cannot file for divorce in New York. However, you might be able to file for divorce in another state, so you should consider where you have lived and where you were married and look into the laws of those states. You also may be able to wait a period of time until you fulfill the New York requirements.

WAYS TO GET A DIVORCE IN NEW YORK

There are several methods you can use to get a divorce in New York. Each of these will be discussed in detail in later chapters, but it is important to have a basic understanding of the choices before reading further in the book.

Uncontested Divorce

An *uncontested divorce* is one in which you file divorce papers and your spouse does not formally respond to the court. He or she has a specific length of time in which to respond. If the court does not receive anything, your divorce stands as uncontested. This means your spouse has no say at all in what happens. This does not mean you can ask for and get everything you want. The judge will still decide if what you are asking for is fair and reasonable.

An uncontested divorce is the simplest and fastest way to obtain a divorce in New York. Many couples decide together to use this process. They agree in advance what will be asked for in the papers. This saves attorney fees and brings a faster resolution. (Read more about uncontested divorce in Chapter 11.)

Contested Divorce

A *contested divorce* is one in which both spouses appear in court. The court must hear from both sides, and if the case does go to trial, each has the opportunity to testify. Contested divorce can be very expensive, but most divorces that start out as contested end up with a *settlement*. This means that both parties agree as to how the case should end. This agreement is submitted to the court for approval. (See Chapter 12 for more information about contested divorce.)

Separation

Separation is an important divorce option in New York. Spouses who become legally separated (most do so using a separation agreement as explained earlier in this chapter) can live apart under the separation agreement for one year and then file for an uncontested divorce. This process takes longer because you have to live under the separation agreement for a full year before you can file to finalize the divorce, but many couples find it to be the best way since it often feels the most amiable.

Mediation

Many couples use *mediation* to help reach a divorce settlement. The couple meets with a *mediator* and discusses everything that needs to be decided in the divorce. The process focuses on cooperative decision making. At the end of the mediation process, the couple can either complete a separation agreement or seek an uncontested divorce. Mediation works well for couples who are unable to reach a compromise on their own, but who do not want to face a contested divorce proceeding. Mediation also offers benefits for the children in a marriage, since it reduces conflict and results in a parenting plan that allows both parents to spend time with their children.

Collaborative Law

Collaborative law is a new trend in legal circles that is gaining popularity. Instead of representing a client in a very adversarial way ("my client is right and yours is wrong"), many attorneys now try to take a collaborative approach when working with the attorney for the other side.

This means that, instead of going into a courtroom and butting heads in front of a judge, the attorneys meet and try to find a solution to the case that will work for each of their clients. This is similar to mediation in that the emphasis is on finding a settlement with which both parties are happy. As in mediation, both sides agree to disclose all information up front so that both sides have the same information. Collaborative law differs from mediation in that a trained party states each party's case. There is no neutral party like there is in mediation. Collaborative lawyers take the case with the intention of settling it. If the case cannot be settled, the parties need to hire new attorneys to take it to court.

To read more about collaborative law, see **www.divorcenet.com/ ca/cafaq10.html**.

GROUNDS FOR DIVORCE

The *grounds* for divorce is the reason for the divorce. Some states have *no-fault divorce*, which means that a couple can be divorced without having to give reasons that blame the other person. No-fault divorce is not available in New York. New York laws require a reason for the divorce. There are only five reasons that can be used for divorce. The five reasons are:

1. cruel and inhuman treatment;

2. abandonment;

3. imprisonment;

4. adultery; and,

5. separation.

Cruel and Inhuman Treatment

Cruel and inhuman treatment is the most common ground used for divorce in New York. It sounds pretty unpleasant, but it is actually the easiest type of ground to use. The technical definition is that one spouse has treated the other cruelly and inhumanly, either physically, mentally, or emotionally, so that it is unsafe or improper for them to live together. In reality, probably any divorcing couple could use this reason.

The couple could argue that that one spouse called the other names, started arguments, or was not affectionate, and that, because of this, they should no longer live together. In legal language, these same complaints are often described as, "The Defendant called the Plaintiff names, provoked arguments, and withheld affection, making it unsafe and improper for the parties to continue to reside together."

In order to prove cruel and inhuman treatment, you should be able to point to at least two specific incidents, and these must have occurred within the last five years. The complaint must go on to describe the conduct in this way: "The conduct of the Defendant was cruel and inhuman and so endangered the physical or mental well-being of the Plaintiff as to render it unsafe or improper for the Plaintiff to cohabit with the Defendant."

Abandonment   In order to cite *abandonment* as grounds for divorce, the defendant must have left *without provocation*. This means that the plaintiff did not tell or ask the defendant to leave, and that the defendant left without the plaintiff's consent. Furthermore, the plaintiff in some way must have asked the defendant to return.

There are two other kinds of abandonment. A *lock out* is when your spouse has locked you out of the home and has not allowed you back in for one year prior to the case. The other kind is *constructive abandonment*. This occurs when your spouse refuses to have sexual relations with you for at least one year prior to the case, and has no consent or justification to do so.

Imprisonment   To use *imprisonment* as a reason, the defendant must be in prison and have been there for at least three consecutive years during the marriage. The imprisonment must have begun after the marriage. There is a five-year time limit on this, beginning in the third year of imprisonment.

Adultery   For *adultery*, the defendant had extramarital sexual intercourse (or "deviant sexual intercourse," which means homosexual sex) during the marriage. If their spouse has cheated on them, many people think they want to use this as their grounds for divorce. In reality, adultery is difficult to prove since you need testimony from someone other than yourself and your spouse.

There are some circumstances in which a divorce will be denied even if adultery is proven:

- ✪ if the adultery was in some way set up by the plaintiff;

- ✪ if adultery occurs and the plaintiff forgives the defendant;

- ✪ if the adultery occurred more than five years prior to the filing of the divorce; or,

- ✪ if the plaintiff is also guilty of adultery.

Separation   For *separation*, the parties have lived apart under a separation agreement or separation decree (court order) for at least one year. During the year apart, the parties cannot live together or have sex in order to qualify for this ground.

While divorce cases are decided by judges, parties can request a jury trial to determine if there are grounds for a divorce. In this situation, a judge would still decide how things will be divided and what kind of parenting plan will be in place.

NOTE: *There is one other way to get a divorce in New York. If your spouse has been missing for over five years and is believed to be dead, a special proceeding can be filed with the court seeking to have the marriage dissolved, without following any of the other procedures in this book. Speak to an attorney if you need to use this method.*

chapter 3

Working with an Attorney

We have all heard the jokes and complaints about attorneys, but if you decide to hire an attorney, he or she will serve as your voice in the courtroom. Because your attorney will speak for you, it is very important that you choose an attorney you are comfortable with, and that you have a clear understanding of what his or her job is.

DECIDING IF YOU NEED AN ATTORNEY

Some people do not question the fact that they will need an attorney for a divorce, while others wonder if they could handle the proceedings on their own. This is a decision each person needs to make individually.

You probably need a lawyer if:

- ✪ you or your spouse is hiding income;

- ✪ there has been domestic violence in your family;

- ✪ you or your spouse owns a business;

- ✪ you or your spouse earned a degree or professional license during the marriage;

- ✪ adultery is the grounds for divorce;

- ✪ child abuse or neglect is going to be an issue;

- ✪ an annulment instead of divorce is being sought;

- ✪ you or your spouse is in the military;

- ✪ you or your spouse is seeking a large amount of spousal support;

- ✪ you want your spouse to take on a lot of debt;

- ✪ you cannot agree about custody;

- ✪ your spouse does not agree that you should get divorced; or,

- ✪ you want to get a portion of your spouse's retirement account.

To be able to handle your own divorce, you need to be able to:

- ✪ read and complete the forms in this book neatly and carefully;

- ✪ be sure of your rights;

- ✪ stand up in a courtroom and talk to a judge or matrimonial referee;

- ✪ have a basic understanding of New York divorce laws;

- ✪ keep documents organized;

- ✪ ask questions of court personnel; and,

- ✪ act confidently.

FINDING AN ATTORNEY

There are many ways to find a good attorney. If you have used an attorney for something else in the past (traffic violation, home purchase, etc.), call him or her and ask if he or she handles divorces. If the attorney is someone you are comfortable with and trust, and he or she has experience in handling divorce cases, you may be all set. If he or she does not handle divorces, does not handle many of them, or is someone you are not comfortable with, ask for a referral to a matrimonial attorney.

Ask friends and family for the names of attorneys with whom they have worked. Some people like to look in the phone book and see who has the largest ad for divorce law. While this can be a way to find an attorney who devotes a lot of his or her time to divorce cases, you are generally better off if you select someone based on a personal referral.

Referral services are another good way to find an attorney. See the listing in Appendix A of county bar association lawyer referral programs. You can also contact the New York State Bar Association Lawyer Referral and Information Service at 800-342-3661. You can also find lawyer referrals on their website at **www.nysba.org**. Click on the "Public Resources" button on the right side of the page and then click on the "Lawyer Referral" section on the left side. The services require attorneys to apply to be on their list and have strict requirements about the attorneys' experience levels in the areas of law in which they are listed.

CHOOSING AN ATTORNEY

Once you have the names of a few attorneys, it is a good idea to shop around. Set up a free consultation with attorneys you are interested in hiring. Interview attorneys and ask them questions about their experience, how they handle cases, and what their costs are. Too often people are intimidated by attorneys and are afraid to question them. You are going to be paying this person a lot of money and sharing some personal things with him or her. It is a good idea to make sure the attorney is someone you like and trust. Use the following list of questions to help you evaluate attorneys.

Office Observations

- ✪ Is the staff friendly?

- ✪ Is the office well organized?

- ✪ Do the other clients who are waiting appear to be satisfied?

Questions to Ask the Attorney

- Where did you go to law school?

- How long have you been practicing law?

- How long have you been with this firm?

- Do you focus your practice on matrimonial and family law? If not, what percentage of your cases are matrimonial?

- Do you belong to any committees or organizations?

- Do you charge a retainer? How much?

- Do you bill hourly? At what rate?

- Is there a reduced rate for work done by your staff?

- Do you offer payment plans?

- How quickly are phone calls returned?

- Does another attorney or paralegal handle your cases when you are unable to be reached?

- How much do you estimate this case will cost?

- How good are my chances of getting what I am asking for?

- Do you think what I am asking for is reasonable?

- Do you suggest clients use mediation?

- Do you settle or try most of your divorces?

Questions to Ask Yourself after Your Meeting

- Did the attorney make you feel comfortable?

- Was he or she impatient or too quick with you?

✪ Did you feel like your questions were answered satisfactorily?

✪ Did the attorney inspire confidence and trust?

✪ Do you feel this person is experienced and professional?

✪ Are you comfortable with his or her approach to your case?

✪ Can you afford his or her services?

UNDERSTANDING ATTORNEY CHARGES

Most attorneys charge a *retainer* (an up-front fee) and then bill at an hourly rate. Work is first charged against the retainer. Once that is used up, you are billed on a monthly basis. Some attorneys will charge a *flat fee* (or one-time cost) for an uncontested divorce or separation agreement. When attorneys bill by the hour, this means that you are charged by the amount of time spent on your case. Billing actually is done in *increments*, or parts of the hour. For example, if your attorney spends fifteen minutes on the phone for your case, this would be billed as .25 hours (or one quarter of an hour) and you would be charged one fourth of the normal hourly rate for that time.

Attorneys charge extra for expenses. All court fees will be paid by you. You will also be required to pay for experts your attorney has to hire, such as appraisers. Some attorneys also pass along costs of large photocopying bills and other office expenses for trial preparation.

AFFORDING AN ATTORNEY

If you find that you simply cannot afford the attorney's fees you are quoted, you may qualify for free legal assistance. Check the list of legal aid agencies in Appendix A and call to find out if you qualify. Unfortunately, there are a lot of people who cannot afford legal assistance, yet do not qualify for legal aid. If you find yourself in this situation, consider asking an attorney if he or she will work out a payment plan for you. Some attorneys will accept payment plans, so it is always a good idea to ask if one can be established. You can also handle your case on your own and pay an attorney an hourly rate if you want to consult on a few questions as you work your way through the case.

Many people borrow money from family members in order to pay their attorneys. Another option to consider is that you might be able to have the court order your spouse to pay your attorney's fees. Talk to attorneys you interview about this possibility in your case.

LEARNING LAW OFFICE PROCEDURES

Lots of clients express frustration with the way their attorneys handle their cases. While there are attorneys who do not return calls, and do not move cases forward, most of the time attorneys are working as quickly as they can to move cases along.

When you call to talk to your attorney, it is likely that he or she will be out of the office. Attorneys spend a lot of their time in court and try to return phone calls at the beginning of the day, during lunchtime, or at the end of the day. If you call your attorney and leave a message, make sure to say why you are calling. You are more likely to get a call back more quickly if you have a specific question or problem. If you have called and left a message and the attorney does not call back within twenty-four hours, call again and explain that you have not heard back and would like to speak to your attorney. If he or she still does not return your call, express your frustration to the secretary and ask if someone else in the office can help you. If you still do not receive a call back, you should think about switching attorneys.

Your attorney will need a lot of information from you. Try to provide it as quickly as possible and in an organized fashion. Your attorney will be completing the forms at the end of this book. If you can provide him or her with the answers to the questions, you will be saving yourself time and money.

Your attorney will meet extensively with you when he or she first takes you on as a client. You will be asked to sign a *retainer agreement* or *engagement letter* (which sets out the information about the attorney's fees), as well as a statement of your rights as a client. After these initial meetings, you may not hear from your attorney for some time. It takes a while to complete and file papers and to satisfy waiting periods. Be patient, but if you have not heard anything within the period of time the attorney suggested, call and find out how things are going.

Your attorney is your guide to the legal system in your case. He or she will help you prepare to testify (if necessary), and tell you what to do while in court. He or she may also have advice for you about things you can do to improve your case. Listen to what your attorney suggests and try to follow it.

COOPERATING WITH YOUR ATTORNEY

To make your case go smoothly, you need to work with your attorney. Provide the information and paperwork he or she requests. Be honest and do not try to hide things from him or her. Be on time for appointments. Be on time for court.

Be proactive and ask questions, but give your attorney your full cooperation. Clients often feel great resentment at the way the divorce process works, at how slow the court system is, and at the way their spouse treats them. It can be easy to bundle all of that up into resentment toward your attorney when none of it is actually his or her fault.

IDENTIFYING PROBLEMS WITH YOUR ATTORNEY

If you have a fee dispute with your attorney, contact your local bar association. Most have a fee conciliation committee, which will help you resolve your problem. Attorneys are required to follow the *Code of Professional Responsibility*, which provides guidelines for how they must treat clients and conduct themselves. If you feel your attorney has done something wrong—has not represented you completely, has made an important mistake, or has done anything else that you believe is a serious problem—you can file a complaint with an attorney grievance committee. To read more about grievance committees, go to **www.nysba.org** and search for "attorney grievance committee."

CHANGING YOUR ATTORNEY

If you hire an attorney and decide you do not like him or her, you can fire that attorney and get a new one. Usually there is no real problem in doing so, other than the delay it will cause. However, if the judge believes that doing so is a delaying tactic, or that your lawyer has been representing you effectively, he or she might not permit you to change attorneys. For the most part, however, there should be no problem if you make a change before your case goes to trial.

To change attorneys, first interview new ones, then select who you want, and let him or her handle the formalities of the changeover with the court.

REPRESENTING YOURSELF

It used to be unheard of for people to represent themselves in a divorce, but self-representation is now becoming more and more common. People who represent themselves are described as *pro se*, which means "for yourself." It is completely possible to handle your own divorce in New York. If your divorce is contested, it will be more difficult, but an uncontested divorce can be handled by almost anyone.

This book is designed to show you how to handle your own case if that is what you choose to do, or to help you be an effective client if you choose to hire an attorney.

Alternative Procedures to Divorce

Mediation is an alternative to traditional divorce that takes a more personal and nonaggressive approach. Most couples can benefit from mediation and reduce their attorneys' fees when they use it. So far, *arbitration*, a more formal procedure involving attorneys, is only offered in one county in New York.

MEDIATION

Mediation is designed to be a process that takes place in a neutral environment, in a reasonable and cooperative atmosphere. The goal of mediation is to help the divorcing couple make the decisions involved in a divorce without facing off in court or letting lawyers do the talking for them. It puts the decision-making power in the hands of the people who have to live with the consequences. The result of mediation is an agreement that has been custom designed by the parties to fit their lives and their circumstances.

The *mediator* acts as a neutral third party who helps to direct the conversation, and to educate the couple about the law and the choices they need to make. The mediator does not make any decisions in the case, and is not there to judge or rule on anything. Some mediators are attorneys, while some are social workers or therapists. There is no licensing of mediators in New York state.

Mediation is usually a face-to-face process, which means the couple sits down together in the same room and talks. Some mediators offer *shuttle mediation* for couples who are unable to stay in the same room with one another. This means the parties sit in separate rooms and the mediator goes back and forth between them. Sometimes more than one mediator can work on a case; this is particularly helpful in shuttle mediation.

The goal of mediation is to help couples decide how to resolve their divorce, by giving them conflict resolution skills to resolve problems on their own. It shows couples how to discuss problems, look for solutions, and offer compromises.

NOTE: *Couples who have experienced domestic violence are not considered appropriate for mediation.*

When mediation is successfully completed, you have a complete agreement about how you will end your marriage. Depending on what kind of mediator you use, you might end up with one of two kinds of agreements. A **MEMORANDUM OF UNDERSTANDING** is a document prepared by a mediator who is not an attorney. This document states everything you have agreed to and is signed by both of you. This document is then given to your attorney, who uses it to create a legal **SEPARATION AGREEMENT**. (see form 27, p.224.)

If your mediator is an attorney, he or she might just prepare the **SEPARATION AGREEMENT**. This is a legally binding agreement. (See Chapter 10 for more information.)

Mediators always recommend that both parties hire independent attorneys. A mediator can only give legal information, and cannot give either spouse legal advice, even if he or she is an attorney. The parties see their own individual attorneys to learn what their options would be in court and what kind of judgment they would likely receive. The attorneys also read and approve the **SEPARATION AGREEMENT** or **MEMORANDUM OF UNDERSTANDING**. One of them files it with the court and finalizes the divorce.

Benefits of Mediation

Mediation allows people the opportunity to work out a solution to their divorce that meets their needs. In mediation, you can choose unconventional solutions, or creative solutions, that work for you. Mediation also helps you make decisions and solve problems that attorneys generally do not address. For example, a mediator can help you create a plan for when and how you are going to physically separate, or how you will tell your children about the divorce. It can also deal with small details that can make all the difference for some people.

Mediation is also less expensive than hiring separate attorneys. Instead of hiring two attorneys who each bill over $100 an hour and put in dozens of hours on the case, the couple hires one mediator who charges significantly less. Then they pay two attorneys for brief consultations, and only one attorney to finalize the divorce in an uncontested manner.

Detriments of Mediation

Most couples who choose mediation do so because they feel more comfortable having control over their own finances, living arrangements, and parenting plans. However, some couples simply cannot handle mediation.

For example, mediation is not appropriate if there has been any kind of domestic violence, because the threat of more violence means the abused spouse cannot make truly voluntary choices. Other couples who avoid mediation want to be divorced and have nothing to do with each other ever again. The thought of spending hours in a room together working out conflicts is unbearable. Furthermore, some people enter mediation willingly but find that they are unable to speak up for themselves, that they cannot ask for what they want, or that they refuse to give in on important points. If either party is intimidated, mediation does not work. For mediation to be successful, both parties must be able to speak for themselves and stand up for what they want.

Additionally, mediation requires complete *financial disclosure*. This means both parties agree to be completely honest about their finances, income, debts, assets, and belongings. While attorneys in a court proceeding can *subpoena* financial information, a mediator does not have this power and must rely upon voluntarily provided information. If one spouse suspects the other is hiding something or is not being completely honest, the process will not work.

Your Role in Mediation

As a participant in mediation, you are expected to attend scheduled sessions, provide all the financial information the mediator requests, and approach the process with an open mind and willingness to work toward a solution that will benefit both you and your spouse. Mediation is not for those who want to win. The goal of mediation is for everyone to win.

Mediation is often scheduled in one- or two-hour sessions. An average divorce mediation might take seven sessions to complete. Depending on the schedules of all the parties involved, this might take one to three months.

Choosing a Mediator

If you are interested in using mediation, the best way to find a mediator is to contact the New York State Council on Divorce Mediation at 800-894-2646 or **www.nysmediate.org**. This is an organization of New York mediators that can provide a list of mediators in your area. Be aware that mediators on the list are not screened—anyone who joins the organization is listed. Your local bar association lawyer referral program may be able to refer you to a mediator as well. If you have already spoken with an attorney about your divorce, ask him or her who he or she recommends for mediation.

Once you have some names of mediators in your area, call to schedule a free consultation. Both you and your spouse need to go. Since a mediator remains neutral, he or she usually will not meet with either of you separately. When you go to the consultation, use the following list of questions to help you evaluate the mediator.

Office Observations

- Do you feel comfortable and relaxed in the office?

- Does the office lend you a feeling of privacy so you do not worry about being overheard?

- Is the staff friendly?

- Are appointments available at convenient times for you?

Questions for the Mediator

- ✪ How long have you practiced divorce mediation?

- ✪ What kind of training do you have?

- ✪ What background do you have (law, social work, psychology, etc.)?

- ✪ How much do you charge?

- ✪ What does your fee cover?

- ✪ Do you create a separation agreement or memorandum of agreement?

- ✪ How many sessions do you estimate will be needed?

- ✪ How frequently can we schedule the sessions?

Observing the Mediator

- ✪ Did the mediator seem pleasant and reasonable?

- ✪ Did you feel he or she treated you and your spouse equally and fairly?

- ✪ Was the mediator someone you will feel comfortable discussing private matters with?

Personal Observations

- ✪ Do you feel comfortable going to mediation with your spouse?

- ✪ Do you trust your spouse to provide accurate financial information in the mediation session?

- ✪ Are you willing to compromise and make decisions that work best for the two of you?

Once you have found a mediator with whom both you and your spouse feel comfortable, the mediator will have you sign an *agreement to mediate*. This sets out fees, your agreement to cooperate fully in mediation, and your right to end mediation at any time. The agreement will advise both of you to retain separate attorneys for legal advice. It will also explain what kind of document the mediator will prepare at the end of the mediation process.

Costs of Mediation   Most mediators require a *retainer*—a sum of money up front. Fees will be deducted from that until it is used up, and then you will be billed at an hourly rate. Rates range from $90 to $200 an hour, depending on a mediator's training and experience. Mediators charge not only for the time spent in actual sessions, but also for phone calls, document preparation, correspondence, and any other time spent on the case. Mediation costs are almost always less than the cost of litigating the issues with attorneys.

ARBITRATION

Arbitration is currently only available in New York County as part of a court-annexed state program. This means the court runs the program and refers cases to it. A case may be referred to arbitration by the judge (and if a judge mandates that you go, you have no choice), or the parties and their attorneys can volunteer to attend arbitration. This must be approved by the judge. The entire process is confidential, and none of the proceedings are shared with the judge in the case. Cases involving domestic violence or child abuse will not be sent to arbitration. You must be represented by an attorney to qualify for the program.

In arbitration, a neutral third party (the *arbitrator* or *evaluator*) hears the case. This *neutral* is an experienced matrimonial attorney who has been trained by the court to handle arbitration. The role of the neutral is to hear how the parties will present their cases and then to provide an evaluation as to how the case would be decided if it were to go to court. The hope is that this evaluation will help the parties reach a settlement more easily and avoid a trial. There is no fee for New York County's arbitration program, but you will need to pay your attorney to go through the arbitration process on your behalf.

How the Program Works

The first meeting must occur within twenty days after the paperwork for the program is completed. Copies of all documents in the case must be given to the evaluator. After attending the first session, either party can decide not to continue in the program and can return to court without any repercussions. In most cases, the program is completed in a few sessions. The process must be completed within seventy-five days. If not, arbitration ends and the parties return to court.

Evaluation

After the meetings have concluded, the evaluator will provide an evaluation of how the case would most likely be resolved in court. This helps the parties and attorneys know what result they can expect from the judge, and helps them reach a settlement.

Custody and Visitation

If you have children, they are probably one of your greatest concerns as you go through a divorce. You and your spouse may already have a good sense of how you want to arrange your schedules with the kids or you may not. Everyone will benefit if you can work this out on your own. However, many couples are not able to do this and must ask a court to decide for them. If you believe you are going to have a hotly contested custody case, then you should seriously think about getting a lawyer. If you are at risk of losing your children, you are being cut out of their lives, or you feel they will be in danger if they are with the other parent, it is important to hire an attorney who can present your concerns to the court.

THE LANGUAGE OF CUSTODY

There are many different words and terms you will probably run across as you work through court or mediation to resolve your custody case. Most people are familiar with the words *custody* and *visitation*. Generally, *custody* refers to the parent with whom the child lives. *Visitation* refers to the other parent's scheduled time with the child.

In recent years there has been a movement among children's rights advocates and organizations to stop using the words *custody* and *visitation*. Custody has the ring of ownership or of prison time to it. Visitation makes the nonresidential parent sound like a stranger who has formal, stiff visits with his or her child. Parents do not own or visit children. They live with them, share their lives with them, and love them. In many states, the terms *parenting time* or *parenting access* have legally replaced the terms *custody* and *visitation*. So far, this is not true in New York. However, many judges, mediators, and attorneys in New York use these terms on a regular basis.

While these terms are gaining acceptance, the law in New York uses only a few specific terms. There are two kinds of custody that are decided by the court. *Physical* or *residential custody* is used to refer to where the child will live primarily. This kind of custody can be *sole*, meaning the child primarily lives with one parent and spends time with the other, or *joint*, which means the child splits his or her time equally between the parents.

Legal custody refers to whether one or both parents will have decision-making authority in the child's life. If one parent is given this authority, it is called *sole legal custody*. If both parents are given this authority, it is called *joint legal custody*.

It is important to understand that physical and legal custody are separate terms. For example, both parents may be given joint legal custody, meaning they must make decisions together about the child, but only one of them may be given physical custody, meaning the child will live primarily with that parent.

You may also have heard the term *supervised visitation*. Supervised visitation is used in extreme cases when a parent has been violent, has demonstrated an inability to care properly for a child, or has a serious drug or alcohol abuse problem. Supervised visitation means that the parent without residential custody of the child is permitted to spend time with the child only in the presence of someone else who can make sure the child is safe and well cared for. Supervision can be provided by a relative or friend, or at a formal supervised visitation center where social workers or other trained professionals are present.

THINKING ABOUT CUSTODY

It is easy to turn custody into a battle against the other parent. Obviously, you feel very emotional about your children. When it becomes clear that a divorce is coming, some parents react by using custody as a way to hurt the other parent. They will try to punish him or her for the reasons behind the divorce. Others may also use custody as a way to try to hold tight to what remains of the family.

Instead of thinking of custody as a struggle against the other parent, it is a much better idea to think of it as a joint venture. You and your spouse were parents together before the divorce and you will continue to be parents together after the divorce. Even if you want to, you cannot erase your spouse from your child's life. You can never undo what is done. Your child has both parents and needs both parents. Even if you think your spouse is a miserable parent with no parenting skills and a terrible attitude, he or she is still your child's parent and your child has to have some kind of meaningful contact with him or her. You are going to be parents together for the rest of your child's life, whether you like it or not. It is better to accept this and find some way to work cooperatively together than to fight it.

Of course, there are certainly instances where you must fight for your child, particularly if the other parent has abused your child or abuses drugs or alcohol. If this is the case, you need to get an attorney to help you work out some way to keep your child safe. This might mean reduced or supervised contact for the other spouse until he or she receives treatment.

However, in most cases, a child needs both parents. Your child will benefit if you and your spouse can work out a way to continue to be parents together. Try to think about custody in a cooperative way, instead of a combative way. If you can find a way to cooperate, everyone wins. If you end up dealing with it in a combative way, no one wins, no matter what the final court order is.

UNDERSTANDING HOW CUSTODY IS DECIDED

The laws about custody in New York are mostly contained in case law. This is because each case is unique, and it would be difficult to create a solid rule to govern how a case should be decided. The important New York cases about custody are not new. This book includes references to the big, important cases that set the standards about custody. Later cases about custody exist, but are not as important. While the dates on the cases in this chapter are old, the standards and rules they set out are current and used by New York courts.

Basically, custody is supposed to be based on the *best interest* of the child. (*Bennett v. Jeffreys*, 40 N.Y.2d 543, 387 N.Y.S.2d 821 (1976).) This means that the court is supposed to make a decision based on what is best for that child. This is referred to as the *best interest analysis*.

Understanding Best Interest

Judges look at many factors when considering the best interest analysis. A judge considers the *totality of the circumstances*, which includes:

- which parent is most likely to allow the other to spend time with the child and encourage a relationship between the child and the other parent;

- the love, affection, and emotional ties between the child and each parent;

- each parent's ability and willingness to support and provide for the child (including clothes, food, medical care, etc.);

- the length of time the child has lived with each parent in a stable environment;

- how permanent each parent's home is;

- the moral fitness of each parent;

- the child's special needs;

- any domestic violence that has affected the child;

✪   the home, school, and community record of the child;

✪   the child's preference about custody (as long as he or she has sufficient intelligence and understanding to have such a preference); and,

✪   any other factor the judge finds relevant.

It is considered important to keep siblings together whenever possible. Courts rarely assign them custody in separate homes. (*Ebert v. Ebert*, 38 N.Y.2d 584, 407 N.Y.S.2d 472 (1976).)

There is no preference for mothers over fathers, or for working parents over nonworking parents. (*Linda R. v. Richard E.*, 561 N.Y.S.2d 29 (1990).) However, a parent's availability is something the court can consider as part of the best interest analysis. Alcohol or drug abuse by a parent is an important factor. A parent's sexual identity or sexual activities are not considered, unless they negatively affect the child. Interfering with the other parent's right to spend time with the child can be used as a reason to grant residential custody to the other parent. (*Finn v. Finn,* 176 A.D.2d 1132 (1991).)

There is a presumption in New York that shared or joint residential custody has a negative impact on children. (*Dintruff v. McGreevy*, 34 N.Y.2d 887, 359 N.Y.S.2d 281 (1974).) However, a judge may still order this arrangement if he or she is convinced it would be best for the children.

NOTE: *If your custody case involves an issue of relocation (one parent who wants physical custody and has already moved or plans to move away), you need to be aware of a line of cases including* ***Tropea v. Tropea, 87 N.Y.2d 727 (1996)*** *and* ***Browner v. Kenward, 86 N.Y.2d 702 (1995)***, *which state that the court must decide if the relocation is in the best interest of the child.*

The Child's Role   Because custody is an important part of a child's life, children are given a role in this part of a divorce case. A *law guardian* is appointed to represent the children in a divorce case. Law guardians are attorneys paid by the state and chosen by the judge. The law guardian's role is to get to know the child, understand the situation, investigate any claims or allegations, and make a recommendation to the court as to what he or she believes to be in the child's best interest. When the child or children involved in the case are old enough to form an intelligent opinion, the law guardian often will present this opinion for consideration by the court. (*Barry v. Glynn,* (1969), 59 Misc.2d 75, 297 N.Y.S.2d 786.)

Law guardians are very important in a custody case. It is essential to develop a good relationship with your child's law guardian. Be polite to him or her and make yourself available for appointments and home visits.

Children never appear in court, but may speak with the judge privately in his or her chambers. This is called an *in camera interview*. The law guardian accompanies him or her, and a court reporter is also present. The interview is *transcribed* (written down) but is not available for anyone other than the appellate court to read.

PREPARING FOR A CUSTODY CASE

If you think that you and your spouse are not going to be able to agree about custody and visitation, first consider whether you would be able to try mediation together to work out the problem. Problems that seem insurmountable can often be solved in mediation. If mediation is not going to work and you are certain you are going to have a custody battle on your hands, there are some preliminary steps you need to take.

Gather Evidence

Start gathering evidence immediately. The more you can gather, the stronger your case will be. You want to gather evidence that will show that you are a good parent and your spouse is not. You will also want to gather evidence that demonstrates special needs or problems your child faces. Do this in the following ways.

- ✪ Keep a journal. This will permit you to record incidents in detail that you might forget.

- ✪ Keep a clear record of the time both you and your spouse spend with your child. This can be important if you need to show that your spouse fails to show up for visitation or is regularly late.

✪ Take photographs. There are some circumstances in which photos can be very helpful. If your child is ever physically harmed by the other parent, obtain care for the child and then make sure there is photographic evidence. If your child regularly comes home in very dirty clothes or clothes that are torn or ripped, take photos.

✪ Keep a telephone log. Keep written records of phone conversations you have with your spouse about the child and what was said.

✪ Get copies of medical and school records that may show the child has special needs or problems, or requires special care. (See Chapter 6 for more information about how to get these documents admitted into court.)

✪ Find witnesses. Determine who has seen, heard, or experienced something that will help your case. Talk to neighbors, friends, and family members. (See Chapter 12 for more information about witnesses.)

Be on Your Best Behavior

If you are gathering ammunition for a court case, you know your spouse is too. Give him or her nothing with which to work. Put your best foot forward and make an effort to put your child first in your life.

Do not shower your child with gifts, suddenly take him or her to all sorts of special places, or relax the rules in your house. Those things will make a judge suspicious. Instead, try to spend real time with your child, exercise your very best parenting skills, and be pleasant and cooperative with the other parent as much as possible.

If you are experiencing a problem with alcohol or drug abuse, or find that you are having some serious emotional problems, it is essential that you obtain help. Doing so will not make you look like a bad parent. It will show that you care enough to try to solve your problems so that you can be a good parent. Hiding the problem or ignoring it can cause a lot of problems, especially once it is revealed to the judge.

TALKING TO YOUR CHILD ABOUT CUSTODY

It can be difficult to talk to your child about a custody case. The most important thing you can do is to be honest—but that does not mean baring your soul. Explain to your child that you and the other parent do not agree about where the child should live and how he or she should share time with both parents. Explain that the judge is going to listen to both sides, and make a decision that will work for everyone. It is important to emphasize to your child that none of this is his or her fault, that there is nothing he or she can do to change things, that there will always be two parents that love and care for him or her, and that both of you will always be an important part of his or her life.

COURT PROCEDURES

Custody is one part of a divorce case. The court decides the issue of custody, along with everything else on which the spouses do not agree. When a court has to hear evidence about custody, specific days and times are set aside to deal just with this issue. Evidence about financial matters is often heard separately.

In most situations, a judge will issue a temporary or preliminary order about custody at the beginning of the case, to get things organized and give the family some basic structure to follow. (To find out more about temporary orders, see Chapter 9.)

SETTLEMENTS

It is possible to settle the custody issue without settling any of the other questions in a divorce. Attorneys often work up until the last minute to help a couple reach a settlement. Many custody cases settle before they are heard in court. Sometimes it takes the threat of a trial to get people to settle.

In considering any settlement offers, you should think about what it is you really want, what you will agree to, and what is not negotiable for you. Keep in mind that custody and visitation plans need to change as children get older. What works for a 3-year-old may not work for a 16-year-old. What you agree to today probably will not work when your child is older, and you will need to modify your agreement at some point. (see Chapter 14.)

VISITATION SCHEDULES

Your parenting plan can follow any schedule to which you and your spouse agree. There are many creative options you can consider, but remember that a court will only approve a schedule if it seems to be in the best interest of the child.

If you and your spouse make up the schedule through a settlement or mediation process, you will need to first decide where your child will primarily live. One of your homes needs to be the child's base. Children usually feel most comfortable if they can remain in the home where they lived prior to the divorce, but if it works best to have the child move, then that is what you should do. It makes the most sense for the child to have his or her home base with the parent who is home more often.

When determining how you will share the child's time, remember that your child's age should play a factor. Younger children need shorter and more frequent contact with each parent, while older children can handle longer absences and extended visits. However, if you both believe it is better for your child to adopt some other plan, you should do so.

Consider your child's schedule when making plans. Does he or she participate in sports or extracurricular activities? You want to make sure he or she will still be able to do so. Consider both your and your spouse's schedules. Does one of you work weekends or evenings? It makes sense to schedule parenting time when a parent is actually home. It does not make sense to schedule time and then leave the child with a sitter on a regular basis.

When deciding visitation, many judges fall back on a standard visitation plan in which the non-custodial parent sees the child every other weekend and once evening on a weekday. The weekend might include any time between Friday afternoon and Sunday night. The weekday evening is often on a Wednesday from after school until after dinner-time. The standard schedule also allows parents to alternate holidays. A list of holidays is agreed upon (this usually includes New Year's Day, Easter or Passover, Memorial Day, Fourth of July, Labor Day, Thanksgiving, Christmas Eve, and Christmas Day or Hanukkah) and the parents agree that they will take turns with the holidays. For example, one parent has Thanksgiving this year while the other parent has Thanksgiving next year. The mother has the child on Mother's Day, while the father has the child on Father's Day. Parents usually alternate time with the child on his or her birthday. The nonresidential parent also normally gets additional time with the child during school vacations, often two weeks in the summer and some time over winter or spring vacation.

You and your spouse can create any plan that works for you, but it must appear to be fair and designed to benefit your child. Sit down together and try to plan out how you will share time over the course of a month. Remember that nothing is written in stone and that you can make changes to the schedule later. Once you have a sense for how you want to handle things on a daily basis, consider holidays and vacations. If you are unable to agree about how you will share time with your child, you will have to let the court decide.

EXPERTS FOR CHILD AND PARENT EVALUATIONS

In some contested divorce cases, attorneys bring in psychologists or social workers to evaluate the child and parents and to make a recommendation about custody. Each side can hire its own expert, as can the law guardian. If an expert is involved in your case, it can be easy to resent another person's power to make recommendations about your situation. Your best avenue is to cooperate as best you can and be honest about your parenting qualities.

Child Support

If you have children, you are probably concerned about *child support*—in particular, how much you will have to pay or how much you will be able to get.

CHILD SUPPORT LAWS

Child support is governed by Domestic Relations Law Section 240, which is called the *Child Support Standards Act* (CSSA). Child support only applies to children who are the legal children of both spouses. If you have a child from a previous relationship and your spouse did not adopt him or her, that spouse would not have to pay child support. Children who are born during a marriage are legally considered to be the legal children of both parents. If you have a child born during the marriage who is not—or who you suspect is not—the biological child of both parents, you need to see a family law attorney to receive help in disproving paternity. An adopted child is covered by the child support laws.

Child support must be paid until the child is age 21 or until he or she is *emancipated*. A child is emancipated if he or she:

- ✪ is married;

- ✪ is in the military;

- ✪ is self-supporting; or,

- ✪ is over age 17 and leaves the parents' home and refuses to obey the parents' reasonable commands.

The parent who does not reside with the child pays child support to the parent who does reside with the child. The purpose of the payments is to help provide the child with the standard of living he or she had before the divorce. The parent receiving the money can use it for any purpose, and need not provide any proof that it was used to support the child.

DETERMINING CHILD SUPPORT

Later in this book, you will complete a form that you will submit to the court to determine child support. For now, begin with a basic understanding of how it is calculated. Most people think that child support is based on the paying parent's income. Actually, both parents' incomes are used when determining the amount.

Calculate Income

The first step is to calculate each parent's income. *Income* includes:

- ✪ wages, dividends, interest, business and investment income, and capital gains;

- ✪ voluntarily deferred income or compensation (money you could have received but you had paid to someone else or you did not accept);

- ✪ cash benefits from workers' compensation, disability, unemployment insurance, Social Security, and veteran's benefits (public assistance or Supplemental Security Income (SSI) are not included in this category);

- ✪ payment from pensions and retirement benefits;

- fellowships and stipends; and,

- annuity payments.

A court may include other things when calculating income, such as:

- money, goods, or services provided by friends or family;

- fringe benefits of employment compensation (like meals, lodging, memberships, or cars) that result in personal economic benefit;

- self-employment or business deductions that reduce personal expenses (for example, writing off a car or home computer); or,

- a parent's former income or resources if there was a reduction in order to avoid paying child support.

The following one-time payments can be considered income as well:

- life insurance policy benefits;

- discharges of indebtedness;

- recovery of bad debts and delinquency amounts; and,

- gifts and inheritances.

Once income is calculated, the following things are deducted from it, where applicable:

- FICA (Social Security and Medicare);

- New York City or Yonkers income or earning taxes;

- child support paid for another child or maintenance (alimony) paid to a former spouse;

- maintenance (alimony) paid to the other parent (only if child support is set to increase when alimony or maintenance ends); and,

✪   un-reimbursed employee business expenses, unless the expenses reduce personal expenditures.

You can calculate income in weekly, monthly, or yearly amounts, but child support payments are always made on a weekly or monthly basis.

Combined Income   Next, total both parents' incomes to reach the *combined parental income*. Then multiply this number by one of the following percentages, based on the number of children you have together:

✪   One child: 17%

✪   Two children: 25%

✪   Three children: 29%

✪   Four children: 31%

✪   Five or more children: 35%

NOTE: *You are only considering the number of children you have together. If you or your spouse has children from another relationship, these children are not counted for this calculation.*

So far you have completed these equations:

> *Parent A's income + Parent B's income = Combined income*
> *Combined income x Percentage = Total parental child support*

The next step is to separate out the amount for which each parent is responsible. To do so, divide each parent's individual income by the combined income. This is that parent's percent of the total child support. Next, multiply that percent by the total parental child support:

> *Parent A's individual income ÷ Combined parental income = Parent A's percent of child support*

> *Parent A's percent of child support x Total combined child support = Total dollar amount Parent A must pay*

Example:

Shirley and Juan have two children together.

- ✪ Shirley earns $400 per week and Juan earns $600 per week.

- ✪ $400 (Shirley's income) + $600 (Juan's income) = $1,000 combined income.

- ✪ $1,000 (combined income) x 25% = $250 total combined child support.

Shirley's child support is calculated as follows:

$400 (Shirley's income) ÷ $1000 (total combined income) = 40% (Shirley's percent of child support).

$250 (total combined child support) x 40% = $100 per week.

Juan's is calculated the same way:

$600 (Juan's income) ÷ $1000 (total combined income) = 60% (Juan's percent of child support).

$250 (total combined child support) x 60% = $150 per week.

It is important to understand that while you have to calculate the child support amount each parent is responsible for, only the nonresidential parent will pay child support. The residential parent does not pay child support or keep track of how much he or she is supposed to contribute to the support of the child.

Doing all of this math can be confusing. For a quick answer, go to the charts in Appendix A and look up how much child support is required in your case. You can also use the online child support calculator located at **www.divorcelawinfo.com/states/ny/cal/NYCSC.html**.

VARIETIES OF CHILD SUPPORT

The formula explained in the previous section is the basic law about how child support is calculated in New York, but the judge can decide that it is unfair, unjust, or inappropriate to apply the formula. He or she can then set child support at a different amount. You and your spouse can also agree to set child support at a different amount if your agreement contains:

✪   a statement that both of you are aware of the Child Support Standards Act (CSSA) standards;

✪   a statement that any parent without an attorney has been given the CSSA chart;

✪   the basic child support amount as calculated using CSSA; and,

✪   the reasons for using a different amount.

If the combined yearly parental income is over $80,000, there are three ways the case can be decided:

1.   the CSSA percentages are applied to the entire income;

2.   the CSSA percentages are applied to the first $80,000 in income, and then the factors listed in the next section of this chapter are applied to the rest of the income; or,

3.   the factors in the next section of the chapter are applied to all of the income.

(*Cassano v. Cassano*, 85 N.Y.2d 649 (1995) and *Langone v. Langone*, 145 Misc.2d, 340, 546 N.Y.S.2d 535 (1989).)

Factors for Altering the CSSA Amount

The CSSA amount can be altered based on the following factors:

- ✪ financial resources of both parents and of the child;

- ✪ the child's special needs, aptitudes, and physical and emotional health;

- ✪ the standard of living the child would have had if the marriage had not ended;

- ✪ tax consequences;

- ✪ nonmonetary contributions a parent makes toward the child's care and well-being;

- ✪ educational needs of either parent;

- ✪ a substantial difference in the gross income of the parents;

- ✪ needs of the non-custodial parent's other children;

- ✪ extraordinary visitation expenses or expenses of extended visitation, if, as a result, the custodial parent's expenses are substantially reduced (this factor may not be considered if the child is receiving public assistance benefits); and,

- ✪ any other factor the court thinks is relevant.

Parent with Low Income

If the nonresidential parent has a very low income, he or she will not be required to pay the full amount of CSSA child support. The amount can be reduced to no less than $25 per month, the *child support standard reserve amount*. (Although in some cases it could possibly be reduced to zero. (*Commissioner of Social Services on Behalf of L.W. v. R.D.W.*, 160 Misc.2d 836, 610 N.Y.S.2d 996 (1994).)) If your income is low, you probably qualify for a free attorney, so check the website for a list of legal aid offices in Appendix A and call for more information.

Custody and Child Support

Generally, child support cannot be reduced or eliminated if the parents agree to a joint or shared custody plan, under which the child spends equal time with each parent. (*Bast v. Rossoff*, 91 N.Y.2d 723,

675 N.Y.S.2d 19 (1998).) In theory, it makes sense that if a child is spending equal amounts of time with each parent, neither would need to pay the other child support. However, this is only true if the parents share all of the child's expenses equally. *Bast v. Rossoff* holds that when parents have shared custody, the court must first apply the CSSA analysis and can then alter it based on several factors.

It is important to note that child support and visitation are completely separate from each other and do not influence each other in any way. If a parent fails to exercise visitation one week, he or she does not owe more money for child support. Likewise, if a nonresidential parent spends more time with a child than usual, he or she cannot reduce the amount of child support paid. Visitation cannot be denied or cut short because of nonpayment or late payment of child support.

OTHER KINDS OF SUPPORT

In addition to monetary child support, the non-custodial parent must also contribute toward:

- reasonable child care expenses while the custodial parent is working, attending school, or receiving vocational training;

- health insurance for the child if it is available through his or her employer; and,

- reasonable health care expenses for the child that are not covered by insurance.

The non-custodial parent may be required to pay the following:

- accident insurance or life insurance for either parent;

- child care expenses while the custodial parent is looking for work; or,

- the child's school expenses, including sports equipment, field trip costs, tuition, school lunches, school supplies, summer camp, and instrument lessons.

If the custodial parent has health insurance available through his or her employer, the court can order him or her to obtain insurance for the child in addition to, or in place of, the health insurance provided by the non-custodial parent.

TAXES

Child support payments are not tax deductible for the non-custodial parent, and are not included as income for tax purposes for the custodial parent. Additionally, child support obligations cannot be discharged in bankruptcy.

The parents must agree, or the court must decide, which parent will claim the child as a dependent. Parents can alternate this yearly, change it if financial circumstances change, or follow a set rule as to who will take the deduction. Normally the parent who can benefit the most from the deduction should be the one to take it.

PRESENTING A CHILD SUPPORT CASE

If your child support case is contested, you should understand what you need to prove to the court. You want to minimize the income you must report, maximize your reported expenses, and try to show that the other parent has more actual income than he or she is disclosing. Use the factors listed on page 44 to argue for a child support amount higher (if you are the custodial parent) or lower (if you are the non-custodial parent) than is provided by the CSSA guidelines.

Child care expenses may be important to the case. The custodial parent may try to prove these expenses are higher than average, while the non-custodial parent may try to show they are lower. Noncustodial parents should also demonstrate that they support their children in nonmonetary ways, such as coaching a child's T-ball team, volunteering at the child's school, or providing all the transportation for extracurricular events.

CHILD SUPPORT HEARINGS

If you need to have a trial about child support, the judge in your case may decide the terms, or may refer the case to a hearing examiner in Family Court. A *hearing examiner* is an attorney who decides child support cases. He or she acts under the judge's authority and decides the case according to the law. The judge must approve his or her decision (this is usually just a matter of rubber-stamping it). Treat a hearing examiner just as you treat the judge, with respect and courtesy. You can refer to him or her as "sir" or "madam." You can also say "your honor" if it feels more comfortable for you.

Child support hearings require a lot of paperwork. You will need to provide evidence of every scrap of income and expense. If you believe your spouse is hiding income, you will need to provide proof of this. Some testimony is needed in child support cases, but most evidence comes from documents.

Financial Survival

When your marriage ends, the court makes sure that all of your property is divided fairly and considers whether maintenance (also known as alimony) is needed to help one of the spouses survive financially.

MAINTENANCE

Most people know the word *alimony*, but the legal term for alimony in New York is *maintenance*. Maintenance is money paid by one spouse to the other on a regular basis after a divorce. Usually maintenance is *durational*, or for a limited time period, so that one of the spouses can go back to school, receive training, or have time to financially regain his or her footing (also referred to as *rehabilitative maintenance*). Maintenance can also be *permanent*, lasting until death. This usually is only ordered if the spouse receiving it is disabled, ill, or elderly.

Maintenance is not designed to punish one of the spouses. However, it is within a judge's discretion to set maintenance at any amount he or she deems fair. Some judges do take into account the behavior of the parties to each other during the marriage.

How Maintenance Is Decided

When a judge determines the amount of maintenance, he or she considers the following:

- the spouses' income and property (both separate and marital);

- the length of the marriage and the age of the parties;

- the present and future earning abilities of each spouse;

- the ability of the spouse seeking maintenance to become self-supporting (including how long it would take to receive the training or education necessary to become self-supporting);

- whether the spouse seeking maintenance had reduced or lost the ability to earn money by not pursuing or completing education, training, or employment during the course of the marriage (usually because he or she stayed home with the children);

- whether there are children and where they live;

- the tax consequences of the divorce to each spouse;

- contributions by the person seeking maintenance as a spouse, parent, homemaker, and wage earner;

- contributions by the spouse seeking maintenance to the career or career potential of the other spouse;

- whether either spouse has destroyed or used up marital property (this is called *wasteful dissipation*);

- marital assets that have been sold, given away, or used as collateral by either spouse as part of a strategy or plan involving the divorce; and,

- any other factor the court finds just and proper.

Additionally, the court must consider the standard of living that was established during the marriage. (*Hartog v. Hartog*, 85 N.Y.2d 36 (1985).)

Amount and Length of Maintenance

The amount of a maintenance award can vary greatly. If you are considering asking for maintenance, look at the difference between your two incomes and also consider how much income you need to support yourself while you find a job, complete education, or finish training. The amount paid as child support is not considered when deciding maintenance.

Generally, maintenance is awarded for one-third of the length of the marriage. So, if you were married for nine years, the standard order would be for three years of maintenance. This is just a standard, though, and a different length of time can be applied to your case depending on the circumstances. Sometimes a provision is included requiring the party paying maintenance to purchase a life insurance policy that would cover the maintenance requirements.

End of Maintenance

Maintenance ends when the length of time it was ordered for has ended, when either ex-spouse dies, or when the spouse receiving maintenance remarries. Maintenance is not payable to or from a deceased person's estate.

Tax Effect of Maintenance

Maintenance is tax deductible for the spouse paying it and is considered income for the spouse receiving it. Also, while the legal fees and expenses relating to your divorce are not tax deductible, the portion that can be attributed to maintenance is. Your attorney can provide you with a breakdown of the legal fees for tax purposes.

PROPERTY DIVISION

When your marriage ends, the court makes sure that all of your belongings are completely separated and divided.

Types of Property

First, it is important to understand that *property* means any belonging—real estate, vehicle, cash, bank account, jewelry, appliances, furniture, and so on. Property is divided into two main categories: *separate property* and *marital property*. (New York does not use the term community property. Items belonging to both spouses are called *marital property*.)

Separate property includes:

- ✪ property owned by a spouse before marriage;

- ✪ property given to a spouse during marriage as a gift or inheritance;

- ✪ property obtained in a personal injury case during marriage;

- ✪ income from property that was owned before the marriage (such as rent from a duplex or dividends from stock); or,

- ✪ property that was obtained by exchanging or replacing an item of property owned before the marriage (for example, a home that was purchased by selling a condominium owned prior to marriage).

Additionally, if an item of separate property increased in value during the marriage and that increase in value can be attributed in part to something the nonowner spouse did (such as maintaining a rental duplex), then the amount of the increase in value during the marriage is considered a marital asset. (*Hartog v. Hartog*, 85 N.Y.2d 36, 623 N.Y.S.2d 537.)

An item is considered to be marital property if:

- ✪ it was bought or acquired during marriage (whether you bought or acquired it separately or together);

- ✪ it is real estate that has both names on the title; or,

- ✪ it is a degree or professional license earned during the course of the marriage.

NOTE: *Debts are divided into the same categories as property, with the same guidelines for determining their status.*

Division of Property and Debts

Separate property and debts never divided or split up by a judge. Such property remains separate. Marital property and debts are divided by the court. New York laws require that property and debt be divided in a way that is *equitable*, or fair, and describe this division as *equitable distribution*. (DRL Sec. 236, Part B.) This is not the same as equal, which means half-and-half. Judges consider many factors when dividing property and debts, including:

- the total value of all property and debts;

- the income of the parties;

- which parent has residential custody of the children (this is especially important when a court considers the home and furniture);

- how the parties use the property (for example, the judge will probably award the boat to the spouse who regularly uses it);

- which debts are tied to which assets (for example, a home mortgage, a car loan, and so on);

- each spouse's financial situation;

- each spouse's contribution to the asset or debt;

- whether there is any maintenance award;

- tax consequences of the property division;

- length of the marriage;

- child support or maintenance payable from or to a spouse of a previous marriage;

- the contribution of each spouse to the family as homemaker or wage earner, or the support of the other's career; and,

- any wasteful dissipation of assets by either spouse.

You and your spouse can probably divide up much of your marital property and debts on your own. Start by each making a list of the items of property you want, and the debt you agree to assume. You will be able to work your way through many of your belongings and some of your debts in this way, and thus reduce the items that need to be negotiated by your lawyers or decided by a judge.

Collect the following financial information:

- most recent tax returns for you and your spouse;

- recent W-2s for you and your spouse;

- stock, investment, bond, IRA, Keogh, and pension plan statements;

- recent paystubs for yourself and your spouse;

- real estate deeds, titles, and insurance papers;

- automobile and boat deeds and insurance papers;

- life insurance policies for you, your children, and your spouse;

- health insurance policies for you, your children, and your spouse;

- bank account statements;

- Social Security numbers, birth dates, and driver's license numbers for you, your spouse, and your children;

- credit card statements;

- mortgage statements;

- student loan statements;

- personal loan statements;

- names and addresses of your and your spouse's employers;

- bills for utilities and regular expenses;

- child care and educational expenses;

- your and your spouse's wills; and,

- a list of all personal and household belongings.

These documents will help you get a handle on your marital assets and debts. If there are items you cannot agree on, make a list of what they are and try negotiating.

The Court System and Court Procedures

This chapter helps you understand how the courts work, what is expected of you, and how to act while you are in court.

COURT PERSONNEL

There are numerous individuals who work in the court system. As you move through your divorce, you will have contact with many of them.

Court Clerk

The first place you will have contact with the court system is at the court clerk's office. In most of New York state, the *court clerk* is the same as the *county clerk*. The clerk's office is filled with many employees whose job it is to accept papers for filing, check them to make sure they meet requirements, collect fees, and provide filing receipts.

Court clerks also work in the judge's office. These court clerks are mostly behind the scenes, but might on occasion make a phone call to you regarding a document you have filed or a scheduling matter.

Security Guards

Security guards monitor people who come into the courthouse. Most courthouses have metal detectors and people entering the building must pass through them. Usually you will need to lay your purse, briefcase, or anything you are carrying on a conveyor belt to go through an X-ray machine, or hand it to a security guard to be searched.

The security staff is there to protect you. If you are ever in a situation in a courthouse where your spouse harasses or threatens you, seek out a security guard. Some of New York's older courthouses have confusing layouts and lack visible signs for guidance. Feel free to ask for directions from a security guard.

Bailiff

The *bailiff* is a uniformed court worker who provides security inside the courtroom. He or she also may call the cases, notifying you when it is your turn to go inside the courtroom. The bailiff may indicate where you should sit in the courtroom. He or she will also say "all rise" when the judge enters the room.

Court Reporter

The *court reporter* is the person who types everything that is said in the courtroom and creates a written *transcript* of the proceeding. He or she remains silent throughout most of the case, but might ask you to spell your name, give your address, or repeat something that he or she could not hear clearly. If you need to go see a hearing examiner for a child support matter, there may be a tape recorder instead of a court reporter in the room.

Law Clerk

The *law clerk* is an attorney who works as the judge's assistant. He or she does research, handles paperwork, and consults with the judge. Some law clerks handle settlement conferences before a trial and try to help the parties reach a compromise. If you do reach a settlement when you meet with the law clerk, he or she will make it official by placing it on the record—sitting at the bench and presiding while the settlement is read out loud and recorded by the court reporter. You can refer to the law clerk as "sir" or "madam."

Hearing Examiner

A *hearing examiner* is an attorney who works for the state court system. Hearing examiners handle child support cases and act with the authority of a judge. The hearing examiner will make a decision about child support that must then be approved by a judge. Refer to him or her as "sir" or "madam."

Matrimonial Referee

If your case is uncontested, you may be scheduled before a *matrimonial referee* instead of a judge. He or she is an attorney who works for the state and is given the authority of a judge in the courtroom. The referee hears your case and makes recommendations to a judge as to how it should be decided. The judge will almost always agree with the referee. Refer to the referee as "sir" or "madam."

Attorneys   If your spouse hires an attorney, you will need to talk with him or her about the case if you do not have your own attorney. Remember that this attorney is just doing his or her job and has no personal vendetta against you. He or she will probably want to have some talks with you outside the courtroom to try to reach a settlement. Do not let him or her pressure you into something against your wishes, but do not disagree just for the sake of disagreeing either. You can choose not to talk to the attorney if you wish and conduct all discussions in the courtroom. It is polite to refer to the attorney as "Mr." or "Ms." If you have your own attorney, your spouse's attorney is not permitted to speak to you, directly, about the case.

Law Guardian   If you have children and your case is contested, a *law guardian* will be appointed to represent your children's interests. A law guardian is an attorney paid by the state. You should refer to the law guardian as "Mr." or "Ms.", unless he or she tells you to use his or her first name.

Judge   Always refer to the judge as "your honor." If you are seated when the judge enters the room, you must stand until he or she sits. When you speak to the judge, you should stand up (unless you are on the witness stand, in which case you should remain seated). If you have an attorney, he or she will speak for you and you should only talk when specifically directed to by the judge or your attorney.

COURTROOM MANNERS

There are certain rules of behavior that judges expect you to follow while in court. The rules are mostly common sense, but it helps to know them before you get there.

Where to Sit   In most courtrooms, the plaintiff sits on the left and the defendant sits on the right. The law guardian may have a separate table in the center or off to one side. If you are unsure where to sit, ask the bailiff or other court personnel. If you have an attorney, he or she will tell you where to sit.

Speaking   When you are in the courtroom, there are some basic rules about talking that you should understand. If you have an attorney, let him or her do all the talking. Do not say anything unless he or she tells you to speak. If you are representing yourself, never interrupt the judge. Listen to what he or she says. Answer questions he or she asks. It is acceptable to bring up a matter or ask a question. Do not talk to the other attorney or to your spouse while in the courtroom. Everyone is there to talk to the judge. Try to speak clearly and loudly enough so that the judge can hear you, especially as some of New York's old courtrooms have terrible acoustics.

Appearance   If you are a man, wear a suit, sport coat, or tie if at all possible. If you are a woman, wear a dress, suit, skirt, or dress pants. Avoid sandals, bare legs, revealing clothing, loud clothing, cutting-edge fashion, big jewelry, and hats. Dress neatly and respectfully. Gum, food, and beverages are not appropriate in a courtroom. Cell phones and pagers must be turned off as well. Children should not be brought to court unless the judge or law guardian specifically asks that they be present.

Attendance   It is important that you go to court at your scheduled time. If you are late, you might miss your case being called, and the judge could decide against you.

If you are working with an attorney, make sure you let him or her know of certain dates when you are absolutely unavailable to go to court. If you are representing yourself, bring a calendar with you to court and tell the judge if a scheduled time does not work for you.

If you are scheduled to appear in court and something comes up, you need to make every effort to get there anyway. If you absolutely cannot, you need to notify your attorney as soon as possible (if you are working with an attorney) or notify the judge's office immediately (if you are representing yourself). In this situation, you must give as much notice as possible and give a good reason.

ORGANIZING DOCUMENTS AND MANAGING DEADLINES

If you are working with an attorney, he or she will manage all of the paperwork involved in your case. However, he or she might ask you to bring certain documents at certain times. Remember to bring whatever is requested. If you are representing yourself, you will need to organize and manage all of the paperwork involved in your case.

Make copies of every form or document that you file with the court or give to the other side. Keep copies of filing receipts, and every document given to you by the other side. It helps to keep these in chronological order.

Completing Forms

Follow these instructions if you are representing yourself. If you have an attorney, he or she will complete the forms. It is best if the forms you file are typewritten or printed, but it is acceptable to submit forms that are filled in by hand.

You will notice that the top of every form you will use in your case has the same *heading*. (Refer to the forms in Appendix C.) When you complete the forms, you will need to fill in the county name as well as the names of the plaintiff (you, if you are starting the divorce) and the defendant (you, if your spouse has started the divorce). Each form also has a space to the right for an *index number*. This is the case number assigned by the court. Once you have this number, fill it in on every form you submit.

At the end of most forms you will need to fill in your name, address, and phone number. Some forms must be notarized. You can get forms notarized at no charge at your bank. If you use the forms in this book, make sure you photocopy them before completing them. Judges do not accept forms that have writing on both sides.

Certification

You must attach a **CERTIFICATION** to any paper you file with the court. (see form 15, p.209.) Make several copies of this form and attach it to everything you file with the court. If you have an attorney handling your case, he or she will make sure this form is attached.

This form is important because it promises that you are not filing a frivolous case. A *frivolous case* is one that is filed to annoy or upset someone, and has no legal basis or real chance of winning. This form also promises that all the things you have said in the forms attached to it are true.

Filing

You will need three copies of each completed form—one for you, one for the court, and one for your spouse or his or her attorney. It is usually a good idea to have four copies in case one gets lost, the court needs another copy, or you decide to hire an attorney at a later point. You can file papers by mail, in person, or by fax.

Before you file a document, make sure you fill it out completely. Some forms require a fee. There are several ways to file papers with the court clerk.

By mail. Mail two copies of the form to the county clerk—one for the clerk to keep, and one for him or her to stamp as filed and return to you. Enclose the filing fee and a stamped, self-addressed envelope so the filed document can be returned. Make sure you use enough postage. If you file by mail, a document with an error on it will simply be returned to you without explanation.

In person. When you file in person, go to your clerk's office and look at the signs for direction. Go to the window for filing court papers, and tell the clerk you would like to file papers. He or she will ask for the fee, and you can pay via check, money order, or credit card. Make sure you get a receipt and a stamped copy of the filed document.

By fax. In order to fax your papers to the clerk's office, you must use a **FACSIMILE TRANSMISSION COVER SHEET**. (see form 44, p.282.) Complete this form with your name, address, phone number, date of fax, number of pages (no more than fifty are accepted), case name and number, and the type of document being filed. You must also enclose a **CREDIT CARD COLLECTION AUTHORIZATION FORM**. (see form 43, p.281.) This authorizes the court to charge your credit card for filing fees in the case. Fill in your card number and expiration date, your name, address, and phone and fax numbers, and sign the form. You also need to enclose **CONFIRMATION OF RECEIPT OF FACSIMILE TRANSMISSION**. (see form 45, p.283.) Fill in your name after the "to" heading as well as your address, fax number, and case name and number. This form will be faxed back to you as a filing receipt.

Serving Papers

All papers in a divorce case must be given to the other party. These papers can be mailed, except for the **SUMMONS** (form 2, p.163) and some other forms indicated later in the book, which must be served on your spouse in person. Instructions for this are included on page 80. Most people use a process server—a professional whose job it is to serve papers in court cases. You cannot serve documents yourself, but you can ask a friend or family member to do it for you.

TRIALS AND HEARINGS

It is a long road to get from the first filing of papers to the final hearing in a divorce case. The road will be shorter if your case is uncontested. You will only need to appear in court once, if at all, to give testimony before a matrimonial referee. You will have more appearances if your case is contested. You might have four or five court dates before any testimony is actually given. These initial court dates might deal with temporary orders (see Chapter 9), and settlement proceedings.

Opening Statements

Once your case is scheduled for a trial, each side has the opportunity to give an *opening statement*. This is an introduction to each person's case. If you are representing yourself, you do not need to give an opening statement, but can if you want. If you do, it should be short and to the point.

Testimony

The plaintiff always begins a case and presents all of his or her witnesses and evidence before the defendant presents his or her case. To call a witness, simply tell the judge the name of the person you are calling. He or she must be there that day. The witness sits on the witness stand and promises to tell the truth. The plaintiff or plaintiff's attorney then asks him or her questions.

If you are representing yourself, call witnesses who can prove important points to the court (for example, that your spouse is hiding assets or that you are a better parent).

Have a list of questions prepared to ask the witness. If you are working with an attorney, write down a list for him or her in advance so that the attorney knows what information this witness has. It is not a good idea to rehearse too much with witnesses. Their testimonies should sound honest and spontaneous.

After the plaintiff finishes questioning a witness, the defendant has the chance to cross-examine him or her. This means the defendant can ask questions about the things to which the witness testified.

If you are going to testify and you represent yourself, simply tell the judge you are calling yourself. Sit on the stand and simply tell the judge the information that you want to share.

Testimony That Is Not Permitted

If you are representing yourself, listen to the testimony the other side offers. If you think something should not be allowed, stand up and say "I object," and then explain why. You do not need an expert knowledge of the law. If you are wrong, the judge will tell you that the objection is denied and the case will continue. It is better to object and be wrong, than to keep your mouth shut and miss the chance to keep out some testimony or evidence that hurts your case.

Reluctant Witnesses

Most of the witnesses that you or your lawyer call will want to help you. Sometimes, however, you might want to ask someone to testify who is unwilling. To get these people to come to court, you need a *subpoena.* Only an attorney or the court can issue a subpoena. If you have an attorney, he or she will handle this. If you do not, you need to tell the judge that you would like to subpoena some witnesses. The court clerk's office will then prepare the documents and instruct you in how to serve them. The subpoena will tell the witness he or she must come to court.

Physical Evidence

In addition to testimony, you might have documents or other pieces of evidence you want to show the court. *Physical evidence* is generally accepted by the court only when accompanied by testimony or an affidavit. If you want to show the court torn clothing that came back with your child after he or she spent time with the other parent, you would need to get on the witness stand and tell the court what the evidence is, how you got it, and what you know about it. If you want to submit documents such as bank statements, school records, or employment records, you need to ask the court to subpoena these documents from the person who prepares them. He or she must either come to court and explain that these records are made in the normal course of business, or he or she must send the documents with an affidavit stating this.

Closing Statements

After both sides have presented witnesses and evidence, each has the opportunity to give a *closing statement,* a short statement in which you ask the court for what you want. So, if you want maintenance, child support, and custody, you would say something such as, "Based on the evidence presented, I am asking the court for residential custody of my children, child support in accordance with the CSSA, and maintenance in the amount of $600 dollars per month."

NOTE: *Most people think that the judge will issue his or her decision as soon as the trial is completed. Judges almost never rule from the bench. You will receive the judge's decision by mail within a few weeks.*

Temporary Assistance

As you have read this book, you have probably come to the conclusion that the divorce process takes a long time. The court system recognizes that it does take a long time to completely decide a divorce, and so judges can issue temporary orders in a case. A *temporary order* is a decision made by the judge about some of the issues in the case—such as custody, child support, and maintenance. It is in effect only for the duration of the trial. Its purpose is to give the parties and children some structure to their lives, to allow both parents to have time with the children, and to make sure both parties can survive financially until the case is over. Another kind of temporary order gives *exclusive occupancy* of the marital residence to one of the parties. This in effect forces one of you to move out. You can also seek a temporary order *freezing* marital assets while the case is being decided so that your spouse cannot take the assets.

DETERMINING IF YOU NEED A TEMPORARY ORDER

Some people feel that they do not need a temporary order. Often couples are able to work out a temporary custody and visitation agreement, and feel that the court need not be involved. Most couples physically separate, and can work out together which one of them will stay in the marital residence. Even if you are in agreement, however, it is a good idea to have the court issue an order that outlines the terms of your agreement. For the sake of preventing future confusion, it is just a good idea to have the arrangement in writing, and signed by the court, so that no one can try to twist words or make changes.

SEEKING A TEMPORARY ORDER

If you are working with an attorney, discuss your situation with him or her. Talk about those things that need to be decided to make life manageable for you. In many cases, things like custody, occupancy of the home, and child support can be worked out between the parties. This temporary settlement can be described to the judge at the first court appearance, and issued by the court as a temporary order.

If you do not have an attorney and are representing yourself, you need to know that some judges automatically issue temporary orders in every case. These orders freeze the assets and debts of the marriage so that neither party can sell them or take on a lot of joint debt, and also prohibit certain things like taking the children out of state during the case.

To seek a temporary order, you need to first begin your divorce case. You can file the forms in this chapter when you file the **SUMMONS** (form 2, p.163), but you must also file a **REQUEST FOR JUDICIAL INTERVENTION**. (see form 30, p.262.) Once the case has been initiated, you can file a request for a temporary order by filing the following two documents:

1. **AFFIDAVIT IN SUPPORT OF MOTION FOR TEMPORARY RELIEF** (form 46) and

2. **ORDER TO SHOW CAUSE** (form 42).

Use the following instructions to complete the **AFFIDAVIT IN SUPPORT OF MOTION FOR TEMPORARY RELIEF**. (see form 46, p.284.)

⇨ ***At line 1:***

List the temporary requests you are making of the court, such as:

✪   a temporary order of custody and visitation;

✪   an order giving you exclusive possession of the marital home;

✪   an order giving you exclusive possession of a car;

✪   an order directing child support; and,

✪   an order directing temporary maintenance.

⇨ ***At line 2:***

Leave this section as is.

⇨ ***At line 3:***

Fill in your date of marriage, age, spouse's age, number of children, names of children, date of physical separation, and where the children reside.

⇨ ***At line 4:***

If you are seeking temporary custody, complete the reasons why. If not, leave this blank or cross it out.

⇨ ***At line 5:***

If you are seeking child support, complete this section. If not, leave it blank or cross it out.

⇨ ***At line 6:***

If you are seeking any kind of financial order (child support or maintenance), complete this section. If not, leave it blank.

➔ *At line 7:*

Complete this section if you are seeking financial assistance. If not, leave it blank or cross it out.

➔ *At line 8:*

If you are seeking maintenance, complete this section. If not, leave it blank or cross it out.

➔ *At line 9:*

If you are requesting exclusive use of a car, identify it (make, model, and year) and give your reasons. If not, leave this blank or cross it out.

➔ *At line 10:*

If you are seeking exclusive occupancy of the home, fill in this section. If not, leave it blank or cross it out.

➔ *At line 11:*

If you are requesting that your spouse pay certain bills, explain why and list the bills. If not, leave this blank or cross it out.

➔ *At line 12:*

If you are requesting anything else, ask for it here and give your reasons. If not, leave it blank or cross it out.

➔ Sign the form before a notary.

Use the following instructions to complete the **ORDER TO SHOW CAUSE**. (see form 42, p. 279.)

➔ Fill in your name and the date you signed the form on the first line. Leave the court date blank (the court will fill this in for you). After "Granting," fill in your requests.

⬧   In the paragraph beginning with "ORDERED," list assets that you want frozen.

⬧   Leave the blanks in the last paragraph and at the end of the form empty for the court to complete.

File these forms together with the court (and file a **REQUEST FOR JUDICIAL INTERVENTION**, form 30, page 262) and serve a copy on your spouse or his or her attorney. You will be given a hearing date. The court will fill in the court date on the papers and notify everyone in the case. Appear in court at the designated time.

Temporary Hearings

In order for the court to make a decision on your request, it needs to hear some evidence. You need to present the judge with some reasons to do what you ask. If you are able to reach agreement about how to handle the issues on a temporary basis, both you and your spouse will appear in court and explain your agreements. If you are unable to agree, you will need to give some brief testimony to the court about the reasons for your requests. Essentially, this means you will just tell the judge your side of the story.

You should prepare well for a *temporary hearing* because judges do not like to make a lot of changes to children's lives. If the children currently live with you, it is more than likely that a judge will want them to remain there until the entire case has been resolved. Additionally, if a judge feels there is enough evidence to make a temporary order of custody, he or she has already developed some preconceptions about the case. Temporary orders are likely to become permanent orders.

Temporary Relief in Family Court

If you need to determine custody or receive child support or maintenance *before* your divorce case begins, go to your local Family Court, and file papers there for these things. If you attempt to file papers in Family Court after your divorce papers have been filed, you will be instructed to deal with these issues in Supreme Court.

Separation

While at first glance it might seem to be more complicated to separate and then to divorce, it is actually the preferred method for many couples. In New York, you can prepare a *separation agreement* that lays out all of your decisions about custody, support, maintenance, and property division, and then submit it to the court and wait one year from the date you both signed the agreement. After one year, you can *convert* the separation to a divorce with very little trouble. Many couples prefer this method because there is no need to give testimony about what the other spouse did or did not do, or to blame the other person.

The other benefit to using a separation procedure is that you and your spouse can decide all of the terms of your divorce yourselves ahead of time, without going to court.

UNDERSTANDING THE MEANING OF SEPARATION

Once you and your spouse are legally *separated*, you will still be married to each other. However, you will live under the terms of your separation agreement. All of your decisions about parenting time, child support, maintenance, and property division will immediately go into effect, and you will be bound by the terms of your separation agreement. You will be divorced in all senses, except you will not have a piece of paper saying your marriage has been dissolved.

Many people say they are separated when they have decided to live apart. It is important to understand that you are only *legally separated* once the court accepts your *separation agreement*. You can only seek a divorce, using separation as a grounds, if you have lived separately for one year under the terms of a separation agreement.

GETTING A SEPARATION

There are two ways to get a legal separation. Most people use the first method, which involves signing a separation agreement. You can also get a separation by beginning a court proceeding asking for one, but in most cases, it makes more sense to use a separation agreement.

If you want to get a judgment of separation (but not a divorce yet), you can begin this procedure. Follow the instructions in this book for obtaining a divorce, and instead of the word "divorce," substitute the word "separation" in all of the documents. Note that you will be asking the court to make all the decisions for you as it would in a regular divorce.

To file a separation agreement, which you can then use one year later as a basis for a simplified divorce, you will first need to create one. Separation agreements are very long and complicated documents. If you want to have a separation agreement, it is best to have an attorney or mediator prepare one for you. However, a blank **SEPARATION AND PROPERTY AGREEMENT** is included in Appendix C as a guide. (see form 27, p.224.)

SEPARATION AGREEMENT

A *separation agreement* completely determines all of the terms of your divorce, including parenting, child support, maintenance, and property and debt division. You and your spouse have to be in complete agreement about everything that is contained in the agreement. You also need to be aware that the agreement must appear to be fair to the judge. If not, he or she can reject it.

The terms of the separation agreement will be lifted exactly and become the terms of your **Judgment of Divorce**. (see form 14, p.200.) It is essential that the terms be worded precisely and correctly.

Before you complete the separation agreement, you and your spouse need to complete and exchange a **Statement of Net Worth** (form 29, p.242), as well as any supporting documents such as tax returns, pay stubs, account statements, and so on. Both of your statements must be filed with the separation agreement.

If you create your own agreement, make sure it is typed, and that both you and your spouse initial any handwritten changes. You can use the sample at the back of this book, but it is a good idea to have one created for you to fit your specific situation.

You can have a mediator who is an attorney draft the separation agreement, or you can have an attorney draft it. It is always recommended that you and your spouse use separate attorneys. Have your own attorney review the document with you, fully explaining it to you before you sign it and informing you of the rights you would have if you were to go to court. Both parties must be fully informed before signing a separation agreement. Most attorneys consider it to be unethical to draft a separation agreement for a couple that has not retained separate attorneys, although some will do so if one of the parties signs a waiver saying he or she waives the right to have a separate attorney.

FILING FOR SEPARATION

If you are working with an attorney, he or she will file the paperwork for you. If you are representing yourself, follow the instructions below for filing the document with the court.

You can either file the complete **Separation and Property Agreement** (form 27) with the court clerk or file a shorter **Memorandum of Separation Agreement** (form 28) instead. If you file a **Memorandum**, you must show the signed separation agreement to the clerk at the time of filing, and then keep it yourself for one year. It is usually a better idea to file the completed agreement so you have no worry of losing it.

If you file a **MEMORANDUM**, complete your names and addresses as well as the date the separation agreement was written (the date in the first paragraph of your agreement). Fill in the dates each of you signed it. Have the form notarized and file it with the clerk.

If you file the **SEPARATION AND PROPERTY AGREEMENT** instead, simply take the completed form to the county clerk and ask to file it. Keep a copy for each of you, as well a copy of the date of filing.

CONVERTING SEPARATION TO DIVORCE

You and your spouse must live separately for one full year after the date the separation agreement is signed. When you do file for the divorce, you will have to swear that you have lived *separate and apart* for one year. Part of this means you have refrained from having sex with each other.

To convert the separation agreement to a divorce (a *conversion divorce*), you can follow the instructions in Chapter 11 for filing an uncontested divorce using separation as your grounds. Once that process is complete and you receive a **JUDGMENT OF DIVORCE**, your marriage is legally dissolved. (see form 14, p.200.)

Uncontested Divorce

An *uncontested divorce* is one in which only one party appears before the court. This means either that the other spouse does not respond to court papers or that he or she files papers indicating that he or she does not contest the divorce. An uncontested divorce is the simplest procedure for divorce in New York.

This chapter guides you through the steps involved in an uncontested divorce. If you are working with an attorney, he or she will complete the forms for you but will require information from you as well as your signature. Even if you have an attorney, this chapter is important because it will help you understand the information your attorney needs, and the process your case will undergo. If you decide to handle the divorce on your own, you can follow the steps explained in this chapter and use the forms included in Appendix C.

UNCONTESTED DIVORCE FORMS

If you plan to handle your divorce yourself, read the instructions in this chapter and follow them carefully. If you are working with an attorney, it is helpful if you read all of the forms anyway so that you understand what your attorney is going to ask of you and what you will be signing.

NOTE: *Remember to attach a* **CERTIFICATION** *(form 15) to every document you file with the court. Remember to make copies of the forms and only file forms with printing on one side. Make sure you always keep a copy of each form for yourself.*

Request for Index Number

To begin your divorce case, the first step is to apply for a *case number* or *index number*. You must obtain this form from your county clerk because it is printed on legal-size, colored paper and has a perforation.

To complete the *Request for Index Number*, do the following.

⟡ Fill in "Supreme" on the blank line under "Title of action or proceeding."

⟡ Place your name above the "v." and your spouse's name under it.

⟡ Fill in your information on the plaintiff's line and your spouse's information on the defendant's line.

⟡ Fill in the case name on both perforated sections at the bottom of the form.

There is a $210 fee for filing this document. When you file it, the bottom perforated section will be returned to you with the index number that will be your *case number*. You will fill in this number on every other form you file with the court.

Summons

Once you have a case number, you can actually begin your case. The **SUMMONS** is a document delivered to your spouse, informing him or her that you are filing for divorce and giving him or her a chance to respond. There are two types of **SUMMONS** that you can use.

✪ **SUMMONS** (form 2, p.163) accompanied by a complete **VERIFIED COMPLAINT** (form 3, p.164). If you and your spouse have reached an agreement about your divorce, this is the form to use.

✪ **SUMMONS WITH NOTICE** (form 1, p.162) is to be used if you have not reached an agreement with your spouse, or he or she is not aware you are filing for divorce. This is because this form goes into much less detail than a **Summons** with a **Verified Complaint**. The **Verified Complaint** spells out your reasons for the divorce. If you and your spouse have not reached an agreement about the divorce, the **Complaint** could make him or her upset and make it more difficult for you to resolve your divorce quickly.

NOTE: *When this book refers to* **Summons**, *it means whichever summons you have chosen to use.*

Use the following instructions to complete a **Summons With Notice**. (see form 1, p.162.)

⬥ At the top right hand of the form, fill in the index number and the name of the county in which you live.

⬥ Fill in the heading for the case and your address to the right.

⬥ In the paragraph beginning with, "You are hereby summoned," check "Plaintiff."

⬥ Fill in the date and fill in your name, address, and phone number and check "Plaintiff."

⬥ At "Notice," fill in the grounds for divorce you are using, choosing the section number from the bottom of the page.

⬥ At the bottom of the page, fill in everything you are requesting:

  ✪ custody and visitation (specify how you want this divided);

  ✪ child support (including health insurance, child care and educational expenses, and un-reimbursed medical expenses);

  ✪ maintenance;

  ✪ equitable division of property and debts;

- a declaration that all your property be declared your sole and separate property;

- a declaration that all debts in your spouse's name be declared his or her sole and separate responsibility;

- an incorporation, but not a merger, of a stipulation (agreement) or Separation and Property Agreement (if you are converting a Separation and Property Agreement to divorce);

- payment for costs and fees of the action (if you want your spouse to have to pay for the divorce); and,

- the right to resume use of a premarital name.

It is important that you think very carefully about your requests. If you are using a **SUMMONS WITH NOTICE**, this is your one chance to ask the court for these things. You cannot change your mind and later ask for something else without filing an amended **SUMMONS WITH NOTICE** and serving it on your spouse. You can ask for something on this form and change your mind later. It is best to ask for everything you might want here.

At this point, you also need to consider strategy. If you and your spouse do not have an agreement, and you are filing this divorce in hopes that he or she does not respond, you do not want to ask for all the marital property, $1,000 a week in maintenance, and custody with no visitation. Your spouse will probably be outraged by this. Instead, ask for something realistic that you think your spouse might not have a problem with, so that he or she will not respond to the **SUMMONS** and your divorce can proceed as uncontested. Otherwise, be prepared to hire an attorney and deal with a contested divorce.

To complete the **SUMMONS** (form 2) just fill in the index number, date, and case name. Fill in your name, address, and phone number at the bottom. Circle the word "Plaintiff" in the text and at the bottom of the form.

Service   If you are using a **SUMMONS WITH NOTICE**, you will serve only that document. If you are using the **SUMMONS**, you must also complete the **VERIFIED COMPLAINT** (form 3, p.164) and serve that at the same time.

Once you have your **SUMMONS WITH NOTICE** or **SUMMONS** and **VERIFIED COMPLAINT** ready to go, you must first file it with the clerk. You then have twenty days to serve it on your spouse. You should know that if you serve the form before filing it, it is not valid.

If you are asking for child support, your spouse must also be served at the same time with a copy of the *Child Support Standards Chart*. (See the clerk of the court to obtain a copy of the chart.)

To *serve* the documents, you can use the local sheriff, a professional process server, or a family member or friend. You cannot do it yourself, but you can go along with someone else while they do it. If you have a friend or family member do it, make sure he or she reads the **AFFIDAVIT OF SERVICE** (form 4) first so that he or she understands what to do.

Affidavit of Service   If you use the sheriff or a process server, they will provide you with a completed form. If a family member or friend does the serving for you, he or she must complete the **AFFIDAVIT OF SERVICE**. (see form 4, p.169.) Fill in the case heading and give the form to the person who served your spouse. He or she must then complete the following.

⬦ Fill in his or her name above paragraph 1.

⬦ Fill in his or her address in paragraph 1.

⬦ Fill in the date, time, and place of service in paragraph 2, and circle what was served.

⬦ Select the method of service in paragraph 4 and the description of the defendant in paragraph 5.

⬦ Complete paragraph 6.

⬦ Sign the **AFFIDAVIT** in front of a notary.

The **AFFIDAVIT** must be filed with the court within 120 days of the date of service.

Your spouse has twenty days to respond to the **SUMMONS**. If you receive no written, formal response, you can go ahead with the uncontested divorce procedure. This is your spouse's one chance to take part in the court procedure, and if he or she does not act, you may proceed without him or her. In this case, he or she will not see any of the documents you file from here on out, and will only receive the **JUDGMENT OF DIVORCE** (form 14).

If you or your attorney receive an *Answer* or a *Notice of Appearance*, then he or she is taking part in the procedure and you will follow the contested procedure set forth in Chapter 12.

Verified Complaint

The **VERIFIED COMPLAINT** is the document that you use to tell the court what you are requesting and why your marriage should be dissolved. (see form 3, p.164.)

Use the following instructions to fill out this form.

◈   Complete the heading. In the first section, if you are not using an attorney, cross out "by __."

◈   In the section labeled "Second," choose the section that best describes your situation and check all necessary boxes within that section.

◈   In the third section, fill in the date and place of marriage. Check your marriage certificate to get the town or village correct if you are unsure. If you were married by clergy, cross out the word "not" at the top of the second page. You do not need to do anything else in the third section. If you were not married by clergy, you leave the word "not" as is and then check one of the three boxes.

◈   Fill in the fourth section with the names and information for any children of the marriage—whether biological or adopted. Do not include children from another relationship. If you have no children, check the first box. Fill in addresses and health insurance information.

◈   In the fifth section, indicate the grounds for your divorce. Fill in the details of your situation as explained on page 14.

◈ After "Wherefore," list everything you are asking the court to do. If you filled out a **Summons With Notice**, ask for the same things you did there. If you did not file a **Summons With Notice**, read the list on pages 81–82 that details all the things you can ask a court to give you. You must be very specific on this form. Instead of asking the court to divide property, you have to list what property you want with a description of it that includes its value. Instead of asking the court to divide debts, you must list which debts you want your spouse responsible for, and name the creditor and balance. If you are asking for maintenance, give an amount. If you are asking for child support, state whether you are asking for the amount indicated by the CSSA guidelines, or if you are asking the court to go outside the guidelines. If you have children and you are asking that your spouse provide health insurance for them, you must indicate this. If you are seeking to convert a **Separation and Property Agreement** to a divorce, or if you and your spouse have completed a stipulation or other binding settlement agreement, you must indicate this and attach the agreement.

◈ Check the first box for Plaintiff and include your address and phone number. Sign the form before a notary and make sure you attach the **Certification** (form 15) to this and all other forms you submit.

Sworn Statement of Removal of Barriers to Remarriage

The **Sworn Statement of Removal of Barriers to Remarriage** (form 5) is required only if you were married in a religious ceremony. If you were married by a judge or justice of peace, you do not need to complete this form. This form states that you agree to take any steps needed in your religion to allow your spouse to remarry in the church or to get a divorce in the eyes of the church.

Use the following instructions to complete the **Sworn Statement of Removal of Barriers to Remarriage**. (see form 5, p.171.)

◈ Complete the heading and index number.

◈ Cross out whichever statement does not apply to you.

◈ Sign this before a notary and attach a **Certification** (form 15).

⬥ Have this document served on your spouse and have the server complete and file the Affidavit of Service that is on the last page of the document.

Affirmation (Affidavit) of Regularity

The **AFFIRMATION (AFFIDAVIT) OF REGULARITY** informs the court that your spouse has been notified of the divorce proceeding and indicates whether he or she has responded. (see form 6, p.173.)

Use the following instructions to complete the **AFFIRMATION OF REGULARITY**.

⬥ Complete the heading and index number.

⬥ Fill in the state and county where you live.

⬥ After "the undersigned," check "plaintiff" and then check which kind of summons you used and whether the defendant was served in New York or outside of New York.

⬥ Check the box to indicate if your spouse has an attorney or is self-represented. If your spouse has not appeared in this case at all so far, check the box for the section under the large "OR."

⬥ Sign the form before a notary and attach the **CERTIFICATION** (form 15).

Statement of Net Worth

The **STATEMENT OF NET WORTH** will share all of your financial information with the court. (see form 29, p.242.) The court needs this information in order to make decisions about child support, maintenance, property, and debt division. Even if you are working with an attorney, he or she will probably ask you to complete this form, or a form like it.

Use the following instructions to complete the **STATEMENT OF NET WORTH**.

⬥ Complete the case heading and index number.

⬥ For "Action Commencement" date, fill in the date when you filed the **SUMMONS**.

⬥ After "an accurate statement as of" in the first numbered paragraph, fill in your name and the date.

◈ Fill in the information in the *Family Data* section. "Date of separation" refers to the date you and your spouse stopped living together. If you are still living together, write "n/a". Item G refers to H/W/J, which means husband, wife, or joint. Check the applicable letter. This will appear throughout the form, so check the appropriate letter wherever this appears.

◈ In the *Expenses* section, fill in monthly figures in both columns. If an expense is listed that does not apply to you, leave it blank. Use estimates if you do not have an actual number. Total each category in the right hand column. At the end of the section, total all sections to get the total monthly expenses. Multiply by 12 to get annual expenses.

◈ List income as well as paycheck deductions in the *Gross Income* section. This must be done in monthly amounts. If you have other types of income, fill in the appropriate sections. Item "o" applies if you live with someone other than your spouse who has income and with whom you share expenses and support one another. You do not need to include any income your children might have. Get a monthly total by adding or subtracting the numbers in the columns. Multiply by 12 to get a monthly total. Note that many people find their monthly income to actually be less than their monthly expenses. You do not need to rework your numbers if this happens.

◈ In the *Assets* section, list all items of value and their estimated value. Some ask for "title owner" or "title holder." This is the person whose name is on the account or paperwork showing ownership. Give a year for "date opened." "Lien unpaid" refers to the amount of a loan on the item that is unpaid.

◈ List all of your debts, including credit cards, medical bills, student loans, and so on, in the *Liabilities* section. "Notes payable" refers to loans and "note holder" is the bank or person from whom you borrowed.

◈ Under the *Net Worth* section, subtract your total debts from your total assets. Again, do not panic if this is a negative number.

◈ In the *Assets Transferred* section, list any large or valuable assets that you have given away or transferred in the last three years. List their fair market value at the time of transfer. You do not need to list items you sold for a fair price.

◈ Skip the *Support Requirements* section if you are not seeking child support or maintenance. To complete this section, check the first box if you are neither paying, nor receiving, child support or maintenance from this spouse. If you are paying or receiving either of these, fill in the amounts and how often it is paid or received. If you received or paid these prior to separating, fill in that section. Indicate if payment is being made due to a court order or if it is voluntary. If there are *arrears* (missed payments that are owed), indicate the amount; if not, check the box for no outstanding arrears.

If you are seeking child support, check the box for the third paragraph. If you are seeking maintenance, check the box for the fourth paragraph and then indicate how much you would like and how often you want to be paid. In the last paragraph, indicate when you would like payments to be due.

◈ Complete *Counsel Fee Requirements* if you are asking that your spouse pay for your attorney or court costs. Check the box that corresponds to what you are requesting. If you do not have an attorney, you can only receive the amounts you paid to the court, process server and court stenographer. Check the third box if you have agreed to pay your spouse's attorney fees.

◈ In the *Account and Appraisal Fee Requirements* section, you may ask for your spouse to pay for appraisal costs (such as for appraising the value of a business or a home). Check the first box if you are not seeking reimbursement of an appraiser's fees. Check the second box if you are seeking reimbursement of an accountant's fees. Indicate the cost involved and whether the expert bills by the hour or by the job. Check the third box if you are seeking reimbursement of an appraiser's fees and fill in the fee information. Complete the fourth or fifth boxes to explain why an expert was needed.

⬧ In the *Other Data* section, you can fill in other important financial information that did not fit anywhere else on the form. The last paragraph allows you to attach additional pages. Place a check in the brackets if you have done so, and indicate the number of pages attached.

⬧ Complete the *Client Certification* and sign the form before a notary.

Affidavit of Defendant

The defendant completes an **AFFIDAVIT OF DEFENDANT** if he or she wants to consent to the proceedings without appearing in court. (see form 8, p.180.) If you are the plaintiff, an uncontested divorce will probably be simpler and to your advantage, so you may wish to help the defendant by filling in the form as you are able.

These instructions are given as if you are the plaintiff filling out the **AFFIDAVIT OF DEFENDANT** form for the defendant.

⬧ Fill in the case heading and index number.

⬧ Fill in the name of the defendant and his or her address.

⬧ In paragraph 1, check the kind of summons used, the date of service, and the grounds used.

⬧ Check the appropriate sentence in paragraph 3.

⬧ Check the appropriate sentence in paragraph 4. This choice is up to your spouse. If he or she checks the second sentence, you must send the requested papers to him or her.

⬧ If you have a written stipulation (agreement) about property division, leave paragraph 5 as it is. If not, cross out the italicized words.

⬧ Leave paragraph 6 as is if your spouse agrees to do this.

⬧ Paragraph 7 deals with child support. If your spouse will not have residential custody, check 7a. If he or she will have residential custody, check 7b and choose one of the sentences labeled 1–4. If your spouse selects 1 or 4, a separate sheet must be attached with the information requested.

◈   The defendant must sign this before a notary.

Complete the **Child Support Worksheet** if child support is part of your case. (see form 9, p.182.)

Child Support Worksheet

Use the following instructions to complete the **Child Support Worksheet**.

◈   Fill in the heading and index number.

◈   Fill in the name of the person who prepared the document and circle "Plaintiff."

NOTE: *You should use yearly figures when filling out the sheet.*

◈   Step 1 deals with income. Each question has a line for each parent's information. Fill in your information accurately, and estimate as best you can for the other parent. Total the income at "A."

◈   Fill in further income information in *Step 2*. Line 15 refers to assets or belongings that do not produce income (for example, a rental home produces income, but a classic car sitting in the garage does not). Line 16 would include items like meals that are reimbursed or provided by an employer. Line 17 would include things such as free samples, clothing, and so on provided by an employer. Line 18 refers to items provided by family or friends, such as regular gifts or financial support.

◈   Total both columns in *Step 2* at "B." At "C," total line "A" and line "B."

◈   Items in *Step 3* will be deducted from income. Total these at "D."

◈   Follow the instructions on the form for lines "E," "F," "G," and "H."

◈   Follow the instructions for *Step 6* and *Step 7*.

◈ On line "K," indicate an amount for child support that is to come out of income over the $80,000 threshold.

◈ Follow the instructions on line "L."

◈ Line "M" is for child care expenses needed by the parent with custody. Fill in only those reasons that apply.

◈ Follow the instructions for line "N."

◈ List health care expenses for the children that are not covered by insurance at line "O."

◈ Follow the instructions on line "P."

◈ Fill in line "Q" if your child has unusual educational expenses, such as special education needs.

◈ *Step 10* should be completed only if the parent who will not have residential custody has a very low income and is seeking to have child support lowered because of this.

◈ Sign this form before a notary.

Support Collection Unit Information Sheet

Complete the **SUPPORT COLLECTION UNIT INFORMATION SHEET** only if you are seeking for child support to be paid through the *Support Collection Unit*. If child support is going to be paid directly to you by the other parent, do not complete this form.

Use the following instructions to complete **SUPPORT COLLECTION UNIT INFORMATION SHEET**. (see form 10, p.188.)

◈ Fill in the heading and index number.

◈ Fill in the names, addresses, dates of birth, and Social Security numbers for you and your spouse.

◈ Fill in the date and place of marriage.

➔ Circle the name of the custodial parent, and whether or not he or she is receiving public assistance.

➔ List the names and birth dates of children still living at home.

➔ Fill in the amounts of child support and maintenance you are seeking, and the way you want them paid.

➔ Indicate the person to whom the payments will be made (they would go to a third party only if the custodial parent is receiving welfare).

➔ Fill in the name and address of the non-custodial parent's employer.

Qualified Medical Child Support Order

Complete the **QUALIFIED MEDICAL CHILD SUPPORT ORDER** if you have children that you want covered by your spouse's medical insurance. Once the form is signed by the judge, you must give it to your spouse's employer.

Use the following instructions to complete the **QUALIFIED MEDICAL CHILD SUPPORT ORDER**. (see form 11, p.189.)

➔ Fill in the heading and index number.

➔ List the names, addresses, dates of birth, and Social Security numbers of the children.

➔ Fill in your spouse's name and information for "participant."

➔ If you are going to have custody, fill in your name and information after "Dependents' Custodial Parent."

➔ Fill in the name of the health plan and the information required.

➔ Fill in the name of the administrator of the plan. This is the person at your spouse's place of employment who handles the health insurance. Usually it is the office manager or human resources office. Call and find out if you do not know.

⟡ Fill in the types of coverage—medical, dental, prescription, vision, and so on.

⟡ Leave the rest of the form blank.

Note of Issue

There is a $30 filing fee for the **NOTE OF ISSUE**, which is a form used by the court to help sort your case. (see form 12, p.191.)

Use the following instructions to complete the **NOTE OF ISSUE**.

⟡ Fill in the case heading and index number.

⟡ If you had a hearing in which you gave oral testimony, cross out "no trial."

⟡ Circle who is filing for divorce (circle "Plaintiff" if you are filing).

⟡ Fill in the date the summons was filed and on line 8 fill in the date it was served.

⟡ Circle "waiver" if your spouse completed the **AFFIDAVIT OF DEFENDANT**. Circle "default" if he or she never responded to the summons. If you are submitting a stipulation or separation agreement, circle the appropriate words.

⟡ Fill in your name and address and your spouse's name and address.

Postcard

When you file your forms, enclose a self-addressed stamped **POSTCARD** with your case name and index number written on it. The clerk will use this to notify you if you need to make any changes to the forms or if there is any problem with them. (A sample **POSTCARD** is in Appendix C as form 20, page 216.)

Request for Judicial Intervention

The **REQUEST FOR JUDICIAL INTERVENTION** (RJI) gets a judge assigned to your case. There is a $95 fee to file the **REQUEST FOR JUDICIAL INTERVENTION**. This form must be filed within forty-five days of the date the **SUMMONS** was served.

Use the following instructions to complete the **REQUEST FOR JUDICIAL INTERVENTION**. (see form 16, p.210.)

⬥ Leave the box blank for court personnel to complete.

⬥ Fill in the case heading and index number as well as the date you purchased the index number (the date you filed your **REQUEST FOR INDEX NUMBER**).

⬥ If you are not using an attorney, cross out "Attorneys for" prior to the word "Plaintiff." Fill in your name, address, and phone number.

⬥ If your spouse has an attorney, fill in that contact information. If not, fill in your spouse's contact information.

⬥ If you have previously been to Family Court for cases with your spouse, fill in the *Related Cases* section. For each case, write the name of the case, the docket number (this is under the index number), the name of the court, and the type of case.

⬥ Sign the form and fill in your name at the bottom.

NOTE: *You are only required to give oral testimony at a hearing if you use adultery as grounds for divorce. If you are not giving oral testimony, complete the following forms and file them with the forms previously described.*

Affidavit of Plaintiff   The **AFFIDAVIT OF PLAINTIFF** can be used in place of appearing in court. It is written testimony. You cannot use this form if you are using adultery as your grounds. If adultery is your grounds, you must appear in court.

Use the following instructions to complete the **AFFIDAVIT OF PLAINTIFF**. (see form 7, p.174.)

⬥ Complete the case heading and index number and the county.

⬥ Fill in your name, address, and Social Security number in paragraph 1. Fill in your spouse's name, address, and Social Security number, and to show that you meet the residency requirement, check any of the boxes that apply in paragraph 2.

◈   In paragraph 3, fill in the details about the date and place of your marriage. If you were not married in a religious ceremony, check one of the boxes. On the second page, select one of the three options and cross out the remaining two.

◈   Indicate whether or not there are children of the marriage and provide the information requested if there are children. At the end of the section, there are three "yes" or "no" questions. Answer "yes" to the first one if there has been any prior case involving custody of these children. The second question asks about custody cases in other states. The third question asks if someone other than you or your spouse has custody of your children, such as a grandparent or the state Department of Social Services. Fill in health insurance information.

◈   In paragraph 5, fill in the things you are requesting from the court. These must be the same as in your **VERIFIED COMPLAINT** (form 3).

◈   In paragraph 6, copy the requested information from your **VERIFIED COMPLAINT**.

◈   Complete paragraph number 7. In paragraph number 8, cross out the word "not" in the first sentence if you are receiving public assistance. Cross out the word "not" in the second sentence if your spouse is receiving public assistance.

◈   Complete paragraph 10 only if a photograph is attached to the **SUMMONS** (form 2).

◈   Select the appropriate choice in paragraph 11. Attach an additional sheet of paper with the information requested if you choose 11b 1–4. Fill in the information for prior surname if you or your spouse had a maiden name prior to the marriage.

◈   Fill in your name in the "Wherefore" section and sign the document before a notary.

Oral Testimony   If you are going to give oral testimony, file the forms described up to this point, except for the **AFFIDAVIT OF PLAINTIFF**, and include a self-addressed, stamped envelope with your case name and index number on it. The court will contact you with your hearing date. You will complete the rest of the forms in this chapter after the court appearance.

If you are going to have a hearing, prepare by reading over your complaint and knowing the facts in it. Try to remember the particulars of your financial situation as best you can. If you are working with an attorney, you will follow his or her directions at the courthouse.

If you are representing yourself, you will be in charge of your own testimony. First, make sure you know how to get to the courthouse so you are not late. When you appear for your court date, check in with the clerk. Wait until your case is called. When it is, go into the courtroom and sit on the witness stand, where you will be sworn in. Then the matrimonial referee may ask you some questions, or he or she may ask you to testify on your own behalf. If you are asked questions, answer them as best you can. Add anything important that the referee has not mentioned. If he or she does not ask you questions (and this would be rare), simply state you are seeking a divorce and explain your grounds, and what you are asking the court to do. At the end of the hearing, the referee will tell his or her recommendations to the judge. You will then be able to leave.

Wait until you receive information that your *transcript* (written record of the hearing) is ready. This is usually ready within a week or two. Send the correct amount of payment to the *stenographer*. The transcript is important because it contains the written recommendations the referee has made. Find this section in the transcript and copy it into your **FINDINGS OF FACT AND CONCLUSIONS OF LAW** (form 13, p.192) and the **JUDGMENT OF DIVORCE** (form 14, p.200).

Income Deduction Order

File the **INCOME DEDUCTION ORDER** if you are asking that child support or maintenance be automatically deducted from your spouse's pay and sent to the *Support Collection Unit*. (see form 23, p.219.)

Follow the instructions on the form. Choose "direct payment" if money is being deducted for child support. Choose "forwarded payment" if money is being deducted for maintenance. Fill in your information for "creditor" and your spouse's information for "debtor."

If the money is for both child support and maintenance, you must fill in this address under "creditor" instead of your own:

Office of Temporary Disability Assistance
P.O. Box 15365
Albany, NY 12212-5365

New York State Case Registry Filing Form

Fill out the **NEW YORK STATE CASE REGISTRY FILING FORM** if child support is NOT going to be paid through Child Support Collection and will instead be paid directly to you. (see form 24, p.220.) "Payor" refers to your spouse and "payee" refers to you.

75-J Affidavit

The **AFFIDAVIT PURSUANT TO DOMESTIC RELATIONS LAW SECTION 75-J** must be filed if you have children from the marriage whose custody or visitation has never been decided in court. If this has already been decided, do not complete this form.

Use the following instructions to complete the **AFFIDAVIT PURSUANT TO DOMESTIC RELATIONS LAW SECTION 75-J**. (see form 39, p.275.)

⬦   Fill in the case heading and index number.

⬦   Fill in your name before "being duly sworn deposes and states."

⬦   Fill in the number of children and their names, dates of birth, addresses, and any other places they have lived.

⬦   Indicate how long the children lived with you and your spouse in the same home.

⬦   Sign the form before a notary.

Notice of Settlement

The **NOTICE OF SETTLEMENT** must be served on your spouse if the judge or referee tells you to do so, or if your spouse indicates in his or her affidavit that he or she wants to receive court papers.

Use the following instructions to complete the **NOTICE OF SETTLEMENT**. (see form 22, p.218.)

⬦   Fill in the case heading and index number.

⬦   Check the document attached and fill in the location of the courthouse and date it will be presented to the court.

Serve this form on your spouse by personal service at least five days before the date the judge will receive the papers, or mail it to your spouse at least ten days before the date the papers are to be submitted to the court.

Findings of Fact and Conclusions of Law

Use the **FINDINGS OF FACT AND CONCLUSIONS OF LAW** (Referee's Report) to record the things ordered by the referee at your hearing. If you submitted an **AFFIDAVIT** instead of having a hearing, copy the language from that.

Use the following instructions to complete the **FINDINGS OF FACT AND CONCLUSIONS OF LAW** form. (see form 13, p.192.)

➔ Fill in the case heading and index number.

➔ In the first paragraph that is not numbered, check "been submitted to" if you submitted an affidavit, or "been heard" if you gave testimony. Fill in the county and the date the testimony was given or the date the forms were sent. Check "reading and considering the papers submitted" if you sent an affidavit or check "hearing the testimony" if you testified.

➔ At "Second," check the section that you used for your residency requirement.

➔ At "Third," fill in the date and place of your marriage, and check whether it was a civil or religious ceremony.

➔ At "Fifth," check the type of **SUMMONS** you used and how it was served. Check whether your spouse did not respond ("defaulted in appearance"), filed an **AFFIDAVIT OF DEFENDANT** ("appeared and waived his/her right to answer"), or filed an **ANSWER** (if he or she filed a document in order to appear in court for the case—read Chapter 12 about contested proceedings to learn more about this).

➔ At "Sixth," check whether your spouse is in the military. If he or she is, indicate if your spouse sent an **AFFIDAVIT**, or if he or she did not appear at all.

➬ At "Seventh," check whether or not there are children from the marriage, and fill in the information requested.

➬ At "Eighth," check and fill in the section that matches the grounds included in your **VERIFIED COMPLAINT** (form 3).

➬ At "Ninth," check the selection that applies to you.

➬ At "Tenth," check whether you and your spouse have agreed to maintenance or if the court has ordered it. Check who is going to pay it, how much it will be, and how often it will be paid.

➬ At "Eleventh," check the person with whom the children live. Indicate which parent will have visitation and which parent will have custody. If you will be sharing or splitting custody, use the "other custody arrangement" line to explain your agreement.

➬ At "Twelfth," check whether your property is being divided in accordance with an agreement you have made, if it is to be divided by the court, or if it does not need dividing.

➬ At "Thirteenth," check "no unemancipated children" if child support does not apply to any of your children, or if you have no children. Check "the award of child support is being based upon the following" if child support will be paid for your children. Fill in their names and dates of birth in "A." In "B," complete 1 if a prior Family Court order directing child support is to be continued. Check and complete 2 if the Supreme Court is ordering child support. Use the numbers from your **CHILD SUPPORT WORKSHEET** (form 9) to complete this section. Check 3 if you and the defendant have an agreement about child support. Complete the details of your agreement.

➬ At "Fourteenth," fill in the information requested. Check the first choice if you have no children involved in the case. Check the second choice if health insurance is not available through you or the defendant. Check the third choice and complete the information if one or both of you has health insurance. Check whether you have agreed, or whether the court is ordering, that one of you provide health insurance, and check how long the responsibility will last.

⬦   Complete "Fifteenth" only if you have prior court orders, such as from Family Court.

⬦   At "Sixteenth," check whether one of you will resume use of a premarital name and what that name is.

⬦   At the bottom of the form at "Second," check "Plaintiff" or "Defendant" and fill in the subsection number of your grounds.

Judgment of Divorce

The **JUDGMENT OF DIVORCE** will be signed by the judge and makes your divorce final.

Use the following instructions to complete the **JUDGMENT OF DIVORCE**. (see form 14, p.200.)

⬦   Fill in the case heading and index number.

⬦   Check "Applicable" if child support is being paid through Support Collection.

⬦   At "This action was submitted to," check whether you had a referee or a judge, and circle "this court." Check "consideration" if you submitted an **AFFIDAVIT** and "inquest" if you testified. Fill in the appropriate date.

⬦   At "The Defendant was served," indicate how your spouse was served and whether service was inside or outside of the state.

⬦   At "Plaintiff presented," check the forms you used.

⬦   At "The defendant has," check whether your spouse did not appear, sent an **AFFIDAVIT OF DEFENDANT** ("appeared and waived his or her right to answer"), sent a **VERIFIED ANSWER** (form 38), signed a stipulation or agreement, or agreed to a stipulation in court ("oral stipulation").

⬦   At "The court accepted," check "written" if you sent an **AFFIDAVIT**. Check "oral" if you testified.

⬦   At "The plaintiff's address," fill in the information requested.

◈ At "Now on motion," fill in your name and check "Plaintiff."

◈ At the second "Ordered, adjudged and decreed," fill in your name and the defendant's name and check the grounds and fill in the details.

◈ At the next section, check who will have custody and list the information about the children. If you have no children, check "there are no children of the marriage."

◈ Check who will have visitation and whether this is based on a written agreement. If you do not have a written agreement, fill in a schedule on the blank lines. If there are no children or if there is no visitation, check "Visitation is not applicable."

◈ At the next section, fill in information about previous court orders that are to be continued. Check the sentence about no court orders if you have none.

◈ At the next section, fill in information about child support if you have a prior order that is to be continued.

◈ At the next section, fill in information about maintenance.

◈ At the next section, fill in the names and birth dates of the children and the details of the child support. Check whether additional amounts will be paid for child care, education, or health care, and whether these are based on your agreement or on the court's decision. Circle the first indented paragraph if child support is in accordance with the child support guidelines. Circle and complete the second paragraph if child support is to be paid in accordance with the guidelines. If there are no children, check the last sentence.

◈ At the next section, complete the details of child care expenses paid by one parent to the other or check "Not Applicable."

◈ At the next section, fill in details about payments for the child's health care, or check "Not Applicable."

◈ At the next section, complete the information about payments for the child's education, or check "Not Applicable."

◈ Complete the next section if you or your spouse is being awarded exclusive occupancy of the marital residence, or check "Not Applicable" if neither of you will live there.

◈ Fill in the next section if you have a settlement or have reached one orally in court. Check "copy" if you have written agreement or "transcript" if your settlement was made orally in court.

◈ At the next section, circle the first choice if a **QUALIFIED MEDICAL CHILD SUPPORT ORDER** is being completed, or "Not Applicable" if it is not.

◈ At the next section, check whether you and the defendant have an agreement, or if the court is making the decision about a **QUALIFIED DOMESTIC RELATIONS ORDER**. This is an order that will divide pensions and retirement funds—this should not apply to you, and if it does, you should have used an attorney as indicated in Chapter 3. In most cases, you will check "Not Applicable."

◈ At the next section, indicate whether an income deduction order is being signed, or check "Not Applicable" if it is not.

◈ At the next section, fill in the person who will be resuming a prior name.

◈ Check "Defendant" if you are required to serve a copy of this on your spouse (if he or she requested this in the **AFFIDAVIT OF DEFENDANT**). Leave the number of days blank.

UCS-113   The **UCS-113** is used by the court for basic recordkeeping. (see form 26, p.223.) Fill in the basic information requested and file it with the previously mentioned forms.

Certificate of Dissolution

File the **CERTIFICATE OF DISSOLUTION** (form 21, p.217) and a $5 fee with the above forms at the clerk's office. The information requested is straightforward.

Now file the following documents with the court to finalize your divorce (they will be returned to you once they are signed):

- **AFFIDAVIT OF PLAINTIFF** (form 7);

- **INCOME DEDUCTION ORDER** (form 23);

- **NEW YORK STATE CASE REGISTRY FILING FORM** (form 24);

- **AFFIDAVIT PURSUANT TO DOMESTIC RELATIONS LAW 75-J** (form 39);

- **NOTICE OF SETTLEMENT** (form 22);

- **FINDINGS OF FACT AND CONCLUSIONS OF LAW** (form 13); and,

- **JUDGMENT OF DIVORCE** (form 14).

Then file the following with the clerk:

- **FINDINGS OF FACT AND CONCLUSIONS OF LAW** (form 13);

- **JUDGMENT OF DIVORCE** (form 14);

- Transcript;

- **VERIFIED COMPLAINT** (form 3);

- **AFFIRMATION OF REGULARITY** (form 6);

- **STATEMENT OF NET WORTH** (form 29);

- **UCS-113** (form 26); and,

- **CERTIFICATE OF DISSOLUTION OF MARRIAGE** (form 21).

The clerk will stamp the **JUDGMENT OF DIVORCE** and return certified copies to you.

Child Support Summary Form (UCS-111)

Complete the **CHILD SUPPORT SUMMARY FORM (UCS-111)** only if you are requesting child support. (see form 25, p.221.) Follow the instruction sheet that precedes the form. Be sure to mail it to the address indicated.

Notice of Entry

Complete the **NOTICE OF ENTRY** (form 17, p.211) if you are serving your spouse with the **JUDGMENT OF DIVORCE**. Attach it to the **JUDGMENT OF DIVORCE** and fill in the date the **JUDGMENT OF DIVORCE** was filed in the clerk's office (not the date it was signed by the judge). Send it to your spouse with the judgment attached. You are now officially divorced.

DEFENDANTS

If you are the defendant in a divorce, and you do not wish to contest it, you have several choices. You can do nothing, and the judge will award your spouse everything he or she has requested. You can choose to file an **AFFIDAVIT OF DEFENDANT** (form 8, p.180) stating that you consent to the divorce. Or, when you receive the **SUMMONS**, you can file a **NOTICE OF APPEARANCE** or **ANSWER**. This last choice allows you to keep your options open.

If you file a **NOTICE OF APPEARANCE** or an **ANSWER**, you are officially appearing in the divorce case. You will have the opportunity to read all of the papers, and decide if you agree with them. If you do, you and your spouse can reach an agreement and tell the judge the terms. If you choose to do nothing, or to file an **AFFIDAVIT OF DEFENDANT**, you give the judge the right to make decisions without your input.

STEP-BY-STEP PROCEDURE FOR UNCONTESTED DIVORCE

The following is a step-by-step review of the procedure you need to follow to finalize an uncontested divorce.

1. File **REQUEST FOR INDEX NUMBER**.

2. File your **SUMMONS** or **SUMMONS WITH NOTICE** with the Child Support Standards Act Chart attached if you have children and are seeking child support.

3. Have the **Summons** with **Verified Complaint** or **Summons With Notice** served. Serve a copy of the Child Support Standards Act Chart with the papers if you are seeking child support.

4. File the **Affidavit of Service** within 120 days of service.

5. Wait twenty days from the date of service for a response. If you receive no response, the case is uncontested and you can continue the uncontested divorce procedure. (If you do receive a response, go to Chapter 12 and follow the contested divorce procedure.)

6. File the following documents:

    a. **Verified Complaint** (form 3);

    b. **Sworn Statement of Removal of Barriers to Remarriage** (form 5);

    c. **Affirmation (Affidavit) of Regularity** (form 6); and,

    d. **Statement of Net Worth** (form 29).

7. Have the **Sworn Statement of Removal of Barriers to Remarriage** served on your spouse and file an **Affidavit of Service** for it.

8. File the **Affidavit of Plaintiff** (form 7) if you are not planning to give oral testimony. If you do plan to appear in court and testify, you do not need to complete this form.

9. The **Affidavit of Defendant** must be filed if your spouse completed it. If he or she does not complete it, your divorce will proceed without him or her.

10. File the **Child Support Worksheet** (form 9) if you have children from the marriage. File a **Support Collection Unit Information Sheet** only if you want child support paid to the state and not paid directly to you, and a **Qualified Medical Child Support Order** if you want a child from the marriage to be covered by your spouse's medical insurance.

11. File the **INCOME DEDUCTION ORDER** (form 23) if you want child support deducted from your spouse's paycheck.

12. File:

   a. **NOTE OF ISSUE** (form 12);

   b. **REQUEST FOR JUDICIAL INTERVENTION** (form 16) within forty-five days of the service of the **SUMMONS**;

   c. **AFFIDAVIT PURSUANT TO DOMESTIC RELATIONS LAW 75-J** (form 39);

   d. **FINDINGS OF FACT AND CONCLUSIONS OF LAW** (form 13);

   e. Transcript (only if you had a hearing);

   f. **JUDGMENT OF DIVORCE** (form 14);

   g. **UCS-113** (form 26); and,

   h. **CERTIFICATE OF DISSOLUTION OF MARRIAGE** (form 21).

13. Send the following to the clerk:

   a. **JUDGMENT OF DIVORCE** (form 14);

   b. **FINDINGS OF FACT AND CONCLUSIONS OF LAW** (form 13);

   c. Transcript (if any);

   d. **VERIFIED COMPLAINT** (form 3);

   e. **AFFIRMATION (AFFIDAVIT) OF REGULARITY** (form 6);

   f. **STATEMENT OF NET WORTH** (form 29);

   g. **CERTIFICATE OF DISSOLUTION OF MARRIAGE** (form 21); and,

   h. any exhibits used in a hearing get **JUDGMENT OF DIVORCE** stamped.

14. Buy two certified copies of the **JUDGMENT OF DIVORCE**.

15. Attach a **NOTICE OF ENTRY** to a certified copy of the **JUDGMENT OF DIVORCE** and mail it to your spouse.

16. Mail a certified copy of the **JUDGMENT OF DIVORCE** (form 14, p.200) to the *Support Collection Unit* in your county if you will be using their services to collect child support.

Contested Divorce

A *contested divorce* is one in which both parties appear in court and file papers with the court. Many divorces start out contested, meaning that both parties file papers and come to court, but most of these end up with a settlement. Once you reach a settlement, the divorce then continues as uncontested.

This chapter is designed to help you understand the process in a contested divorce. It contains descriptions of forms that are needed and explanations for handling a basic contested divorce. It should be understood, however, that if your divorce is contested, you are best served by hiring an attorney. There are many nuances and complicated procedures that can arise in a contested divorce. If your spouse has an attorney, he or she will be more experienced and knowledgeable about divorce than you are. To fully protect yourself and your rights, you need an attorney.

If you are working with an attorney, this chapter will help you understand what to expect from the contested divorce process and make you better able to assist your attorney. Most of the chapter will focus on how to proceed if you are the plaintiff. The latter part of the chapter will address how to handle the case as a defendant.

AVOIDING A CONTESTED DIVORCE

If it seems that your divorce is going to be contested, do not panic. There are many things you can do to prevent the case from becoming an expensive trial.

Try to talk with your spouse. Plan a business-type meeting to discuss your divorce. Come with a list of suggestions for how you can divide things. Try to talk in an unemotional way, and work for a compromise.

See a mediator. Even if you think there is no room for compromise, you will be surprised by the compromises that mediation can help you reach.

Tell your attorney (if you are working with one) that you want to avoid a long trial, and want to find a way to settle the case. Press your attorney to reach a fair settlement. Request that he or she try to do this in advance of the first court date. Many attorneys wait until the first court appearance, and try to work out a settlement in the hallway. This is not usually the best method for reaching a well-thought-out settlement.

If none of this works, do not give up hope. Even if you have to appear in court more than once, it is likely that the court will encourage a settlement and that you will eventually reach one.

DIFFERENCES FROM AN UNCONTESTED DIVORCE

In a contested divorce, the biggest difference is that you must justify all your requests. In an uncontested divorce, the court is probably going to go along with much of what you ask for if it seems fairly reasonable. In a contested divorce, you have to prove that your requests are fair, and that your spouse's requests are unfair. You need evidence to prove your points, and you also have to make sure you keep copies of all the documents that your spouse or his or her attorney files with the court.

Remember that if you choose to represent yourself, you can always change your mind at any point along the way and hire an attorney.

If you are representing yourself in a contested divorce, you should read Chapter 11 for the complete instructions on when and how to fill out and file the forms for a divorce. Note, however, that there are two main procedural differences in a contested divorce, as well as some other smaller issues. First, you will have a formal trial with direct questioning and cross-examination. Second, you will not prepare the *Referee's Report*, since the case will be heard by the judge.

NOTE: *In a contested divorce, you must file the **contested** versions of some forms. These are explained in the next section.*

Request for Judicial Intervention (Contested)

You must use the contested version of the REQUEST FOR JUDICIAL INTERVENTION. This form must be completed in order to schedule your trial or pretrial conference, or whenever you need a judge assigned to your case. If you are seeking a temporary order, file this with the motion papers to get a judge assigned to the case. File this form now if you have not already done so.

Use the following instructions to complete the REQUEST FOR JUDICIAL INTERVENTION. (see form 30, p.262.)

- ◈ Fill in the case heading and index number. Mark whether a *Bill of Particulars* was served by either of you. (If you do not know what this is, the answer is no.)

- ◈ Under *Nature of Judicial Intervention*, check "request for preliminary conference" if you want to meet with the judge's law clerk to try to work out a settlement. Check "order to show cause" if you are filing for a temporary order.

- ◈ Under *Nature of Action or Proceeding*, check "contested" under Matrimonial.

- ◈ Complete the "yes" or "no" questions on the second page, checking "no" for all but the question about equitable relief. For this question, check "yes" if your case involves property that has to be distributed. Otherwise, check "no."

- ◈ Fill in the names and addresses of any attorneys. If there are none, fill in the names and addresses for you and your spouse.

◈ Leave *Insurance Carriers* blank.

◈ Sign and date the form, and pay the filing fee when filing.

Note of Issue (contested)

File the contested version of the **NOTE OF ISSUE** when you are ready for a trial. You are not ready for a trial if discovery is still going on, or if you are scheduled for a pretrial conference.

Use the following instructions to complete the **NOTE OF ISSUE**. (see form 31, p.264.)

◈ Fill in the case heading and index number.

◈ Check "trial without jury." (You have the right to a jury trial to determine grounds, but that situation is too complicated for this book to address. If you want a jury for your grounds trial, you need an attorney to handle it for you.)

◈ Fill in your name after "Filed By." Fill in the date the summons was served and the date service was completed (in some instances these dates can be different).

◈ Check "Contested Matrimonial" under *Nature of Action or Special Proceeding*.

◈ Fill in your and your spouse's names and addresses, or those of your attorneys.

◈ On the second page, in the second column, indicate how this document was served. Try to get your spouse to admit service of this document (bottom left). If he or she will not, then it must be personally delivered, and the top part must be completed by the server.

◈ In the right column for items 1–7, check whether each item is "completed," "waived," or "required." Check "completed" for 1, 6, and 7. For the other numbers, check "completed" if it was done and "not required" if it was not done.

⟡ For number 8–10, check "yes." Leave 11 blank and check "yes" for 12.

⟡ Sign and date the form, filling in your address. Ask your spouse to sign at the bottom right. You must sign there as well.

NOTE: *Once a judge is assigned to your case, you file all the papers (except the* **NOTE OF ISSUE** *(form 31), the* **JUDGMENT** *(form 14), and papers that are filed with the signed* **JUDGMENT***, with the judge's office, not the clerk's office. Remember that if a law guardian is assigned to the case, you must send him or her copies of all papers filed with the court.*

UNDERSTANDING DISCOVERY

Discovery is a period of time in a case between the filing of initial papers (such as the Summons) and the trial. During this time you gather information to prove your case. There are many different kinds of discovery methods. This chapter covers a few of the methods you are most likely to need if you are handling the case yourself.

The kind of information you might need to obtain through discovery includes financial records, debt records, school records, insurance information, medical records, and investment records. You must obtain copies directly from the company or from the person who produces them.

Release of these forms requires a **SUBPOENA DUCES TECUM**. Since you are not an attorney, you cannot issue a subpoena, and you must ask the court to do this for you.

Notice of Motion for Subpoena Duces Tecum

To complete a **NOTICE OF MOTION FOR SUBPOENA DUCES TECUM** (form 32, p.266), fill out the heading and the name of your spouse or his or her attorney in the "To" section. The court will fill in the date the motion is to be heard. Fill out the affidavit attached to the motion. Fill in the names of the people or businesses, and the information you need. Sign it before a notary and attach it to the **NOTICE OF MOTION FOR SUBPOENA DUCES TECUM**. There is a $45 filing fee to file a Notice of Motion.

Subpoena Duces Tecum

Use the following instructions to complete the **SUBPOENA DUCES TECUM** (form 33, p.268).

◈ Fill in the case heading and index number.

◈ Fill in the name of the person or business you need information from after "TO."

◈ Attach a separate sheet and list everything you need from that person. Remember to fill out a separate subpoena form for each person or business.

◈ If you want the person to testify in person (if he or she has something that can be added only through oral testimony), cross out the second paragraph. Otherwise, the person can send the documents and need not appear in court. If you want the person to testify about something NOT related to the documents, you must use **SUBPOENA FOR APPEARANCE**. (see form 35, p.271.)

Serving the Subpoena

File the papers with the court. They will be returned to you with the date of the court appearance. Send a copy of this to your spouse. Appear in court on the correct day, and explain to the judge why you need these documents. Once the judge signs the **SUBPOENA**, have it served on the person or business, using a process server. Be aware that a business or medical office can require you to pay a copying fee for records.

If the person or business subpoenaed does not respond, call the judge's office and explain the situation and ask what the judge would like you to do next. (He or she can require that the subpoena be followed using law enforcement.)

Witness Subpoena

If you need witnesses to testify in your case, but know some of them will not come willingly on your behalf, you need to subpoena them. Use the **NOTICE OF MOTION FOR SUBPOENA FOR APPEARANCE** (form 34, p.269) and the **SUBPOENA FOR APPEARANCE** (form 35, p.271). See Chapter 8 for more information about selecting witnesses.

Complete the **NOTICE OF MOTION FOR SUBPOENA FOR APPEARANCE** and explain which people you need to testify and why. Complete the **SUBPOENA FOR APPEARANCE** (one for each witness) and file it with the court. Once the **NOTICE OF MOTION** is signed, send it to your spouse or his or her attorney. Appear in court and explain why you need each witness. Once the subpoenas are signed, have them served on the witnesses by a process server.

Other Discovery Methods

Other discovery methods include *depositions* (taking testimony outside of court), inspections, demands for witness lists, interrogatories (a list of questions to answer), and demands for statements. If you want to pursue these methods, see an attorney.

If You Are Served With Discovery Papers

If your spouse has an attorney, you may be served with discovery papers, requiring you to provide information or facts. If you are unsure about whether you need to respond to these, see an attorney. It is possible sometimes to quash or stop certain discovery requests.

PROPERTY AND DEBT IN A CONTESTED CASE

Property and debt are divided *equitably* in New York. This means they may be divided fairly, but not necessarily equally. In a contested case, you need to have a very clear sense as to what property you really need, what property you would like, and what you are willing to sacrifice. If you end up going to trial over property division, you should ask for everything first, but you should be willing to compromise when negotiating. The court can only divide what it considers *marital property*, not *separate property*.

CUSTODY AND VISITATION

If you have a custody trial, you are going to need a lot of witnesses who can support your point of view. Many cases also involve *psychological evaluations* of the child and parents. If your case involves this, get an attorney. (See Chapter 5 for more information about custody and visitation.)

CHILD SUPPORT

A child support hearing is a numbers game. The person seeking child support will probably attempt to show that he or she has very little income or assets, and that the other parent has a lot. The parent who will pay child support will probably attempt to prove the opposite.

For your trial you will need to subpoena all relevant financial documents, or provide the information to your attorney so he or she can do this. (See Chapter 6 for more information about child support.)

MAINTENANCE

If you have a contested maintenance case, you probably need an attorney. The law about maintenance can be complicated, and this situation can require expert witnesses.

If you are handling your own case and are seeking temporary maintenance, you will want the court to hear testimony about:

  ◈ your current skills;

  ◈ how much money you earn now;

  ◈ how much money you will need to earn to be self-supporting; and,

  ◈ the type and length of the training necessary to achieve self-support.

You also want to prove the ways that you contributed to the marriage—for example, raising children or taking care of the household chores. If you are the spouse who would be paying maintenance, you want to prove that your spouse does not need it, has a decent earning potential, and is, or easily could be, self-supporting.

GROUNDS

In most contested cases, the parties agree that they should get a divorce but argue over custody, or how to divide property.

Uncontested Grounds If you and your spouse agree about the grounds, the plaintiff will testify to them in a closed hearing without the defendant present (although his or her attorney can stay). This is a separate part of the trial.

Contested Grounds Occasionally spouses cannot agree about grounds, and a full trial is necessary to decide if there are grounds for divorce. It is very important to have an attorney handle a grounds trial. If you do not use one, you need to provide very specific details in your testimony. You may also need witnesses. If you are using adultery as your grounds, you absolutely need an attorney. It is possible to have a jury for a grounds trial.

SETTLING

At any point in the course of your contested divorce, you and your spouse can reach a settlement. If one or both of you is represented by an attorney, a written settlement can be submitted to the court. If neither of you is represented by an attorney, you can simply tell the court you have reached a settlement, and then explain what it is. The court reporter will take it down, and the judge will include it in the **JUDGMENT OF DIVORCE**. Be aware that the judge can reject a settlement that he or she feels is not fair.

NOTE: *If you have a law guardian in the case, he or she must agree to the terms of the settlement that apply to custody, or the court will not accept the settlement.*

JUDGMENT OF DIVORCE

When a contested case goes to trial, the court will usually prepare the **JUDGMENT OF DIVORCE**. (see form 14, p.200.) Wait to receive it in the mail before following the steps in Chapter 11 for filing and serving it. You will need to file all other papers listed on page 105 as you would in an uncontested divorce.

DEFENDANTS

If you are the defendant in the divorce case, you are probably wondering what all of the information in this chapter means to you. This chapter has outlined the procedure that a plaintiff follows. If you are the defendant and want to contest the divorce, you must file either a **NOTICE OF APPEARANCE: MATRIMONIAL ACTION** (form 37, p.273) or a **VERIFIED ANSWER** (form 38, p.274) once you receive the **SUMMONS**. You have twenty days to file one of these documents so that you can appear and contest the divorce. If you do not file one of these two documents, the case will proceed according to the uncontested procedure in Chapter 11.

Notice of Appearance: Matrimonial Action

File a **NOTICE OF APPEARANCE: MATRIMONIAL ACTION** if you receive a **SUMMONS WITH NOTICE**. This document tells the court you are appearing in the case to contest it.

Use the following instruction to complete the **NOTICE OF APPEARANCE**. (see form 37, p.273.)

◈ Fill in the heading.

◈ If you are representing yourself, cross out "represented by the undersigned."

◈ Fill in your name and address.

◈ If your spouse or his or her attorney will accept service (in other words, will agree the document was served if you just mail it), you do not need to serve it. If your spouse is trying to make things difficult and will not accept service, you will have to use a process server.

Verified Answer

If you have already filed a **NOTICE OF APPEARANCE** and wish to continue to contest the divorce, you will need to file a **VERIFIED ANSWER** once you receive the **VERIFIED COMPLAINT**. If you have not filed a **NOTICE OF APPEARANCE**, you must file an **ANSWER** in response to a **SUMMONS WITH VERIFIED COMPLAINT**. Note that the **ANSWER** is a form that really should be completed by an attorney, so if you get to this point, and do not have an attorney, you may want to hire one.

Use the following instructions to complete the **VERIFIED ANSWER**. (see form 38, p.274.)

◈ Fill in the heading.

◈ For number 1, go through the complaint and list the paragraph numbers for things that are untrue.

◈ List all other paragraph numbers in number 2.

⬦   In the affirmative defenses section, indicate reasons why the things the plaintiff listed are legally wrong. For example, if abandonment is the grounds and you have not been away a full year, this would be an affirmative defense. (You really need an attorney to help you with this section.)

⬦   List the things you are asking from the court in the counter-claim section. For example, if you want residential custody, state that you request it. If you are requesting possession of the car or home, state this. Also list any marital property you are seeking.

⬦   Sign the form before a notary.

Discovery   Read the section on discovery that appears earlier in this chapter. You can follow any of the procedures and use any of the forms described in order to obtain documents or compel witnesses.

Other Forms and Procedures   There are other forms and procedures that you can use as a defendant. If you simply file a **Verified Answer** and then go to trial, you put your spouse in the position of having to prove everything. However, if you do this, you cannot ask the court for anything yourself. In order to ask the court to do something, such as award property or custody to you, you will need to file a *Cross-Complaint*. You can use the **Verified Complaint** form described in Chapter 11 and fill it in as the defendant, renaming it "Cross-Complaint." It is a good idea to retain an attorney to handle this for you.

You can also file papers with the court asking for a temporary order on your behalf. See Chapter 9 for more information about this.

Trial   Remember to indicate that you are the defendant when you complete any forms. Most of the instructions in this book are designed to instruct the plaintiff on how to fill out forms.

As the defendant, you will sit back and let your spouse go first at trial. You have the opportunity to cross-examine witnesses. Once your spouse has concluded his or her case, you can present your own witnesses. Read Chapter 8 for more information about trials.

You have the right to appeal any decision made by the judge with the **NOTICE OF MOTION FOR SUBPOENA FOR APPEARANCE** (form 34, p.269) described earlier in this chapter.

APPEALS

When a judge decides a case, you always have the right to appeal the judge's decision if you disagree with it. An appeal is a long and expensive process, so it is best to discuss the case in depth with an attorney before deciding to pursue it. If you think you might want to appeal, you need to file the **NOTICE OF APPEAL** (form 36, p.272) within the thirty- day time period. You can easily withdraw your appeal at any time if you choose not to pursue it.

Notice of Appeal

Remember that when you appeal, you are asking the next highest court to review the way the judge applied the law in your case. You can complete the **NOTICE OF APPEAL** on your own, but if you wish to pursue the appeal, you will need an attorney experienced in appellate practice. There is a $65 filing fee to file the Notice of Appeal.

Use the following instructions to complete the **NOTICE OF APPEAL**. (see form 36, p.272.)

◈ Fill in the case heading and index number.

◈ Fill in your name after "please take notice that."

◈ Ask the clerk in the county where you filed your paperwork which judicial department you are in and fill this in before "Department."

◈ Fill in the county where your case was filed. Fill in the judge's name after "Hon. J." and fill in the name of the county again.

◈ Date the form and fill in your name and address on the bottom right.

◈ After "To," fill in your spouse's name and address or that of his or her attorney, as well as the names of the court clerk and law guardian. Mail a copy of this form to each of these people. There is a $65 filing fee.

Special Situations

Not everyone's case fits the mold of a typical divorce. You might have special concerns or you may be facing a situation that falls outside the realm of divorce proceedings covered so far. This chapter is designed to address some of those concerns and problems.

DOMESTIC VIOLENCE

Domestic violence can be physical or emotional. If you are in a situation where you believe that you or your children are in danger from your spouse, you need to get out immediately. Call the police or a local domestic violence shelter for assistance, or ask a friend or family member to take you to safety. Your first consideration must be for your own and your children's safety.

If domestic violence is a concern in your divorce, you need an attorney. If you cannot afford one, domestic violence shelters can put you in touch with legal aid services.

If your divorce has not yet been filed, you can go to Family Court and seek an *Order of Protection*, which is a court order directing your spouse to stay away from you. This order is filed with the police, and will help you get protection quickly if your spouse should try to violate it. To get an Order of Protection, go to the Family Court intake office and explain what you need. The clerks there will help you complete the needed forms, and get you a temporary order of protection that same day. If your divorce has been filed, you can ask your judge for an Order of Protection.

CHILD ABUSE

If you know or believe that your child is being abused, call the New York State Child Abuse Hotline at 800-342-3720. You can also call your local police department. The most important thing is to get your child to safety. Use a domestic violence shelter if you believe that, by rescuing your child, you are putting yourself in jeopardy.

PARENTAL KIDNAPPING

Unfortunately, parental kidnapping is a real problem. The first thing to do to prevent parental kidnapping is to get a temporary order of custody (see Chapter 9), and request that the judge order that the other parent not remove the child from the state. If you do not have an order giving you custody, the other parent has just as much right to time with your child as you do, and would not violate any court orders by removing the child from the state.

If the other parent kidnaps your child, the very first thing you must do is call the police. Report it immediately. Next, you need to find an attorney experienced in this kind of case.

If you are worried about parental kidnapping, there are several things you can do to prevent the situation. Get a passport for your child, and place it in a safe-deposit box at the bank. Only one passport can be issued per person, so this prevents your spouse from taking your child out of the country using his or her real identity. It is, of course, possible to obtain false documents under an alias.

Keep a current photo of your child and, if possible, have your child fingerprinted. The New York State Police often do free fingerprinting at fairs, store openings, and other events. Call your local state police and ask about programs, or for a free kit for fingerprinting at home. You might also want to keep a recent videotape of your child, as well as pieces of his or her hair for DNA. Let your child's school or caregiver know that the child is never to be released to the other parent without your written permission.

POOR PERSON STATUS

If you cannot afford to pay the filing fees for your divorce, you can ask the court to waive the fees. In order to qualify, you need to be *indigent*. There is no real definition of what this means, but you probably qualify if you are receiving financial assistance from the state. However, if you are in this difficult financial position, then you probably will qualify for free legal assistance from a local legal aid bureau. It might make more sense to go there first and ask for a free lawyer, rather than having the court fees waived and trying to handle the divorce on your own.

To seek to have court fees waived, you will need to file a **NOTICE OF MOTION FOR PERMISSION TO PROCEED AS A POOR PERSON WITH AFFIDAVIT IN SUPPORT OF APPLICATION TO PROCEED AS A POOR PERSON** (form 18, p.212), and a **POOR PERSON ORDER** (form 19, p.215). File these forms when you file your **SUMMONS** with the court.

To complete the **NOTICE OF MOTION FOR PERMISSION TO PROCEED AS A POOR PERSON**, you only need to fill in the header on the form. Leave the rest blank.

To complete the **AFFIDAVIT IN SUPPORT OF APPLICATION TO PROCEED AS A POOR PERSON** section, follow these instructions.

- ◈ Fill in your name.

- ◈ In paragraph number 1, fill in your complete address and the length of time you have lived there.

- ◈ In paragraph number 2, fill in the type of grounds you are using for your divorce.

⟡ In paragraph number 3, fill in information about your income.

⟡ In paragraph number 4, list items you own (other than clothing, food, and small household objects) and their value.

⟡ At paragraph number 7, leave the next line blank, unless you have previously filed this document with the court.

⟡ Sign this document in front of a notary.

Use the following instructions to complete the **POOR PERSON ORDER**.

⟡ Fill in the heading.

⟡ Fill in your name in the blank after "annexed affidavit of" and the date of your complaint.

⟡ Fill in your name after "Plaintiff."

⟡ Fill in the grounds section you are using.

⟡ Fill in your name after "Now in motion of."

⟡ Fill in you name after "ordered that" and the name of your spouse after "against."

NOTE: *You can be held in contempt of court if anything you list on the form is untrue.*

Once the papers are filed, you will be notified of the date of the court appearance. At this appearance, the judge will probably ask you a lot of questions about your financial situation. If he or she decides to waive the court fees for you, you will get a copy of the **POOR PERSON ORDER** with the judge's signature on it. You will need to file a copy of this in the clerk's office, and give a copy to the sheriff so that the sheriff's office will serve the divorce papers on your spouse at no cost. However, the fees for a private process server are not waived. Also, if you need to publish notice in the newspaper in the case of a missing spouse (see the next section in this chapter), that fee cannot be waived.

DIFFICULTY LOCATING YOUR SPOUSE

You have read through this book and seen all the requirements about serving papers on your spouse. What do you do if you do not know where your spouse is? It is not uncommon for one spouse to take off when a couple splits up, and sometimes there can be no way to contact him or her. Fortunately, you can still get a divorce even if you do not know where your spouse is.

How to Find a Missing Spouse

Before you can use *alternative service* (service other than personal service), you must use *due diligence*. To meet this requirement, talk to family, friends, employers, landlords, and neighbors and see if they know where your spouse is. Check the phone book or directory assistance. Check with the post office to see if he or she left a forwarding address. You can also check with the Department of Motor Vehicles to see if he or she has registered a car.

If these methods turn up an address or current place of employment, then use personal service. It will be faster and less expensive. If you cannot find your spouse, be prepared to be able to list for the court the steps you have taken to try to find him or her.

Alternative Service

This section describes several additional ways to serve your spouse, along with the necessary paperwork.

If you know where your spouse lives or works, but a server cannot seem to catch him or her:

> In this case, the documents can be served upon someone who lives with the spouse or works at his or her place of employment, as long as this person is over 18 and seems competent. If this method is used, the document must also be mailed by first-class mail. The envelope must be marked *personal and confidential* and must not indicate on the outside what is inside. It must be mailed within twenty days of the personal delivery, and the **AFFIDAVIT OF SERVICE** must be filed within twenty days of the mailing or the personal service, whichever was done last.

If you know where your spouse lives or works, but there is no one there to receive the document:

In this case, the document can be affixed to the door (this is sometimes called *nail and mail*). Attach the document to the door of the residence using tape or a thumbtack, and mail another copy by first-class mail. Both must be addressed to your spouse, must be marked *personal and confidential*, and must not indicate what is inside. You have twenty days to complete the mailing after the *nailing*, and you must file the **AFFIDAVIT OF SERVICE** within twenty days of whichever happens last. You can only use this method if *due diligence* has been used to locate your spouse, or to locate someone else at the residence or workplace who can be served in place of your spouse.

If you have no clue where to find your spouse:

In this case, you can serve your spouse by publishing a notice in a newspaper once a week for three consecutive weeks. Publish the **SUMMONS WITH NOTICE** (form 1, p.162) in the English-language newspaper most likely to be seen by your spouse. (You can also publish the **SUMMONS** (form 2, p.163) and **VERIFIED COMPLAINT** (form 3, p.164) if you want, but there is no reason to make these details about your life public.)

If you have an address where you think your spouse might be, you must mail the **SUMMONS WITH NOTICE** (form 1) and a *Notice of Publication* (which you will obtain from the newspaper) to him or her at this address before the first day of planned publication. The first publication must happen within thirty days of the court order allowing service by publication. You must file the **AFFIDAVIT OF SERVICE** (form 4, p.169) within twenty days of the last publication.

If you believe your spouse is dead:

If your spouse has been missing for over five years, and you believe he or she is dead, you can use a special proceeding to divorce on the grounds of absence. (DRL Sec. 220 and 221.) You can qualify for this proceeding if you have lived in New York for one year prior to filing for divorce or if you and your spouse lived together in New York at the time he or she disappeared.

To get a divorce in this manner, you follow a different procedure than that described elsewhere in the book. You need to hire an attorney who will file a special proceeding petition with the court explaining that your spouse has been gone five years and is believed to be dead. If the court agrees that your spouse is probably dead, and believes that you have made a reasonable effort to find him or her, and your attorney has published a notice in a newspaper, the court will dissolve your marriage based upon the petition. You will not need to follow any of the other procedures described in this book.

Filing for Alternate Service

To request alternative service, you will need to file the **NOTICE OF MOTION FOR ALTERNATE SERVICE WITH AFFIDAVIT IN SUPPORT OF MOTION** (form 40, p.276) and **ORDER DIRECTING SERVICE** (form 41, p.278) when you file your **REQUEST FOR JUDICIAL INTERVENTION** (form 30, p.262).

To complete the **NOTICE OF MOTION OF ALTERNATE SERVICE**, follow these instructions.

- ⟡ Leave the date and time blank.

- ⟡ Check the box that describes the type of service you are requesting.

- ⟡ If you choose the third type, indicate the newspaper you would like to use.

Use the following instructions to complete the **AFFIDAVIT IN SUPPORT OF MOTION** section.

- ⟡ Fill in your name on the first line.

- ⟡ Fill in the number of times that service has been attempted and describe each attempt.

- ⟡ Explain why you have not been able to find your spouse (for example, he or she moved with no forwarding address, or no one ever answers the door).

- ⟡ Sign the form before a notary.

To complete the **ORDER DIRECTING SERVICE**, follow these instructions.

- ◈ Fill in your name on the first line and the date you signed the **AFFIDAVIT**.

- ◈ On the second line, fill in the names of anyone else who has submitted an affidavit (such as a process server who has been unable to serve your spouse) and the date of that document.

- ◈ Check the first box if you cannot find your spouse.

- ◈ Check the second box if you know where he or she is, but have not been able to serve him or her.

- ◈ Next, read the three sections with boxes in front of them.

- ◈ Check the box that describes the type of service you want.

- ◈ If you select publication, fill in the name of the newspaper and where it is published.

Once you have completed the forms, file them with your **REQUEST FOR JUDICIAL INTERVENTION**. A hearing will be scheduled. You will need to appear and answer questions from the judge about the problems you are having serving your spouse. Once the judge signs the order and you receive it, go ahead and have your spouse served in the way described.

If you use publication, the newspaper will provide you with a completed **AFFIDAVIT OF SERVICE** that you will file with the court. If you are using another type of alternative service, you will need to have the server complete the **AFFIDAVIT OF SERVICE** (form 4, p.169) as follows.

- ◈ Complete the personal information about the server.

- ◈ Check the box to indicate what documents were served.

- ◈ Check either "suitable person" or "affixing to the door," depending on what type of service was ordered.

- ◈ Fill in the details about the service.

◈ Check the box "Mailing use with" and fill in the address where it was mailed.

◈ If another person was served, a description must be entered describing this person under Description of Recipient.

◈ The process server must sign the form before a notary.

COMMON LAW MARRIAGE

Common law marriage is not recognized in New York. In some states, if you live together and present yourselves as a married couple, you can be considered legally married after a certain number of years. Because New York does not recognize this, you cannot get a legal divorce in New York. You can, however, use Family Court to decide custody and child support.

NO-FAULT DIVORCE

Many people ask about *no-fault divorce* in New York. There is no provision for no-fault divorce in New York (talk to your state assembly representative if you think this is wrong). The closest thing to a no-fault divorce in New York is to get a *conversion divorce* (see Chapter 10) in which you live apart under a separation agreement for one year and then convert it to a divorce.

NOTE: *New York allows divorce on the basis of cruel and inhuman treatment that is defined broadly to include name-calling, arguing, or emotional abuse. These categories fit just about every couple considering divorce.*

COMMUNITY PROPERTY

You have probably heard the term *community property* come up when people talk about divorce. It is a legal term that explains how marital belongings are divided. New York is not a community property state, and uses *equitable distribution* to divide marital property. See Chapter 12 for more information.

CHANGING THE LOCKS

"When can I change the locks?" is one of the most common questions asked by a divorce client. You can change the locks once your spouse moves out, or once the court gives you exclusive occupancy. If you and your spouse are both still living in the martial residence, and there is no court order giving occupancy to either of you, then you both have an equal right to live there.

PRENUPTIAL AGREEMENTS

A *prenuptial agreement* is an agreement signed before you marry, laying out how you will divide your property if the marriage should end in divorce. *Prenups* (as they are commonly called) are becoming more and more common, especially for couples who are entering second marriages or who have children from previous relationships.

If you have a prenup, its terms will decide how your property is divided should you divorce. (DRL Sec. 236 Part B3.) However, if the agreement was not fair and reasonable or was made under duress, it will not be honored. If you have a prenup, you need an attorney to assist you with your divorce.

chapter 14

Life After Divorce

The first thing you will probably feel once your divorce is finalized is relief that the court proceedings and paperwork are behind you, and you can finally start to think about something else.

FINALIZING YOUR DIVORCE

Your divorce is not final and legal until you receive the **JUDGMENT OF DIVORCE** with the judge's signature. Expect this paperwork to come in the mail two to four weeks after your final court appearance, or after you have filed all the papers if you did not testify. If it takes longer than four weeks, call the judge's secretary and ask about the status. Once your divorce is final, all of the decisions laid out in the **JUDGMENT OF DIVORCE** must be put into place, and you are free to marry again.

CHANGING YOUR NAME

If you used a different last name before your marriage, and if the court has given permission for you to go back to using it, you can start using that name immediately. You will need to contact your bank, creditors, insurance companies, employer, child's school, and so on, with the change. If you need to provide proof of the name change (to the Department of Motor Vehicles (DMV), for example), show them your **JUDGMENT OF DIVORCE**. To change your name on your license, complete an *Application for Driver License*, and bring it to your local DMV with your license and proof of name change. To change your registration and title, complete a *Vehicle Registration Application* (both of these forms are available online or at your local DMV office), and bring your current registration and title, as well as proof of the name change. There is a fee for each name change (currently $8 for the license and $3 for each the registration and the title). You can read more about the DMV's requirements at **http://nysdmv.com/ dmvfaqs.htm#CHANGE**.

You can continue to use your married name if you prefer.

COPING WITH CHANGES IN YOUR NEW LIFE

Once that initial feeling of relief washes over you, you will probably go on to experience a host of other emotions and thoughts. It is common to feel grief, sadness, anger, fear, loneliness, and uncertainty. Many people find that talking about their situation helps them feel better. You can talk to friends and family, find a support group in your local area, or talk to a professional counselor, social worker, or clergy member.

The months that follow your divorce will be filled with many adjustments. You may still be adjusting to living alone and handling all the household chores and tasks your spouse might have done. You may be adjusting to a new residence and a new routine. Still, with that change comes great freedom. Now you, and only you, will make choices about your life.

You might also find that your friendships have changed. You might not feel as comfortable around married friends, and might gravitate to those who are single or divorced. Do not expect to be ready to date immediately. Some people feel ready within months, while others take years to feel comfortable with the idea.

Most of all, it is important to be patient with yourself. Give yourself time to adjust to the changes in your life and give yourself time to learn to enjoy them. Do not be frustrated if you find divorce has not made you a happy person. It takes a long time to recover from the trauma of an ended marriage. Give yourself space and time to adjust.

HELPING YOUR CHILDREN COPE

Just as finalization of the divorce may not mean sudden happiness for you, your children need time to adjust as well. Kids have a lot to adjust to. They used to have two parents in one home, and now they have two parents in two homes. As the dust settles, probably both you and your former spouse will make some changes in your homes. You might each adjust the rules to suit your own needs, make scheduling changes to your own life and your children's lives, and try new things as part of your newfound freedom. As enlightening as this may be for you, it is confusing and stressful for kids. They need to adjust, not only to the divorce and the idea of viewing their parents as two entirely separate entities, but also to the new rules, the new order of things, and their own emotions.

Learning about an impending divorce brings one traumatic moment in a child's life, but actually living with the changes a divorce creates brings a more long-term change. Make yourself available to your child to listen, and when appropriate, offer support and advice. Some days things will go smoothly, some days your child will prefer one parent over another, and some days he or she will resent both of you. Be patient and give your child time to adjust.

Seek professional help for your child if he or she:

- ✪ is withdrawn for long periods;

- ✪ hurts or talks about hurting him- or herself or others;

- ✪ has difficulty eating or sleeping on a regular basis;

- ✪ regresses in a noticeable and long-term manner;

- ✪ is often extremely angry;

- ✪ refuses to communicate on a regular basis;

- ✪ has continual difficulty in school;

- ✪ has difficulty making or keeping friends; or,

- ✪ does anything else that seriously concerns you.

Your pediatrician can recommend a counselor or therapist.

The best thing you can do for your child is help him or her accept this new reality. Make small adjustments to visitation schedules, extracurricular activities, and house rules if they help him or her cope with things. Reinforce that both you and your former spouse love your child, and that both are a part of his or her life. Make it clear that you will always love your child no matter what. Many children hope their parents will be reconciled. You should be honest in saying that this will probably not happen.

Make the most of the good times, emphasize the positive aspects of your new life, and be patient.

COPING AS A SINGLE PARENT

Whether you have residential custody of your child, or you can only see your child at set access times, you will now be functioning as a single parent. Most married couples divide responsibilities between them, so that one parent might have always done bath time, while the other parent always did bedtime. Now you are solely responsible for everything involving your child at your home.

The biggest adjustment is that there is no downtime. You are on call twenty-four hours a day every day your child is with you. Learn to rely on family members and friends for help if you need it. You cannot do everything all the time, and it is fine to accept help. It is also perfectly acceptable to call upon the other parent. Many parents try to offer each other first right of refusal as a babysitter when needed.

You should expect criticisms and complaints from your child, such as, "Daddy doesn't do it like this" or "Mommy never makes us do this." You are in charge in your household, and while it is usually best if the rules in both households remain similar, you have the final say in your home.

A single-parent household can seem frantic and crazy at times. Not only do you need to manage your own life and schedule, but when your children are with you, you need to manage them as well, without input or assistance from anyone. Do not expect to be perfect, and do not blame yourself when things go wrong. Things were not perfect when you all lived under one roof, so it is not reasonable to expect things to be perfect after the family has split.

SURVIVING FINANCIALLY

Financial difficulties may occur in the aftermath of divorce. Somehow, the income you and your former spouse shared during marriage must now support two separate homes. You probably also have legal bills to pay. You might have additional expenses, such as moving or purchasing new furniture.

The first thing to do is to create a budget. Determine how much money you have coming in on a weekly or monthly basis. Then create a list of your monthly expenses. If your monthly expenses are larger than your income, you need to decide whether you will cut expenses or increase your income. If you are in the position of having more income than expenses, set up a plan that will allow you to save money for things like retirement, college expenses, vacations, and large purchases.

It takes a while to adjust to living on the income available to you after divorce, but within a few months you should feel more certain about what you have coming in and what you have available to spend.

MODIFYING YOUR JUDGMENT OF DIVORCE

You may find after a few years that the parenting arrangement ordered by the court does not work as smoothly as it should. Your children will get older, and both parents' schedules will change. You and the other parent are always able to make changes to the schedule upon which you mutually agree. If you make minor changes, there is little reason to go back to court to get things formally changed. However, if you agree to make major changes or if one of you wants some major changes made and the other does not agree, you will either need to return to court or use a mediator to help you resolve the issues.

If you do return to court, check your judgment of divorce. Many judges put in a requirement that you return to Supreme Court if you are seeking a modification within eighteen months of the divorce. Otherwise, you can go to Family Court and seek a modification there. The Family Court staff can help you file the necessary papers or you can check the list of resources in Appendix A for books and websites that can provide you with the forms you need. Be aware that custody and visitation orders can only be modified if there has been a significant change in circumstances since the **Judgment of Divorce** was made. Examples might include one parent moving out of state, a parent mistreating the child, a change in the parents' work schedules, or a change in the child's needs.

If your child support is paid through the state, rather than directly from one parent to the other, it will automatically be reviewed every two years and increased to meet inflation. You can also seek to have it increased or decreased at any time if you have a very good reason (for example, if you pay child support and have lost your job, or if you receive child support and your child has new needs that require extra expenses). Go to Family Court to file modification papers for child support.

If you worked with an attorney on your divorce, you can go back to him or her to help you resolve modification problems, or you can choose to handle the case on your own.

Glossary

A

abandonment. Legal reason for a divorce in New York; occurs when a spouse has abandoned another for at least one year.

access. Another word for parenting plan, or custody and visitation.

adultery. Legal reason for divorce in New York; consists of having sexual intercourse with someone other than one's spouse during the marriage.

affidavit. Document in which you state facts for the court and swear that they are true.

alimony. *See maintenance.*

annulment. Declaration by a court that a marriage was void at the time it was created and is not legal.

Appellate Division. The court to which Supreme Court cases are appealed in New York.

arbitration. An alternative dispute resolution method available only in one area of New York. A court-approved evaluator hears both sides of the case and makes a recommendation as to which side would likely win in court.

attorney grievance committee. Committee of volunteer lawyers that hears complaints filed by clients against attorneys.

B

bailiff. Court official who calls cases and keeps order in the courtroom.

C

child support. Amount paid by a parent to financially support a child.

collaborative law. Process in which attorneys work together to reach a settlement in a case.

contested divorce. Divorce in which both parties appear in court and ask the court for different things.

Court of Appeals. The highest court in New York.

court reporter. Person who creates a written transcript of what is said in court.

cruel and inhuman treatment. Legal reason for divorce in New York. It happens when a spouse treats the other in such a way (physically or mentally) as to make it unsafe or improper for them to live together.

custody. Legal residency and control of children.

D

decree. Judgment from a court.

defendant. Spouse who did not file for divorce.

F

family courts. Courts in New York that hear custody, visitation, and support cases for couples not currently in a divorce case.

fee conciliation committee. Program of a local bar association that helps clients work out fee (payment) problems with their attorneys.

G

grounds. Legal reasons for divorce in New York.

I

in camera interview. Private talk between the judge and the child in a custody case.

J

judgment. Final decision by a court in a case.

judgment of separation. Decision by a court that a couple should live apart.

L

law clerk. Attorney who works as an assistant to the judge.

law guardian. Attorney appointed by the court to represent a child in a matrimonial or custody case.

legal custody. Refers to how the parents share decision-making authority over their child.

M

maintenance. Spousal support.

matrimonial referee. Attorney that hears uncontested divorce cases.

mediation. Process in which a neutral third party helps a couple reach a resolution to their case.

mediator. A neutral third party who facilitates mediation.

memorandum of understanding. Agreement prepared by a non-attorney mediator that resolves all the issues discussed in mediation. It is used to prepare the separation agreement.

modify. To change a court order after it is issued.

motion. Formal request to the court.

O

order. Decision by a judge, similar to a judgment.

P

paralegal. Trained professional who assists an attorney with legal paperwork.

parental access/parenting time. How parents share time with their children.

parenting plan. Division of how parents will share their time with their children.

parties. People in a divorce case.

physical custody. Refers to where the child of divorced parents primarily lives.

plaintiff. Spouse who files for or asks for the divorce.

prenuptial agreement. An agreement signed before marriage, determining how property will be divided should the couple divorce.

pro se. Term for a person who is representing him- or herself in court.

R

residency requirements. New York's statute that requires people to have some kind of residency in the state before filing for divorce.

residential custody. *See physical custody.*

S

separation agreement. An agreement between two parties that explains how they will divide their assets and debts and share time with their children. It can be converted to a divorce after one year.

settlement. Agreement between the parties about how they are going to end a case without the court making a decision.

shared custody. Equal division of time between the parents with regard to time spent with their child.

shuttle mediation. Mediation that is done with the parties in separate rooms and with the mediator going back and forth between them.

spousal support. Amount paid by one spouse to financially support the other.

subpoena. Document issued by an attorney or court, compelling a witness to come to court or to release certain documents.

supervised visitation. Parental access that is monitored or supervised by someone else.

Supreme Courts. Courts in New York that hear divorce cases.

T

temporary order. Court order made by a judge that is meant to last only while the whole case is being decided.

transcript. Written record of what is said in court.

U

uncontested divorce. Divorce in which only one party appears in court.

Resources

This appendix contains additional resource information to assist the reader with specific areas of concern.

BOOKS

Child Custody, Visitation and Support in New York, by Brette McWhorter Sember

The Divorced Dad's Survival Book, by Knox and Leggett

Helping Children Survive Divorce, by Archibald Hart

How to Parent With Your Ex: Working Together for Your Child's Best Interest, by Brette McWhorter Sember

Live Away Dads, by William C. Klatt

No-Fight Divorce: Spend Less Money, Save Time, and Avoid Conflicts Using Mediation, by Brette McWhorter Sember

HOTLINES

New York State Child Abuse Hotline:
800-342-3720

MAGAZINES

Divorce Magazine
www.divorcemag.com

ORGANIZATIONS

Catholic Annulment
Canon Law Society of America
431 Caldwell Hall
Catholic University
Washington, DC 20064
202-269-3491
www.clsa.org

Lawyers and Legal Aid and Assistance

New York State Bar Association Lawyer Referral and Information Service
800-342-3661
www.nysba.org

Mediation

Family & Divorce Mediation Council of Greater New York (NYC area)
114 West 47th Street
Suite 2200
New York, NY 10036
212-978-8590
www.fdmcgny.org

New York State Council on Divorce Mediation (statewide)
585 Stewart Avenue
Suite 610
Garden City, N.Y. 11530
800-894-2646
www.nysmediate.org

Mental Health

American Association for Marriage and Family Therapy
112 South Alfred Street
Alexandria, VA 22314
703-838-9808
www.aamft.org

New York State Counseling Association
PO Box 12636
Albany, New York 12212
877-692-2462
www.nycounseling.org

New York State Psychological Association
6 Executive Park Drive
Albany, NY 12203
800-732-3933
www.nyspa.org

WEBSITES

Attorney Information
www.nysba.org

Child Support

Child Support Services Home Page
https://newyorkchildsupport.
com/home.html

Child Support Guidelines Chart
https://newyorkchildsupport.
com/child_support_
standards.html

Collaborative Law
www.divorcenet.com/ca/
cafaq10.html

Custody
www.childcustodyattorney.com/
newyorkchildcustody.htm

Legal Aid Agencies
www.lawhelp.org/ny

Family Court
www.nycourts.gov/forms/
familycourt/index.shtml

Forms

Electronic Filing Forms
https://iapps.courts.state.ny.us/
caseTrac/jsp/ecourt.htm

New York State Divorce Forms
www.courts.state.ny.us/
litigants/divorce/index.shtml

New York State Family Court forms
www.nycourts.gov/forms/
familycourt/index.shtml

Legal Research

List of New York State Public Access Law Libraries
www.courts.state.ny.us/
pubacc.html

New York Case Law
www.findlaw.com/11stategov/ny/
laws.html

www.law.cornell.edu/ny/ctap

New York Statutes
http://caselaw.lp.findlaw.com/
nycodes/index.html
http://public.leginfo.state.ny.
us/menugetf.cgi?COMMON
QUERY=LAWS

Mediation
www.courts.state.ny.us/ip/adr/
index.shtml

Process Servers

United States Process Servers Association Online Directory
www.usprocessservers.com

Religious Annulment

Catholic
www.ultimatewedding.com

www.clsa.org

Jewish

www.beliefnet.com/story/75/
story_7563_1.html

www.jlaw.com/Articles/
divorcebeit.html

Supreme Court Locations

www.courts.state.ny.us/
courthelp/cfacts1.html

New York Statutes

This appendix contains portions of the New York Domestic Relations Law. You will note that the legislature has not been consistent in its designation of subsections. For example, in Section 170, the subsections are designated (1), (2), (3), etc., while in Section 170-a, the subsections are a, b, c, etc.

The material has been edited to provide the most commonly needed sections. For additional information, or the complete text of the statutes, visit your local law library.

Domestic Relations Law
Article 10 - ACTION FOR DIVORCE
§170. Action for divorce.
An action for divorce may be maintained by a husband or wife to procure a judgment divorcing the parties and dissolving the marriage on any of the following grounds: (1) The cruel and inhuman treatment of the plaintiff by the defendant such that the conduct of the defendant so endangers the physical or mental well being of the plaintiff as renders it unsafe or improper for the plaintiff to cohabit with the defendant. (2) The abandonment of the plaintiff by the defendant for a period of one or more years. (3) The confinement of the defendant in prison for a period of three or more consecutive years after the marriage of plaintiff and defendant. (4) The commission of an act of adultery, provided that adultery for the purposes of articles ten, eleven, and eleven-A of this chapter, is hereby defined as the commission of an act of sexual intercourse, oral sexual conduct or anal sexual conduct, voluntarily performed by the defendant, with a person other than the plaintiff after the marriage of plaintiff and defendant. Oral sexual conduct and anal sexual conduct include, but are not limited to, sexual conduct as defined in subdivision two of section 130.00 and subdivision three of section 130.20 of the penal law. (5) The husband and wife have lived apart pursuant to a decree or judgment of separation for a period of one or more years after the granting of such decree or judgment, and satisfactory proof has been submitted by the plaintiff that he or she has substantially performed all the terms and conditions of such decree or judgment. (6) The husband and wife have lived separate and apart pursuant to a written agreement of separation, subscribed by the parties thereto and acknowledged or proved in the form required to entitle a deed to be recorded, for a period of one or more years after the execution of such agreement and satisfactory proof has been submitted by the plaintiff that he or she has substantially performed all the terms and conditions of such agreement. Such agreement shall be filed in the office of the clerk of the county wherein either party resides. In lieu of filing such agreement, either party to such agreement may file a memorandum of such agree

ment, which memorandum shall be similarly subscribed and acknowledged or proved as was the agreement of separation and shall contain the following information: (a) the names and addresses of each of the parties, (b) the date of marriage of the parties, (c) the date of the agreement of separation and (d) the date of this subscription and acknowledgment or proof of such agreement of separation.

§170-a. Special action.

a. A spouse against whom a decree of divorce has been obtained under the provisions of subdivision five or six of section one hundred seventy of this chapter, where the decree, judgment or agreement of separation was obtained or entered into prior to January twenty-first, nineteen hundred seventy, may institute an action in which there shall be recoverable, in addition to any rights under this or any other provisions of law, an amount equivalent to the value of any economic and property rights of which the spouse was deprived by virtue of such decree, except where the grounds for the separation judgment would have excluded recovery of economic and property rights. b. In determining the value of the economic and property rights described in subdivision a hereof, the plaintiff's interest shall be calculated as though the defendant died intestate and as if the death of the defendant had immediately antedated the divorce. c. If the defendant shall establish that intervening circumstances have rendered an award described in subdivision a hereof inequitable, the court may award to the plaintiff such portion of such economic and property rights as justice may require. d. If the defendant shall establish that the plaintiff has expressly or impliedly waived all or some portion of the aforesaid economic or property rights, the court shall deny recovery of all such rights, or deny recovery of the portion of such rights as justice may require. e. Actions under this subdivision may be brought: (i) Within two years of the enactment of this section, or (ii) Within two years of the obtainment of the subject divorce, whichever is later.

§171. When divorce denied, although adultery proved.

In either of the following cases, the plaintiff is not entitled to a divorce, although the adultery is established: 1. Where the offense was committed by the procurement or with the connivance of the plaintiff. 2. Where the offense charged has been forgiven by the plaintiff. The forgiveness may be proven, either affirmatively, or by the voluntary cohabitation of the parties with the knowledge of the fact. 3. Where there has been no express forgiveness, and no voluntary cohabitation of the parties, but the action was not commenced within five years after the discovery by the plaintiff of the offense charged. 4. Where the plaintiff has also been guilty of adultery under such circumstances that the defendant would have been entitled, if innocent, to a divorce.

§172. Co-respondent as party.

1. In an action brought to obtain a divorce on the ground of adultery the plaintiff or defendant may serve a copy of his pleading on a co-respondent named therein. At any time within twenty days after such service, the co-respondent may appear to defend such action so far as the issues affect him. If no such service be made, then at any time before the entry of judgment a co-respondent named in any of the pleadings may make a written demand on any party for a copy of a summons and a pleading served by such party, which must be served within ten days thereafter, and he may appear to defend such action so far as the issues affect him. 2. In an action for divorce where a co-respondent has appeared and defended, in case no one of the allegations of adultery controverted by such co-respondent shall be proven, such co-respondent shall be entitled to a bill of costs against the person naming him as such co-respondent, which bill of costs shall consist only of the sum now allowed by law as a trial fee, and disbursements.

§173. Jury trial.

In an action for divorce there is a right to trial by jury of the issues of the grounds for granting the divorce.

Article 11 - ACTION FOR SEPARATION
§200. Action for separation.

An action may be maintained by a husband or wife against the other party to the marriage to procure a judgment separating the parties from bed and board, forever, or for a limited time, for any of the following causes: 1. The cruel and inhuman treatment of the plaintiff by the defendant such that the conduct of the defendant so endangers the physical or mental well being of the plaintiff as renders it unsafe or improper for the plaintiff to cohabit with the defendant. 2. The abandonment of the plaintiff by the defendant. 3. The neglect or refusal of the defendant-spouse to provide for the support of the plaintiff-spouse where the defendant-spouse is chargeable with such support under the provisions of section thirty-two of this chapter or of section four hundred twelve of the family court act. 4. The commission of an act of adultery by the defendant; except where such offense is committed by the procurement or with the connivance of the plaintiff or where there is voluntary cohabitation of the parties with the knowledge of the offense or where action was not commenced within five years after the discovery by the plaintiff of the offense charged or where the plaintiff has also been guilty of adultery under such circumstances that the defendant would have been entitled, if innocent, to a divorce, provided that adultery for the purposes of this subdivision is hereby defined as the commission of an act of sexual intercourse, oral sexual conduct or anal sexual conduct, voluntarily performed by the defendant, with a person other than the plaintiff after the marriage of plaintiff and defendant. Oral sexual conduct and anal sexual conduct include, but are not limited to, sexual conduct as defined in subdivision two of section 130.00 and subdivision three of section 130.20 of the penal law. 5. The confinement of the defendant in prison for a period of three or more consecutive years after the marriage of plaintiff and defendant.

Article 11-A - SPECIAL PROVISIONS RELATING TO DIVORCE AND SEPARATION
§210. Limitations on actions for divorce and separation.

No action for divorce or separation may be maintained on a ground which arose more than five years before the date of the commencement of that action for divorce or separation except where: (a) In an action for divorce, the grounds therefor are one of those specified in subdivision (2), (4), (5) or (6) of section one hundred seventy of this chapter, or (b) In an action for separation, the grounds therefor are one of those specified in subdivision 2 or 4 of section two hundred of this chapter.

§211. Pleadings, proof and motions.

A matrimonial action shall be commenced by the filing of a summons with the notice designated in section two hundred thirty-two of this chapter, or a summons and verified complaint as provided in section three hundred four of the civil practice law and rules. A final judgment shall be entered by default for want of appearance or pleading, or by consent, only upon competent oral proof or upon written proof that may be considered on a motion for summary judgment. Where a complaint or counterclaim in an action for divorce or separation charges adultery, the answer or reply thereto may be made without verifying it, except that an answer containing a counterclaim must be verified as to that counterclaim. All other pleadings in a matrimonial action shall be verified.

Article 12 - DISSOLUTION OF MARRIAGE ON GROUND OF ABSENCE
§220. Special proceeding to dissolve marriage on the ground of absence.

A special proceeding to dissolve a marriage on the ground of absence may be maintained in either of the following cases: 1. Where the petitioner is a resident of this state and has been a resident thereof for one year immediately preceding the commencement of the special proceeding. 2. Where the matrimonial domicile at the time of the disappearance of the absent spouse was within the state.

§221. Procedure.
The petition shall allege that the husband or wife of such party has absented himself or herself for five successive years then last past without being known to such party to be living during that time; that such party believes such husband or wife to be dead; and that a diligent search has been made to discover evidence showing that such husband or wife is living, and no such evidence has been found. The court shall thereupon by order require notice of the presentation and object of such petition to be published in a newspaper in the English language designated in the order as most likely to give notice to such absent husband or wife once each week for three successive weeks; such notice shall be directed to the husband or wife who has so absented himself or herself and shall state the time and place of the hearing upon such petition, which time shall be not less than forty days after the completion of the publication of such notice; said notice must be subscribed with the name of the petitioner and with the name of the petitioner's attorney and with his office address, specifying a place within the state where there is a post-office. If in a city, said notice must also set forth the street and street number, if any, of such attorney's office address or other suitable designation of the particular locality in which said office address is located. In addition to the foregoing requirements said notice must be in substantially the following form, the blanks being properly filled: "Supreme court, _____.county. In the matter of the application of_____..for dissolution of his or her marriage with _____ To_____: Take notice that a petition has been presented to this court by_____, your husband or wife, for the dissolution of your marriage on the ground that you have absented yourself for five successive years last past without being known to him or her to be living and that he or she believes you to be dead, and that pursuant to an order of said court, entered the _____day of _____, 20___, a hearing will be had upon said petition at the said supreme court, _____.term part_____., in the _____.county court house, in the_____ state of New York, on the _____.day of _____, 20___, at _____ o'clock in the _____ noon. Dated_____;" and if the court, after the filing of proof of the proper publication of said notice and after a hearing and proof taken, is satisfied of the truth of all the allegations contained in the petition, it may make a final order dissolving such marriage.

Article 13 - PROVISIONS APPLICABLE TO MORE THAN ONE TYPE OF MATRIMONIAL ACTION
§230. Required residence of parties.
An action to annul a marriage, or to declare the nullity of a void marriage, or for divorce or separation may be maintained only when: 1. The parties were married in the state and either party is a resident thereof when the action is commenced and has been a resident for a continuous period of one year immediately preceding, or 2. The parties have resided in this state as husband and wife and either party is a resident thereof when the action is commenced and has been a resident for a continuous period of one year immediately preceding, or 3. The cause occurred in the state and either party has been a resident thereof for a continuous period of at least one year immediately preceding the commencement of the action, or 4. The cause occurred in the state and both parties are residents thereof at the time of the commencement of the action, or 5. Either party has been a resident of the state for a continuous period of at least two years immediately preceding the commencement of the action.

§231. Residence of married persons.
If a married person dwells within the state when he or she commences an action against his or her spouse for divorce, annulment or separation, such person is deemed a resident thereof, although his or her spouse resides elsewhere.

§232. Notice of nature of matrimonial action; proof of service.
a. In an action to annul a marriage or for divorce or for separation, if the complaint is not personally served with the summons, the summons shall have legibly written or printed upon the face thereof: "Action to annul a marriage", "Action to declare the nullity of a void marriage", "Action for a divorce", or "Action for a separation", as the case may be, and shall specify the nature of any ancillary relief demanded. A judgment shall not be rendered in favor of the plaintiff upon the defendant's default in appearing or pleading, unless either (1) the summons and a copy of the complaint were personally delivered to the defendant; or (2) the copy of the summons (a) personally delivered to the defendant, or (b) served on the defendant pursuant to an order directing the method of service of the summons in accordance with the provisions of section three hundred eight or three hundred fifteen of the civil practice law and rules, shall contain such notice. b. An affidavit or certificate proving service shall state affirmatively in the body thereof that the required notice was written or printed on the face of the copy of the summons delivered to the defendant and what knowledge the affiant or officer who executed the certificate had that he was the defendant named and how he acquired such knowledge. The court may require the affiant or officer who executed the affidavit or certificate to appear in court and be examined in respect thereto.

§234. Title to or occupancy and possession of property.
In any action for divorce, for a separation, for an annulment or to declare the nullity of a void marriage, the court may (1) determine any question as to the title to property arising between the parties, and (2) make such direction, between the parties, concerning the possession of property, as in the court's discretion justice requires having regard to the circumstances of the case and of the respective parties. Such direction may be made in the final judgment, or by one or more orders from time to time before or subsequent to final judgment, or by both such order or orders and final judgment. Where the title to real property is affected, a copy of such judgment, order or decree, duly certified by the clerk of the court wherein said judgement was rendered, shall be recorded in the office of the recording officer of the county in which such property is situated, as provided by section two hundred ninety-seven-b of the real property law.

§235. Information as to details of matrimonial actions or proceedings.
1. An officer of the court with whom the proceedings in a matrimonial action or a written agreement of separation or an action or proceeding for custody, visitation or maintenance of a child are filed, or before whom the testimony is taken, or his clerk, either before or after the termination of the suit, shall not permit a copy of any of the pleadings, affidavits, findings of fact, conclusions of law, judgment of dissolution, written agreement of separation or memorandum thereof, or testimony, or any examination or perusal thereof, to be taken by any other person than a party, or the attorney or counsel of a party, except by order of the court. 2. If the evidence on the trial of such an action or proceeding be such that public interest requires that the examination of the witnesses should not be public, the court or referee may exclude all persons from the room except the parties to the action and their counsel, and in such case may order the evidence, when filed with the clerk, sealed up, to be exhibited only to the parties to the action or proceeding or someone interested, on order of the court. 3. Upon the application of any person to the county clerk or other officer in charge of public records within a county for evidence of the disposition, judgment or order with respect to a matrimonial action, the clerk or other such officer shall issue a "certificate of disposition", duly certifying the nature and effect of such disposition, judgment or order and shall in no manner evidence the subject matter of the pleadings, testimony, findings of fact, conclusions of law or judgment of dissolution derived in any such action. 4. Any county, city, town or village clerk or other municipal official issuing marriage

licenses shall be required to accept, as evidence of dissolution of marriage, such "certificate of disposition" in lieu of a complete copy of the findings of fact, conclusions of law and judgment of dissolution. 5. The limitations of subdivisions one, two and three of this section in relation to confidentiality shall cease to apply one hundred years after date of filing, and such records shall thereupon be public records available to public inspection.

§236.

PART B

NEW ACTIONS OR PROCEEDINGS

Maintenance and distributive award.

1. Definitions. Whenever used in this part, the following terms shall have the respective meanings hereinafter set forth or indicated: a. The term "maintenance" shall mean payments provided for in a valid agreement between the parties or awarded by the court in accordance with the provisions of subdivision six of this part, to be paid at fixed intervals for a definite or indefinite period of time, but an award of maintenance shall terminate upon the death of either party or upon the recipient's valid or invalid marriage, or upon modification pursuant to paragraph (b) of subdivision nine of section two hundred thirty-six of this part or section two hundred forty-eight of this chapter. b. The term "distributive award" shall mean payments provided for in a valid agreement between the parties or awarded by the court, in lieu of or to supplement, facilitate or effectuate the division or distribution of property where authorized in a matrimonial action, and payable either in a lump sum or over a period of time in fixed amounts. Distributive awards shall not include payments which are treated as ordinary income to the recipient under the provisions of the United States Internal Revenue Code. c. The term "marital property" shall mean all property acquired by either or both spouses during the marriage and before the execution of a separation agreement or the commencement of a matrimonial action, regardless of the form in which title is held, except as otherwise provided in agreement pursuant to subdivision three of this part. Marital property shall not include separate property as hereinafter defined. d. The term separate property shall mean: (1) property acquired before marriage or property acquired by bequest, devise, or descent, or gift from a party other than the spouse; (2) compensation for personal injuries; (3) property acquired in exchange for or the increase in value of separate property, except to the extent that such appreciation is due in part to the contributions or efforts of the other spouse; (4) property described as separate property by written agreement of the parties pursuant to subdivision three of this part. e. The term "custodial parent" shall mean a parent to whom custody of a child or children is granted by a valid agreement between the parties or by an order or decree of a court. f. The term "child support" shall mean a sum paid pursuant to court order or decree by either or both parents or pursuant to a valid agreement between the parties for care, maintenance and education of any unemancipated child under the age of twenty-one years. 2. Matrimonial actions. Except as provided in subdivision five of this part, the provisions of this part shall be applicable to actions for an annulment or dissolution of a marriage, for a divorce, for a separation, for a declaration of the nullity of a void marriage, for a declaration of the validity or nullity of a foreign judgment of divorce, for a declaration of the validity or nullity of a marriage, and to proceedings to obtain maintenance or a distribution of marital property following a foreign judgment of divorce, commenced on and after the effective date of this part. Any application which seeks a modification of a judgment, order or decree made in an action commenced prior to the effective date of this part shall be heard and determined in accordance with the provisions of part A of this section. 3. Agreement of the parties. An agreement by the parties, made before or during the marriage, shall be valid and enforceable in a matrimonial action if such agreement is in writing, subscribed by the parties, and acknowledged or proven in the manner required to entitle a deed to be recorded.

Notwithstanding any other provision of law, an acknowledgment of an agreement made before marriage may be executed before any person authorized to solemnize a marriage pursuant to subdivisions one, two and three of section eleven of this chapter. Such an agreement may include (1) a contract to make a testamentary provision of any kind, or a waiver of any right to elect against the provisions of a will; (2) provision for the ownership, division or distribution of separate and marital property; (3) provision for the amount and duration of maintenance or other terms and conditions of the marriage relationship, subject to the provisions of section 5-311 of the general obligations law, and provided that such terms were fair and reasonable at the time of the making of the agreement and are not unconscionable at the time of entry of final judgment; and (4) provision for the custody, care, education and maintenance of any child of the parties, subject to the provisions of section two hundred forty of this article. Nothing in this subdivision shall be deemed to affect the validity of any agreement made prior to the effective date of this subdivision. 4. Compulsory financial disclosure. a. In all matrimonial actions and proceedings in which alimony, maintenance or support is in issue, there shall be compulsory disclosure by both parties of their respective financial states. No showing of special circumstances shall be required before such disclosure is ordered. A sworn statement of net worth shall be provided upon receipt of a notice in writing demanding the same, within twenty days after the receipt thereof. In the event said statement is not demanded, it shall be filed with the clerk of the court by each party, within ten days after joinder of issue, in the court in which the proceeding is pending. As used in this part, the term "net worth" shall mean the amount by which total assets including income exceed total liabilities including fixed financial obligations. It shall include all income and assets of whatsoever kind and nature and wherever situated and shall include a list of all assets transferred in any manner during the preceding three years, or the length of the marriage, whichever is shorter; provided, however that transfers in the routine course of business which resulted in an exchange of assets of substantially equivalent value need not be specifically disclosed where such assets are otherwise identified in the statement of net worth. All such sworn statements of net worth shall be accompanied by a current and representative paycheck stub and the most recently filed state and federal income tax returns including a copy of the W-2(s) wage and tax statement(s) submitted with the returns. In addition, both parties shall provide information relating to any and all group health plans available to them for the provision of care or other medical benefits by insurance or otherwise for the benefit of the child or children for whom support is sought, including all such information as may be required to be included in a qualified medical child support order as defined in section six hundred nine of the employee retirement income security act of 1974 (29 USC 1169) including, but not limited to: (i) the name and last known mailing address of each party and of each dependent to be covered by the order; (ii) the identification and a description of each group health plan available for the benefit or coverage of the disclosing party and the child or children for whom support is sought; (iii) a detailed description of the type of coverage available from each group health plan for the potential benefit of each such dependent; (iv) the identification of the plan administrator for each such group health plan and the address of such administrator; (v) the identification numbers for each such group health plan; and (vi) such other information as may be required by the court. Noncompliance shall be punishable by any or all of the penalties prescribed in section thirty-one hundred twenty-six of the civil practice law and rules, in examination before or during trial. b. As soon as practicable after a matrimonial action has been commenced, the court shall set the date or dates the parties shall use for the valuation of each asset. The valuation date or dates may be anytime from the date of commencement of the action to the date of trial. 5. Disposition of property in certain matrimonial actions. a. Except where the parties have provided in an agreement for the disposition of their property pursuant to subdivision three of this part, the court, in an action wherein all or part of the relief granted is divorce, or the dissolution, annulment or declaration of the nullity of a marriage, and in proceedings to obtain a distribution of marital property following a foreign judgment of divorce, shall determine the respective rights of the parties in their separate or marital property, and shall provide for the disposition thereof in the final judgment. b. Separate property shall remain such. c. Marital property shall be distributed equitably between the parties, considering the circumstances of the case and of the respective parties. d. In determining an equitable disposition of property under paragraph c, the court shall consider: (1) the income and property of each party at the time of marriage, and at the time of the commencement of the action; (2) the duration of the marriage and the age and health of both parties; (3) the need of a custodial parent to occupy or own the marital residence and to use or own its household effects; (4) the loss of inheritance and pension rights upon dissolution of the marriage as of the date of dissolution; (5) any award of maintenance under subdivision six of this part; (6) any equitable claim to, interest in, or direct or indirect contribution made to the acquisition of such marital property by the party not having title, including joint efforts or expenditures and contributions and services as a spouse, parent, wage earner and homemaker, and to the career or career potential of the other party; (7) the liquid or non-liquid character of all marital property; (8) the probable future financial circumstances of each party; (9) the impossibility or difficulty of evaluating any component asset or any interest in a business, corporation or profession, and the economic desirability of retaining such asset or interest intact and free from any claim or interference by the other party; (10) the tax consequences to each party; (11) the wasteful dissipation of assets by either spouse; (12) any transfer or encumbrance made in contemplation of a matrimonial action without fair consideration; (13) any other factor which the court shall expressly find to be just and proper. e. In any action in which the court shall determine that an equitable distribution is appropriate but would be impractical or burdensome or where the distribution of an interest in a business, corporation or profession would be contrary to law, the court in lieu of such equitable distribution shall make a distributive award in order to achieve equity between the parties. The court in its discretion, also may make a distributive award to supplement, facilitate or effectuate a distribution of marital property. f. In addition to the disposition of property as set forth above, the court may make such order regarding the use and occupancy of the marital home and its household effects as provided in section two hundred thirty-four of this chapter, without regard to the form of ownership of such property. g. In any decision made pursuant to this subdivision, the court shall set forth the factors it considered and the reasons for its decision and such may not be waived by either party or counsel. h. In any decision made pursuant to this subdivision the court shall, where appropriate, consider the effect of a barrier to remarriage, as defined in subdivision six of section two hundred fifty-three of this article, on the factors enumerated in paragraph d of this subdivision. 6. Maintenance. a. Except where the parties have entered into an agreement pursuant to subdivision three of this part providing for maintenance, in any matrimonial action the court may order temporary maintenance or maintenance in such amount as justice requires, having regard for the standard of living of the parties established during the marriage, whether the party in whose favor maintenance is granted lacks sufficient property and income to provide for his or her reasonable needs and whether the other party has sufficient property or income to provide for the reasonable needs of the other and the circumstances of the case and of the respective parties. Such order shall be effective as of the date of the application therefor, and any retroactive amount of maintenance due shall be paid in one sum or periodic sums, as the court shall direct, taking into account any amount of temporary maintenance which has been paid. In deter-

mining the amount and duration of maintenance the court shall consider: (1) the income and property of the respective parties including marital property distributed pursuant to subdivision five of this part; (2) the duration of the marriage and the age and health of both parties; (3) the present and future earning capacity of both parties; (4) the ability of the party seeking maintenance to become self-supporting and, if applicable, the period of time and training necessary therefor; (5) reduced or lost lifetime earning capacity of the party seeking maintenance as a result of having foregone or delayed education, training, employment, or career opportunities during the marriage; (6) the presence of children of the marriage in the respective homes of the parties; (7) the tax consequences to each party; (8) contributions and services of the party seeking maintenance as a spouse, parent, wage earner and homemaker, and to the career or career potential of the other party; (9) the wasteful dissipation of marital property by either spouse; (10) any transfer or encumbrance made in contemplation of a matrimonial action without fair consideration; and (11) any other factor which the court shall expressly find to be just and proper. b. In any decision made pursuant to this subdivision, the court shall set forth the factors it considered and the reasons for its decision and such may not be waived by either party or counsel. c. The court may award permanent maintenance, but an award of maintenance shall terminate upon the death of either party or upon the recipient's valid or invalid marriage, or upon modification pursuant to paragraph (b) of subdivision nine of section two hundred thirty-six of this part or section two hundred forty-eight of this chapter. d. In any decision made pursuant to this subdivision the court shall, where appropriate, consider the effect of a barrier to remarriage, as defined in subdivision six of section two hundred fifty-three of this article, on the factors enumerated in paragraph a of this subdivision. 7. Child support. a. In any matrimonial action, or in an independent action for child support, the court as provided in section two hundred forty of this chapter shall order either or both parents to pay temporary child support or child support without requiring a showing of immediate or emergency need. The court shall make an order for temporary child support notwithstanding that information with respect to income and assets of either or both parents may be unavailable. Where such information is available, the court may make an order for temporary child support pursuant to section two hundred forty of this article. Such order shall, except as provided for herein, be effective as of the date of the application therefor, and any retroactive amount of child support due shall be support arrears/past due support and shall be paid in one sum or periodic sums, as the court shall direct, taking into account any amount of temporary child support which has been paid. In addition, such retroactive child support shall be enforceable in any manner provided by law including, but not limited to, an execution for support enforcement pursuant to subdivision (b) of section fifty-two hundred forty-one of the civil practice law and rules. When a child receiving support is a public assistance recipient, or the order of support is being enforced or is to be enforced pursuant to section one hundred eleven-g of the social services law, the court shall establish the amount of retroactive child support and notify the parties that such amount shall be enforced by the support collection unit pursuant to an execution for support enforcement as provided for in subdivision (b) of section fifty-two hundred forty-one of the civil practice law and rules, or in such periodic payments as would have been authorized had such an execution been issued. In such case, the court shall not direct the schedule of repayment of retroactive support. The court shall not consider the misconduct of either party but shall make its award for child support pursuant to section two hundred forty of this article. b. Notwithstanding any other provision of law, any written application or motion to the court for the establishment of a child support obligation for persons not in receipt of family assistance must contain either a request for child support enforcement services which would authorize the collection of the support obligation by the immediate issuance of an income execution for support enforcement as provided for by this chapter, completed in the manner specified in section one hundred eleven-g of the social services law; or a statement that the applicant has applied for or is in receipt of such services; or a statement that the applicant knows of the availability of such services, has declined them at this time and where support enforcement services pursuant to section one hundred eleven-g of the social services law have been declined that the applicant understands that an income deduction order may be issued pursuant to subdivision (c) of section five thousand two hundred forty-two of the civil practice law and rules without other child support enforcement services and that payment of an administrative fee may be required. The court shall provide a copy of any such request for child support enforcement services to the support collection unit of the appropriate social services district any time it directs payments to be made to such support collection unit. Additionally, the copy of any such request shall be accompanied by the name, address and social security number of the parties; the date and place of the parties' marriage; the name and date of birth of the child or children; and the name and address of the employers and income payors of the party from whom child support is sought. Unless the party receiving child support has applied for or is receiving such services, the court shall not direct such payments to be made to the support collection unit, as established in section one hundred eleven-h of the social services law. c. The court shall direct that a copy of any child support or combined child and spousal support order issued by the court on or after the first day of October, nineteen hundred ninety-eight, in any proceeding under this section be provided promptly to the state case registry established pursuant to subdivision four-a of section one hundred eleven-b of the social services law. 8. Special relief in matrimonial actions. a. In any matrimonial action the court may order a party to purchase, maintain or assign a policy of insurance providing benefits for health and hospital care and related services for either spouse or children of the marriage not to exceed such period of time as such party shall be obligated to provide maintenance, child support or make payments of a distributive award. The court may also order a party to purchase, maintain or assign a policy of accident insurance or insurance on the life of either spouse, and to designate in the case of life insurance, either spouse or children of the marriage, or in the case of accident insurance, the insured spouse as irrevocable beneficiaries during a period of time fixed by the court. The obligation to provide such insurance shall cease upon the termination of the spouse's duty to provide maintenance, child support or a distributive award. A copy of such order shall be served, by registered mail, on the home office of the insurer specifying the name and mailing address of the spouse or children, provided that failure to so serve the insurer shall not affect the validity of the order. b. In any action where the court has ordered temporary maintenance, maintenance, distributive award or child support, the court may direct that a payment be made directly to the other spouse or a third person for real and personal property and services furnished to the other spouse, or for the rental or mortgage amortization or interest payments, insurances, taxes, repairs or other carrying charges on premises occupied by the other spouse, or for both payments to the other spouse and to such third persons. Such direction may be made notwithstanding that the parties continue to reside in the same abode and notwithstanding that the court refuses to grant the relief requested by the other spouse. c. Any order or judgment made as in this section provided may combine any amount payable to either spouse under this section with any amount payable to such spouse as child support or under section two hundred forty of this chapter.

§237. Counsel fees and expenses.

(a) In any action or proceeding brought (1) to annul a marriage or to declare the nullity of a void marriage, or (2) for a separation, or (3) for a divorce, or (4) to declare the validity or nullity of a judgment of divorce rendered against a spouse who was the defendant

in any action outside the State of New York and did not appear therein where such spouse asserts the nullity of such foreign judgment, or (5) to enjoin the prosecution in any other jurisdiction of an action for a divorce, the court may direct either spouse or, where an action for annulment is maintained after the death of a spouse, may direct the person or persons maintaining the action, to pay such sum or sums of money directly to the attorney of the other spouse to enable that spouse to carry on or defend the action or proceeding as, in the court's discretion, justice requires, having regard to the circumstances of the case and of the respective parties. Such direction must be made in the final judgment in such action or proceeding, or by one or more orders from time to time before final judgment, or by both such order or orders and the final judgment; provided, however, such direction shall be made prior to final judgment where it is shown that such order is required to enable the petitioning party to properly proceed. Any applications for counsel fees and expenses may be maintained by the attorney for either spouse in his own name in the same proceeding. (b) Upon any application to annul or modify an order or judgment for alimony or for custody, visitation, or maintenance of a child, made as in section two hundred thirty-six or section two hundred forty provided, or upon any application by writ of habeas corpus or by petition and order to show cause concerning custody, visitation or maintenance of a child, the court may direct a spouse or parent to pay such sum or sums of money for the prosecution or the defense of the application or proceeding by the other spouse or parent as, in the court's discretion, justice requires, having regard to the circumstances of the case and of the respective parties. With respect to any such application or proceeding, such direction may be made in the order or judgment by which the particular application or proceeding is finally determined, or by one or more orders from time to time before the final order or judgment, or by both such order or orders and the final order or judgment. Any applications for counsel fees and expenses may be maintained by the attorney for either spouse in counsel's own name in the same proceeding. Representation by an attorney pursuant to paragraph (b) of subdivision nine of section one hundred eleven-b of the social services law shall not preclude an award of counsel fees to an applicant which would otherwise be allowed under this section. (c) In any action or proceeding for failure to obey any lawful order compelling payment of support or maintenance, or distributive award the court shall, upon a finding that such failure was willful, order respondent to pay counsel fees to the attorney representing the petitioner. (d) The term "expenses" as used in subdivisions (a) and (b) of this section shall include, but shall not be limited to, accountant fees, appraisal fees, actuarial fees, investigative fees and other fees and expenses that the court may determine to be necessary to enable a spouse to carry on or defend an action or proceeding under this section. In determining the appropriateness and necessity of fees, the court shall consider: 1. The nature of the marital property involved; 2. The difficulties involved, if any, in identifying and evaluating the marital property; 3. The services rendered and an estimate of the time involved; and 4. The applicant's financial status.

§240. Custody and child support; orders of protection.

1. (a) In any action or proceeding brought (1) to annul a marriage or to declare the nullity of a void marriage, or (2) for a separation, or (3) for a divorce, or (4) to obtain, by a writ of habeas corpus or by petition and order to show cause, the custody of or right to visitation with any child of a marriage, the court shall require verification of the status of any child of the marriage with respect to such child's custody and support, including any prior orders, and shall enter orders for custody and support as, in the court's discretion, justice requires, having regard to the circumstances of the case and of the respective parties and to the best interests of the child and subject to the provisions of subdivision one-c of this section. Where either party to an action concerning custody of or a right to visitation with a child alleges in a sworn petition or com-

plaint or sworn answer, cross-petition, counterclaim or other sworn responsive pleading that the other party has committed an act of domestic violence against the party making the allegation or a family or household member of either party, as such family or household member is defined in article eight of the family court act, and such allegations are proven by a preponderance of the evidence, the court must consider the effect of such domestic violence upon the best interests of the child, together with such other facts and circumstances as the court deems relevant in making a direction pursuant to this section. An order directing the payment of child support shall contain the social security numbers of the named parties. In all cases there shall be no prima facie right to the custody of the child in either parent. Such direction shall make provision for child support out of the property of either or both parents. The court shall make its award for child support pursuant to subdivision one-b of this section. Such direction may provide for reasonable visitation rights to the maternal and/or paternal grandparents of any child of the parties. Such direction as it applies to rights of visitation with a child remanded or placed in the care of a person, official, agency or institution pursuant to article ten of the family court act, or pursuant to an instrument approved under section three hundred fifty-eight-a of the social services law, shall be enforceable pursuant to part eight of article ten of the family court act and sections three hundred fifty-eight-a and three hundred eighty-four-a of the social services law and other applicable provisions of law against any person having care and custody, or temporary care and custody, of the child. Notwithstanding any other provision of law, any written application or motion to the court for the establishment, modification or enforcement of a child support obligation for persons not in receipt of public assistance and care must contain either a request for child support enforcement services which would authorize the collection of the support obligation by the immediate issuance of an income execution for support enforcement as provided for by this chapter, completed in the manner specified in section one hundred eleven-g of the social services law; or a statement that the applicant has applied for or is in receipt of such services; or a statement that the applicant knows of the availability of such services, has declined them at this time and where support enforcement services pursuant to section one hundred eleven-g of the social services law have been declined that the applicant understands that an income deduction order may be issued pursuant to subdivision (c) of section fifty-two hundred forty-two of the civil practice law and rules without other child support enforcement services and that payment of an administrative fee may be required. The court shall provide a copy of any such request for child support enforcement services to the support collection unit of the appropriate social services district any time it directs payments to be made to such support collection unit. Additionally, the copy of any such request shall be accompanied by the name, address and social security number of the parties; the date and place of the parties' marriage; the name and date of birth of the child or children; and the name and address of the employers and income payors of the party from whom child support is sought or from the party ordered to pay child support to the other party. Such direction may require the payment of a sum or sums of money either directly to the custodial parent or to third persons for goods or services furnished for such child, or for both payments to the custodial parent and to such third persons; provided, however, that unless the party seeking or receiving child support has applied for or is receiving such services, the court shall not direct such payments to be made to the support collection unit, as established in section one hundred eleven-h of the social services law. Every order directing the payment of support shall require that if either parent currently, or at any time in the future, has health insurance benefits available that may be extended or obtained to cover the child, such parent is required to exercise the option of additional coverage in favor of such child and execute and deliver to such person any forms, notices, documents or instruments necessary to assure timely payment of any health insurance claims for such child.

1-b. (a) The court shall make its award for child support pursuant to the provisions of this subdivision. The court may vary from the amount of the basic child support obligation determined pursuant to paragraph (c) of this subdivision only in accordance with paragraph (f) of this subdivision. (b) For purposes of this subdivision, the following definitions shall be used: (1) "Basic child support obligation" shall mean the sum derived by adding the amounts determined by the application of subparagraphs two and three of paragraph (c) of this subdivision except as increased pursuant to subparagraphs four, five, six and seven of such paragraph. (2) "Child support" shall mean a sum to be paid pursuant to court order or decree by either or both parents or pursuant to a valid agreement between the parties for care, maintenance and education of any unemancipated child under the age of twenty-one years. (3) "Child support percentage" shall mean: (i) seventeen percent of the combined parental income for one child; (ii) twenty-five percent of the combined parental income for two children; (iii) twenty-nine percent of the combined parental income for three children; (iv) thirty-one percent of the combined parental income for four children; and (v) no less than thirty-five percent of the combined parental income for five or more children. (4) "Combined parental income" shall mean the sum of the income of both parents. (5) "Income" shall mean, but shall not be limited to, the sum of the amounts determined by the application of clauses (i), (ii), (iii), (iv), (v) and (vi) of this subparagraph reduced by the amount determined by the application of clause (vii) of this subparagraph: (i) gross (total) income as should have been or should be reported in the most recent federal income tax return. If an individual files his/her federal income tax return as a married person filing jointly, such person shall be required to prepare a form, sworn to under penalty of law, disclosing his/her gross income individually; (ii) to the extent not already included in gross income in clause (i) of this subparagraph, investment income reduced by sums expended in connection with such investment; (iii) to the extent not already included in gross income in clauses (i) and (ii) of this subparagraph, the amount of income or compensation voluntarily deferred and income received, if any, from the following sources: (A) workers' compensation, (B) disability benefits, (C) unemployment insurance benefits, (D) social security benefits, (E) veterans benefits, (F) pensions and retirement benefits, (G) fellowships and stipends, and (H) annuity payments; (iv) at the discretion of the court, the court may attribute or impute income from, such other resources as may be available to the parent, including, but not limited to: (A) non-income producing assets, (B) meals, lodging, memberships, automobiles or other perquisites that are provided as part of compensation for employment to the extent that such perquisites constitute expenditures for personal use, or which expenditures directly or indirectly confer personal economic benefits, (C) fringe benefits provided as part of compensation for employment, and (D) money, goods, or services provided by relatives and friends; (v) an amount imputed as income based upon the parent's former resources or income, if the court determines that a parent has reduced resources or income in order to reduce or avoid the parent's obligation for child support; (vi) to the extent not already included in gross income in clauses (i) and (ii) of this subparagraph, the following self-employment deductions attributable to self-employment carried on by the taxpayer: (A) any depreciation deduction greater than depreciation calculated on a straight-line basis for the purpose of determining business income or investment credits, and (B) entertainment and travel allowances deducted from business income to the extent said allowances reduce personal expenditures; (vii) the following shall be deducted from income prior to applying the provisions of paragraph (c) of this subdivision: (A) unreimbursed employee business expenses except to the extent said expenses reduce personal expenditures, (B) alimony or maintenance actually paid to a spouse not

a party to the instant action pursuant to court order or validly executed written agreement, (C) alimony or maintenance actually paid or to be paid to a spouse that is a party to the instant action pursuant to an existing court order or contained in the order to be entered by the court, or pursuant to a validly executed written agreement, provided the order or agreement provides for a specific adjustment, in accordance with this subdivision, in the amount of child support payable upon the termination of alimony or maintenance to such spouse, (D) child support actually paid pursuant to court order or written agreement on behalf of any child for whom the parent has a legal duty of support and who is not subject to the instant action, (E) public assistance, (F) supplemental security income, (G) New York city or Yonkers income or earnings taxes actually paid, and (H) federal insurance contributions act (FICA) taxes actually paid. (6) "Self-support reserve" shall mean one hundred thirty-five percent of the poverty income guidelines amount for a single person as reported by the federal department of health and human services. For the calendar year nineteen hundred eighty-nine, the self-support reserve shall be eight thousand sixty-five dollars. On March first of each year, the self-support reserve shall be revised to reflect the annual updating of the poverty income guidelines as reported by the federal department of health and human services for a single person household. (c) The amount of the basic child support obligation shall be determined in accordance with the provision of this paragraph: (1) The court shall determine the combined parental income. (2) The court shall multiply the combined parental income up to eighty thousand dollars by the appropriate child support percentage and such amount shall be prorated in the same proportion as each parent's income is to the combined parental income. (3) Where the combined parental income exceeds the dollar amount set forth in subparagraph two of this paragraph, the court shall determine the amount of child support for the amount of the combined parental income in excess of such dollar amount through consideration of the factors set forth in paragraph (f) of this subdivision and/or the child support percentage. (4) Where the custodial parent is working, or receiving elementary or secondary education, or higher education or vocational training which the court determines will lead to employment, and incurs child care expenses as a result thereof, the court shall determine reasonable child care expenses and such child care expenses, where incurred, shall be prorated in the same proportion as each parent's income is to the combined parental income. Each parent's pro rata share of the child care expenses shall be separately stated and added to the sum of subparagraphs two and three of this paragraph. (5) The court shall prorate each parent's share of future reasonable health care expenses of the child not covered by insurance in the same proportion as each parent's income is to the combined parental income. The non-custodial parent's pro rata share of such health care expenses shall be paid in a manner determined by the court, including direct payment to the health care provider. (6) Where the court determines that the custodial parent is seeking work and incurs child care expenses as a result thereof, the court may determine reasonable child care expenses and may apportion the same between the custodial and non-custodial parent. The non-custodial parent's share of such expenses shall be separately stated and paid in a manner determined by the court. (7) Where the court determines, having regard for the circumstances of the case and of the respective parties and in the best interests of the child, and as justice requires, that the present or future provision of post-secondary, private, special, or enriched education for the child is appropriate, the court may award educational expenses. The non-custodial parent shall pay educational expenses, as awarded, in a manner determined by the court, including direct payment to the educational provider. (d) Notwithstanding the provisions of paragraph (c) of this subdivision, where the annual amount of the basic child support obligation would reduce the non-custodial parent's income below the poverty income guidelines amount for a single person as reported by the federal department of health and human services, the basic child support obligation shall be twenty-five dollars per month or the difference between the non-custodial parent's income and the self-support reserve, whichever is greater. Notwithstanding the provisions of paragraph (c) of this subdivision, where the annual amount of the basic child support obligation would reduce the non-custodial parent's income below the self-support reserve but not below the poverty income guidelines amount for a single person as reported by the federal department of health and human services, the basic child support obligation shall be fifty dollars per month or the difference between the non-custodial parent's income and the self-support reserve, whichever is greater. (e) Where a parent is or may be entitled to receive non-recurring payments from extraordinary sources not otherwise considered as income pursuant to this section, including but not limited to: (1) Life insurance policies; (2) Discharges of indebtedness; (3) Recovery of bad debts and delinquency amounts; (4) Gifts and inheritances; and (5) Lottery winnings, the court, in accordance with paragraphs (c), (d) and (f) of this subdivision may allocate a proportion of the same to child support, and such amount shall be paid in a manner determined by the court. (f) The court shall calculate the basic child support obligation, and the non-custodial parent's pro rata share of the basic child support obligation. Unless the court finds that the non-custodial parents's pro-rata share of the basic child support obligation is unjust or inappropriate, which finding shall be based upon consideration of the following factors: (1) The financial resources of the custodial and non-custodial parent, and those of the child;
(2) The physical and emotional health of the child and his/her special needs and aptitudes; (3) The standard of living the child would have enjoyed had the marriage or household not been dissolved; (4) The tax consequences to the parties; (5) The non-monetary contributions that the parents will make toward the care and well-being of the child; (6) The educational needs of either parent; (7) A determination that the gross income of one parent is substantially less than the other parent's gross income; (8) The needs of the children of the non-custodial parent for whom the non-custodial parent is providing support who are not subject to the instant action and whose support has not been deducted from income pursuant to subclause (D) of clause (vii) of subparagraph five of paragraph (b) of this subdivision, and the financial resources of any person obligated to support such children, provided, however, that this factor may apply only if the resources available to support such children are less than the resources available to support the children who are subject to the instant action; (9) Provided that the child is not on public assistance (i) extraordinary expenses incurred by the non-custodial parent in exercising visitation, or (ii) expenses incurred by the non-custodial parent in extended visitation provided that the custodial parent's expenses are substantially reduced as a result thereof; and (10) Any other factors the court determines are relevant in each case, the court shall order the non-custodial parent to pay his or her pro rata share of the basic child support obligation, and may order the non-custodial parent to pay an amount pursuant to paragraph (e) of this subdivision. (g) Where the court finds that the non-custodial parent's pro rata share of the basic child support obligation is unjust or inappropriate, the court shall order the non-custodial parent to pay such amount of child support as the court finds just and appropriate, and the court shall set forth, in a written order, the factors it considered; the amount of each party's pro rata share of the basic child support obligation; and the reasons that the court did not order the basic child support obligation. Such written order may not be waived by either party or counsel; provided, however, and notwithstanding any other provision of law, the court shall not find that the non-custodial parent's pro rata share of such obligation is unjust or inappropriate on the basis that such share exceeds the portion of a public assistance grant which is attributable to a child or children. In no instance shall the court order child support below twenty-five dol-

lars per month. Where the non-custodial parent's income is less than or equal to the poverty income guidelines amount for a single person as reported by the federal department of health and human services, unpaid child support arrears in excess of five hundred dollars shall not accrue. (h) A validly executed agreement or stipulation voluntarily entered into between the parties after the effective date of this subdivision presented to the court for incorporation in an order or judgment shall include a provision stating that the parties have been advised of the provisions of this subdivision, and that the basic child support obligation provided for therein would presumptively result in the correct amount of child support to be awarded. In the event that such agreement or stipulation deviates from the basic child support obligation, the agreement or stipulation must specify the amount that such basic child support obligation would have been and the reason or reasons that such agreement or stipulation does not provide for payment of that amount. Such provision may not be waived by either party or counsel. Nothing contained in this subdivision shall be construed to alter the rights of the parties to voluntarily enter into validly executed agreements or stipulations which deviate from the basic child support obligation provided such agreements or stipulations comply with the provisions of this paragraph. The court shall, however, retain discretion with respect to child support pursuant to this section. Any court order or judgment incorporating a validly executed agreement or stipulation which deviates from the basic child support obligation shall set forth the court's reasons for such deviation. (i) Where either or both parties are unrepresented, the court shall not enter an order or judgment other than a temporary order pursuant to section two hundred thirty-seven of this article, that includes a provision for child support unless the unrepresented party or parties have received a copy of the child support standards chart promulgated by the commissioner of social services pursuant to subdivision two of section one hundred eleven-i of the social services law. Where either party is in receipt of child support enforcement services through the local social services district, the local social services district child support enforcement unit shall advise such party of the amount derived from application of the child support percentage and that such amount serves as a starting point for the determination of the child support award, and shall provide such party with a copy of the child support standards chart. In no instance shall the court approve any voluntary support agreement or compromise that includes an amount for child support less than twenty-five dollars per month. (j) In addition to financial disclosure required in section two hundred thirty-six of this article, the court may require that the income and/or expenses of either party be verified with documentation including, but not limited to, past and present income tax returns, employer statements, pay stubs, corporate, business, or partnership books and records, corporate and business tax returns, and receipts for expenses or such other means of verification as the court determines appropriate. Nothing herein shall affect any party's right to pursue discovery pursuant to this chapter, the civil practice law and rules, or the family court act. (k) When a party has defaulted and/or the court is otherwise presented with insufficient evidence to determine gross income, the court shall order child support based upon the needs or standard of living of the child, whichever is greater. Such order may be retroactively modified upward, without a showing of change in circumstances. (l) In any action or proceeding for modification of an order of child support existing prior to the effective date of this paragraph, brought pursuant to this article, the child support standards set forth in this subdivision shall not constitute a change of circumstances warranting modification of such support order; provided, however, that (1) where the circumstances warrant modification of such order, or (2) where any party objects to an adjusted child support order made or proposed at the direction of the support collection unit pursuant to section one hundred eleven-h or one hundred eleven-n of the social services law, and the

court is reviewing the current order of child support, such standards shall be applied by the court in its determination with regard to the request for modification, or disposition of an objection to an adjusted child support order made or proposed by a support collection unit. In applying such standards, when the order to be modified incorporates by reference or merges with a validly executed separation agreement or stipulation of settlement, the court may consider, in addition to the factors set forth in paragraph (f) of this subdivision, the provisions of such agreement or stipulation concerning property distribution, distributive award and/or maintenance in determining whether the amount calculated by using the standards would be unjust or inappropriate.

3. Order of protection. a. The court may make an order of protection in assistance or as a condition of any other order made under this section. The order of protection may set forth reasonable conditions of behavior to be observed for a specified time by any party. Such an order may require any party: (1) to stay away from the home, school, business or place of employment of the child, other parent or any other party, and to stay away from any other specific location designated by the court; (2) to permit a parent, or a person entitled to visitation by a court order or a separation agreement, to visit the child at stated periods; (3) to refrain from committing a family offense, as defined in subdivision one of section 530.11 of the criminal procedure law, or any criminal offense against the child or against the other parent or against any person to whom custody of the child is awarded or from harassing, intimidating or threatening such persons; (4) to permit a designated party to enter the residence during a specified period of time in order to remove personal belongings not in issue in a proceeding or action under this chapter or the family court act; or (5) to refrain from acts of commission or omission that create an unreasonable risk to the health, safety or welfare of a child. (6) to pay the reasonable counsel fees and disbursements involved in obtaining or enforcing the order of the person who is protected by such order if such order is issued or enforced. (7) to observe such other conditions as are necessary to further the purposes of protection. b. An order of protection entered pursuant to this subdivision shall bear in a conspicuous manner, on the front page of said order, the language "Order of protection issued pursuant to section two hundred forty of the domestic relations law". The absence of such language shall not affect the validity of such order. The presentation of a copy of such an order to any peace officer acting pursuant to his or her special duties, or police officer, shall constitute authority, for that officer to arrest a person when that person has violated the terms of such an order, and bring such person before the court and, otherwise, so far as lies within the officer's power, to aid in securing the protection such order was intended to afford. c. An order of protection entered pursuant to this subdivision may be made in the final judgment in any matrimonial action or in a proceeding to obtain custody of or visitation with any child under this section, or by one or more orders from time to time before or subsequent to final judgment, or by both such order or orders and the final judgment. The order of protection may remain in effect after entry of a final matrimonial judgment and during the minority of any child whose custody or visitation is the subject of a provision of a final judgment or any order. An order of protection may be entered notwithstanding that the court for any reason whatsoever, other than lack of jurisdiction, refuses to grant the relief requested in the action or proceeding. d. The chief administrator of the courts shall promulgate appropriate uniform temporary orders of protection and orders of protection forms, applicable to proceedings under this article, to be used throughout the state. Such forms shall be promulgated and developed in a manner to ensure the compatibility of such forms with the statewide computerized registry established pursuant to section two hundred twenty-one-a of the executive law. e. No order of protection may direct any party to observe conditions of behavior unless: (i) the party requesting the order of protection has served and filed an action, proceeding,

counter-claim or written motion and, (ii) the court has made a finding on the record that such party is entitled to issuance of the order of protection which may result from a judicial finding of fact, judicial acceptance of an admission by the party against whom the order was issued or judicial finding that the party against whom the order is issued has given knowing, intelligent and voluntary consent to its issuance. The provisions of this subdivision shall not preclude the court from issuing a temporary order of protection upon the court's own motion or where a motion for such relief is made to the court, for good cause shown. Any party moving for a temporary order of protection pursuant to this subdivision during hours when the court is open shall be entitled to file such motion or pleading containing such prayer for emergency relief on the same day that such person first appears at such court, and a hearing on the motion or portion of the pleading requesting such emergency relief shall be held on the same day or the next day that the court is in session following the filing of such motion or pleading. Upon issuance of an order of protection or temporary order of protection or upon a violation of such order, the court may make an order in accordance with section eight hundred forty-two-a of the family court act directing the surrender of firearms, revoking or suspending a party's firearms license, and/or directing that such party be ineligible to receive a firearms license. Upon issuance of an order of protection pursuant to this section or upon a finding of a violation thereof, the court also may direct payment of restitution in an amount not to exceed ten thousand dollars in accordance with subdivision (e) of section eight hundred forty-one of such act; provided, however, that in no case shall an order of restitution be issued where the court determines that the party against whom the order would be issued has already compensated the injured party or where such compensation is incorporated in a final judgment or settlement of the action.

§241. Interference with or withholding of visitation rights; alimony or maintenance suspension. When it appears to the satisfaction of the court that a custodial parent receiving alimony or maintenance pursuant to an order, judgment or decree of a court of competent jurisdiction has wrongfully interfered with or withheld visitation rights provided by such order, judgment or decree, the court, in its discretion, may suspend such payments or cancel any arrears that may have accrued during the time that visitation rights have been or are being interfered with or withheld. Nothing in this section shall constitute a defense in any court to an application to enforce payment of child support or grounds for the cancellation of arrears for child support.

§248. Modification of judgment or order in action for divorce or annulment.
Where an action for divorce or for annulment or for a declaration of the nullity of a void marriage is brought by a husband or wife, and a final judgment of divorce or a final judgment annulling the marriage or declaring its nullity has been rendered, the court, by order upon the application of the husband on notice, and on proof of the marriage of the wife after such final judgment, must modify such final judgment and any orders made with respect thereto by annulling the provisions of such final judgment or orders, or of both, directing payments of money for the support of the wife. The court in its discretion upon application of the husband on notice, upon proof that the wife is habitually living with another man and holding herself out as his wife, although not married to such man, may modify such final judgment and any orders made with respect thereto by annulling the provisions of such final judgment or orders or of both, directing payment of money for the support of such wife.

§253. Removal of barriers to remarriage.
1. This section applies only to a marriage solemnized in this state or in any other jurisdiction by a person specified in subdivision one of section eleven of this chapter. 2. Any party to a marriage defined in subdivision one of this section who commences a proceeding to annul the marriage or for a divorce must allege, in his

or her verified complaint: (i) that, to the best of his or her knowledge, that he or she has taken or that he or she will take, prior to the entry of final judgment, all steps solely within his or her power to remove any barrier to the defendant's remarriage following the annulment or divorce; or (ii) that the defendant has waived in writing the requirements of this subdivision. 3. No final judgment of annulment or divorce shall thereafter be entered unless the plaintiff shall have filed and served a sworn statement: (i) that, to the best of his or her knowledge, he or she has, prior to the entry of such final judgment, taken all steps solely within his or her power to remove all barriers to the defendant's remarriage following the annulment or divorce; or (ii) that the defendant has waived in writing the requirements of this subdivision. 4. In any action for divorce based on subdivisions five and six of section one hundred seventy of this chapter in which the defendant enters a general appearance and does not contest the requested relief, no final judgment of annulment or divorce shall be entered unless both parties shall have filed and served sworn statements: (i) that he or she has, to the best of his or her knowledge, taken all steps solely within his or her power to remove all barriers to the other party's remarriage following the annulment or divorce; or (ii) that the other party has waived in writing the requirements of this subdivision. 5. The writing attesting to any waiver of the requirements of subdivision two, three or four of this section shall be filed with the court prior to the entry of a final judgment of annulment or divorce. 6. As used in the sworn statements prescribed by this section "barrier to remarriage" includes, without limitation, any religious or conscientious restraint or inhibition, of which the party required to make the verified statement is aware, that is imposed on a party to a marriage, under the principles held by the clergyman or minister who has solemnized the marriage, by reason of the other party's commission or withholding of any voluntary act. Nothing in this section shall be construed to require any party to consult with any clergyman or minister to determine whether there exists any such religious or conscientious restraint or inhibition. It shall not be deemed a "barrier to remarriage" within the meaning of this section if the restraint or inhibition cannot be removed by the party's voluntary act. Nor shall it be deemed a "barrier to remarriage" if the party must incur expenses in connection with removal of the restraint or inhibition and the other party refuses to provide reasonable reimbursement for such expenses. "All steps solely within his or her power" shall not be construed to include application to a marriage tribunal or other similar organization or agency of a religious denomination which has authority to annul or dissolve a marriage under the rules of such denomination. 7. No final judgment of annulment or divorce shall be entered, notwithstanding the filing of the plaintiff's sworn statement prescribed by this section, if the clergyman or minister who has solemnized the marriage certifies, in a sworn statement, that he or she has solemnized the marriage and that, to his or her knowledge, the plaintiff has failed to take all steps solely within his or her power to remove all barriers to the defendant's remarriage following the annulment or divorce, provided that the said clergyman or minister is alive and available and competent to testify at the time when final judgment would be entered. 8. Any person who knowingly submits a false sworn statement under this section shall be guilty of making an apparently sworn false statement in the first degree and shall be punished in accordance with section 210.40 of the penal law. 9. Nothing in this section shall be construed to authorize any court to inquire into or determine any ecclesiastical or religious issue. The truth of any statement submitted pursuant to this section shall not be the subject of any judicial inquiry, except as provided in subdivision eight of this section.

Blank Forms

The forms contained in this appendix have been discussed throughout the text and specific instructions are contained therein. Make photocopies of the blank forms and fill in the copies in case you make a mistake or need to make changes. The blank forms can then be used to make additional copies.

Table of Forms

1   **SUPREME COURT OF THE STATE OF NEW YORK**
23   **COUNTY OF** _____

4   ---X
5

6

                                    Plaintiff,

                    -against-

7
8

                                    Defendant.
        ---X

Index No.:_____
Date Summons filed:_____
Plaintiff designates _____
County as the place of trial
The basis of venue is:

_____

SUMMONS WITH NOTICE
Plaintiff/Defendant resides at:

_____
_____
_____

ACTION FOR A DIVORCE

To the above named Defendant:

9   **YOU ARE HEREBY SUMMONED** to serve a notice of appearance on the ❑ *Plaintiff*
OR ❑ *Plaintiff's Attorney(s)* within twenty (20) days after the service of this summons, exclusive
of the day of service (or within thirty (30) days after the service is complete if this summons is not
personally delivered to you within the State of New York); and in case of your failure to appear,
judgment will be taken against you by default for the relief demanded in the notice set forth below.

10, 11 Dated _____

❑ *Plaintiff*
❑ *Attorney(s) for Plaintiff*
   Address:

12

                                    Phone No.:

13   **NOTICE:**   The nature of this action is to dissolve the marriage between the parties, on the
                       grounds: **DRL §170 subd.____ - _____
                                       _____

        The relief sought is a judgment of absolute divorce in favor of the Plaintiff dissolving the marriage
        between the parties in this action. The nature of any ancillary or additional relief demanded is:

14   _____
        _____
        _____
        _____
        _____

**Insert the grounds for the divorce:
DRL §170(1) - cruel and inhuman treatment   DRL §170(4) - adultery
DRL §170(2) - abandonment   DRL §170(5) - living apart one year after separation decree or judgment of separation
DRL §170(3) - confinement in prison   DRL §170(6) - living apart one year after execution of a separation agreement

(Form UD-1 - Rev. 5/99)

1 **SUPREME COURT OF THE STATE OF NEW YORK**   Index No.:_____

2 3 **COUNTY OF** _____   Date Summons filed:_____
4 ---   Plaintiff designates _____

5   County as the place of trial
                                                                    The basis of venue is:
6
                                                                    _____
                                              Plaintiff,
              -against-   **SUMMONS**
                                                                    Plaintiff/Defendant resides at:
7
8   _____
                                                                    _____
                                              Defendant.
      ---X   _____

ACTION FOR A DIVORCE

To the above named Defendant:

9   **YOU ARE HEREBY SUMMONED** to answer the complaint in this action and to serve
a copy of your answer on the ❑ *Plaintiff* **OR** ❑ *Plaintiff's Attorney(s)* within twenty (20) days
after the service of this summons, exclusive of the day of service, where service is made by delivery
upon you personally within the state, or within thirty (30) days after completion of service where
service is made in any other manner. In case of your failure to appear or answer, judgment will be
taken against you by default for the relief demanded in the complaint.

10, 11 Dated _____   • *Plaintiff*
                                            • *Attorney(s) for Plaintiff*
12   Address:

                                              Phone No.:

SUPREME COURT OF THE STATE OF NEW YORK
COUNTY OF _____

---X

Plaintiff,

-against-

Defendant.

---X

Index No.:

VERIFIED COMPLAINT

ACTION FOR DIVORCE

FIRST:

Plaintiff *herein / by* _____, complaining of the Defendant, alleges that the parties are over the age of 18 years and;

SECOND:

❑ The Plaintiff has resided in New York State for a continuous period in excess of two years immediately preceding the commencement of this action.

OR

❑ The Defendant has resided in New York State for a continuous period in excess of two years immediately preceding the commencement of this action.

OR

❑ The Plaintiff has resided in New York State for a continuous period in excess of one year immediately preceding the commencement of this action, and:

    a. ❑ the parties were married in New York State.
    b. ❑ the Plaintiff has lived as husband or wife in New York State with the Defendant.
    c. ❑ the cause of action occurred in New York State.

OR

❑ The Defendant has resided in New York State for a continuous period in excess of one year immediately preceding the commencement of this action, and:

    a. ❑ the parties were married in New York State.
    b. ❑ the Defendant has lived as husband or wife in New York State with the Plaintiff.
    c. ❑ the cause of action occurred in New York State.

OR

❑ The cause of action occurred in New York State and both parties were residents thereof at the time of the commencement of this action.

THIRD: The Plaintiff and the Defendant were married on _____ in (city, town or village; and state or country) _____.

8   The marriage was *not* performed by a clergyman, minister or by a leader of the Society for Ethical Culture.

(If the word "not" is deleted above check the appropriate box below).

    ❑ *To the best of my knowledge I have taken all steps solely within my power to remove any barrier to the Defendant's remarriage.*   **OR**

    ❑ *I will take prior to the entry of final judgment all steps solely within my power to the best of my knowledge to remove any barrier to the Defendant's remarriage.*   **OR**

    ❑ *The Defendant has waived in writing the requirements of DRL §253 (Barriers to Remarriage).*

9   **FOURTH:** ❑ There are no children of the marriage.   **OR**

                  ❑ There *is (are)* _____ child(ren) of the marriage, namely:

Name	Date of Birth	Address
_____	_____	_____
_____	_____	_____
_____	_____	_____
_____	_____	_____
_____	_____	_____

The Plaintiff resides at _____.
The Defendant resides at _____.

11   The parties are covered by the following group health plans:

Plaintiff	**Defendant**
Group Health Plan:_____	Group Health Plan:_____
Address:_____	Address:_____
Identification Number:_____	Identification Number:_____
Plan Administrator:_____	Plan Administrator:_____
Type of Coverage:_____	Type of Coverage:_____

12   **FIFTH:** The grounds for divorce that are alleged as follows:

Cruel and Inhuman Treatment (DRL §170(1)):

❑   At the following times, none of which are earlier than (5) years prior to commencement of this action, the Defendant engaged in conduct that so endangered the mental and physical well-being of the Plaintiff, so as to render it unsafe or improper for the parties to cohabit (live together) as husband and wife.

       (State the facts that demonstrate cruel and inhuman conduct giving dates, places and specific acts. Conduct may include physical, verbal, sexual or emotional behavior.)

_____
_____
_____
_____

_____
_____
_____
_____

(Attach an additional sheet, if necessary).

Abandonment (DRL 170(2):

❑ That commencing on or about _____, and continuing for a period of more than one (1) year immediately prior to commencement of this action, the Defendant left the marital residence of the parties located at _____, and did not return. Such absence was without cause or justification, and was without Plaintiff's consent.

❑ That commencing on or about _____, and continuing for a period of more than one (1) year immediately prior to commencement of this action, the Defendant refused to have sexual relations with the Plaintiff despite Plaintiff's repeated requests to resume such relations. Defendant does not suffer from any disability which would prevent _her / him_ from engaging in such sexual relations with Plaintiff. The refusal to engage in sexual relations was without good cause or justification and occurred at the marital residence located at _____.

❑ That commencing on or about _____, and continuing for a period of more than one (1) year immediately prior to commencement of this action, the Defendant willfully and without cause or justification abandoned the Plaintiff, who had been a faithful and dutiful _husband / wife_ by depriving Plaintiff of access to the marital residence located at _____.
This deprivation of access was without the consent of the Plaintiff and continued for a period of greater than one year.

Confinement to Prison (DRL §170(3)):

❑ (a) That after the marriage of Plaintiff and Defendant, Defendant was confined in prison for a period of three or more consecutive years, to wit: that Defendant was confined in _____ _____ prison on _____, and has remained confined to this date; and

(b) not more that five (5) years has elapsed between the end of the third year of imprisonment and the date of commencement of this action.

Adultery (DRL §170(4)):

❑ (a) That on _____, at the premises located at _____, the Defendant engaged in sexual intercourse with _____, without the procurement nor the connivance of the Plaintiff, and the Plaintiff ceased to cohabit (live) with the Defendant upon the discovery of the adultery; and

(b) not more than five (5) years elapsed between the date of said adultery and the date of commencement of this action.

(Attach a corroborating affidavit of a third party witness or other additional proof).

(Form UD-2 - Rev. 5/99)

Living Separate and Apart Pursuant to a Separation Decree or Judgment of Separation (DRL §170(5)):

❑   (a)   That the _____ Court, _____ County, _____ (Country or State) rendered a decree or judgment of separation on _____, under Index Number _____; and

       (b)   that the parties have lived separate and apart for a period of one year or longer after the granting of such decree; and

       (c)   that the Plaintiff has substantially complied with all the terms and conditions of such decree or judgment.

Living Separate and Apart Pursuant to a Separation Agreement (DRL §170(6)):

❑   (a)   That the Plaintiff and Defendant entered into a written agreement of separation, which they subscribed and acknowledged on _____, in the form required to entitle a deed to be recorded; and

       (b)   that the *agreement / memorandum of said agreement* was filed on _____ in the Office of the Clerk of the County of _____, wherein *Plaintiff / Defendant* resided; and

       (c)   that the parties have lived separate and apart for a period of one year or longer after the execution of said agreement; and

       (d)   that the Plaintiff has substantially complied with all terms and conditions of such agreement.

13   **SIXTH:** There is no judgment in any court for a divorce and no other matrimonial action between the parties pending in this court or in any other court of competent jurisdiction.

14   **WHEREFORE,** Plaintiff demands judgment against the Defendant as follows: A judgment dissolving the marriage between the parties and

❑ _____
_____
_____
_____

AND

❑ equitable distribution of marital property;

OR

❑ marital property to be distributed pursuant to the annexed separation agreement / stipulation;

OR

❑ I waive equitable distribution of marital property;

and any other relief the court deems fitting and proper.

15   Dated:_____

16

             ❑ *Plaintiff*
             ❑ *Attorney(s) for Plaintiff*
             Address:

             Phone No.:

17   STATE OF NEW YORK, COUNTY OF _____ SS:

I _____ (Print Name), am the Plaintiff in the within action for a divorce. I have read the foregoing complaint and know the contents thereof. The contents are true to my own knowledge except as to matters therein stated to be alleged upon information and belief, and as to those matters I believe them to be true.

Subscribed and Sworn to
before me on

_____   _____
                                     Plaintiff's Signature

_____
       NOTARY PUBLIC

SUPREME COURT OF THE STATE OF NEW YORK
COUNTY OF _____
--X

<table>
<tr><td>Plaintiff,</td><td>Index No.:</td></tr>
<tr><td>-against-</td><td></td></tr>
<tr><td></td><td>**AFFIDAVIT OF SERVICE**</td></tr>
<tr><td>Defendant.</td><td></td></tr>
</table>

--X

STATE OF _____   }

                        ss:

COUNTY OF _____   }

_____ being duly sworn, says:

1.   I am not a party to the action, am over 18 years of age and reside at:
_____

2.   On_____, at _____a.m./p.m. at _____
_____ I served the   •   *summons with notice* **OR** •   *summons and verified complaint* on _____,
the Defendant named by delivering a true copy to the Defendant personally.   •   In addition I served a copy of the Child Support Standards Chart.

3.   The notice required by the Domestic Relations Law, Section 232 -- "ACTION FOR A DIVORCE" -- was legibly printed on the face of the summons served on the Defendant.

4.   I knew the person so served to be the person described in the summons as the Defendant. My knowledge of the Defendant and how I acquired it is as follows: (select one)

      •   I have known the defendant for _____ years and_____
_____
_____
OR
      •   I identified the Defendant by a photograph annexed to this affidavit and which was given to me by the Plaintiff.
OR
      •   Plaintiff accompanied me and pointed out the Defendant.
OR
      •   I asked the person served if he/she was the person named in the summons and Defendant admitted being the person so named.

5.   Deponent describes the individual served as follows:

<u>Sex</u>	<u>Height</u>	<u>Weight</u>	<u>Age</u>	<u>Color of Skin</u>	<u>Color of Hair</u>
• Male	• Under 5'	• Under 100 Lbs.	• 14-17 Yrs.	Describe color:	• Black
• Female	• 5'0"-5'3"	• 100-130 Lbs.	• 18-20 Yrs.	_____	• Brown
	• 5'4"-5'8"	• 131-160 Lbs.	• 21-35 Yrs.	_____	• Blond
	• 5'9"-6'0"	• 161-200 Lbs.	• 36-50 Yrs.	_____	• Gray
	• Over 6'	• Over 200 Lbs.	• 51-65 Yrs.	_____	• Red
			• Over 65 Yrs.		• White
					• Balding
					• Bald

Other identifying features, if any:_____.

6a. *At the time I served the Defendant, I asked him/her if he/she was in the military service of this state, any other state, or this nation, and the Defendant responded in the negative.*

  b. *The Defendant stated that he/she is in the following military service* _____.

_____
Server's Signature

Subscribed and Sworn to
before me on

_____

_____
NOTARY PUBLIC

SUPREME COURT OF THE STATE OF NEW YORK
COUNTY OF _____

---X

Plaintiff,	Index No.:_____
-against-	**SWORN STATEMENT OF REMOVAL OF BARRIERS TO REMARRIAGE**
Defendant.	

---X

STATE OF _____ }

                      ss:

COUNTY OF _____ }

I _____ (Print Name), state under penalty of perjury that the parties' marriage was solemnized by a minister, clergyman or leader of the Society for Ethical Culture, and that;

- *To the best of my knowledge I have taken all steps solely within my power to remove all barriers to the Defendant's remarriage following the divorce.*

OR

- *The Defendant has waived in writing the requirements of DRL §253.*

_____
Plaintiff's Signature

Subscribed and Sworn to
before me on

_____

_____
NOTARY PUBLIC

(Form UD-4 - Rev. 5/99)

Affidavit of Service

SUPREME COURT OF THE STATE OF NEW YORK

1 **COUNTY OF** _____

2 _____ being sworn, says, I am not a party to the action, and am over 18 years of age.   I reside at _____.

3 On _____, I served a true copy of the within Removal of Barriers Statement on the Defendant:

- *personally at* _____

OR

- *by depositing a true copy thereof enclosed in a post-paid wrapper, in an official depository under the exclusive care and custody of the U.S. Postal Service within New York State, to the address designated by the Defendant at* _____

    _

    _____

___

4

_____
Server's Signature

Subscribed and Sworn to
before me on

_____

_____
NOTARY PUBLIC

OR

5 Service of the within document is hereby acknowledged.

_____
- *Defendant's Signature*   **OR**
- *Defendant's Attorney's Signature*

(Form UD-4a - Rev. 5/99)

SUPREME COURT OF THE STATE OF NEW YORK
1 **COUNTY OF _____**

--X

2
3   Plaintiff,   Index No.:

              -against-   **AFFIRMATION (AFFIDAVIT)**
                                                    OF REGULARITY

4
                              Defendant.

--X

5 **STATE OF _____ }**

                                          ss:

    COUNTY OF _____ }

6   The undersigned, being duly sworn, deposes and says:

        I am ❑ *the attorney for* **OR** ❑ *the Plaintiff herein.*

        This is a matrimonial action.

        The ❑ *Summons with Notice* **OR** ❑ *Summons and Verified Complaint* was personally served upon the Defendant herein, ❑ *within* **OR** ❑ *outside* the State of New York as appears in the affidavit of service submitted herewith.

7   *Defendant has appeared* ❑ *on his or her own behalf* **OR** ❑ *by the firm of:* _____ _____ *and executed an affidavit agreeing that this matter be placed on the matrimonial*
calendar immediately.

                          OR

    ❑ *Defendant is in default for failure to serve a notice of appearance or failure to answer the complaint served in this action in due time, and the time to answer has not been extended by stipulation, court order, or otherwise.*

        WHEREFORE, I respectfully request that this action be placed on the undefended matrimonial calendar for trial.

        I state under the penalties of perjury that the statements herein made are true, except as to such statements as are based on information and belief, which statements I believe to be true.

8   Dated: _____
                                            ❑ *Plaintiff*
                                            ❑ *Attorney(s) for Plaintiff*

        Subscribed and Sworn to
        before me on

        _____

        _____
              NOTARY PUBLIC

SUPREME COURT OF THE STATE OF NEW YORK
COUNTY OF _____
---X

Plaintiff,   Index No.:_____

-against-   **AFFIDAVIT OF PLAINTIFF·**

Defendant.
---X

STATE OF _____   }
                                        ss:
COUNTY OF _____   }

_____ being duly sworn, says:

1.   The Plaintiff's address is _____,
      and social security number is _____. The Defendant's address is _____
      _____, and social security number is _____
      .

2.❑   The Plaintiff has resided in New York State for a continuous period in excess of two years
       immediately preceding the commencement of this action.
                                    OR
❑   The Defendant has resided in New York State for a continuous period in excess of two years
       immediately preceding the commencement of this action.
                                    OR
❑   The Plaintiff has resided in New York State for a continuous period in excess of one year
       immediately preceding the commencement of this action, and:

              a. ❑ the parties were married in New York State.
              b. ❑ the Plaintiff has lived as husband or wife in New York State with the
                    Defendant.
              c. ❑ the cause of action occurred in New York State.
                                    OR
❑   The Defendant has resided in New York State for a continuous period in excess of one
       year immediately preceding the commencement of this action, and:

              a. ❑ the parties were married in New York State.
              b. ❑ the Defendant has lived as husband or wife in New York State with the
                    Plaintiff.
              c. ❑ the cause of action occurred in New York State.
                                    OR
❑   The cause of action occurred in New York State and both parties were residents thereof
       at the time of the commencement of this action.

9 3.   I married the Defendant on _____, in the City, Town or Village of
        _____, County of _____, State or Country of _____. The
        marriage was *not* performed by a clergyman, minister or by a leader of the Society for
        Ethical Culture.

10 (If the word "not" is deleted, check one of the following below:)

❑   *To the best of my knowledge I have taken all steps solely within my power to remove any barrier
     to the Defendant's remarriage.*   **OR**

❑   *I will take prior to the entry of final judgment all steps solely within my power to the best of my
     knowledge to remove any barrier to the Defendant's remarriage.*   **OR**

❑   *The Defendant has waived in writing the requirements of DRL §253 (Barriers to Remarriage).*

11 4.   There is (are) _____ child(ren) of the marriage:

Name & Social Security Number   _Date of Birth_

_____   _____
_____   _____
_____   _____
_____   _____
_____   _____

*The present address of each child under the age of 18 and all other places where each child
has lived within the last five (5) years is as follows:*

Child   _Present Address_

_____   _____
_____   _____
_____   _____
_____   _____

Child   _Other Address Within Last 5 years_

_____   _____
_____   _____
_____   _____
_____   _____

*The name(s) and present address(es) of the person(s) with whom each child under the age
of 18 has lived within the last five (5) years is:*

_____   _____
_____   _____
_____   _____
_____   _____

12 I have participated in other litigation concerning the custody of the child(ren) in this or another
    state.   Yes ❑ No ❑
    I have information of a custody proceeding concerning the child(ren) pending in a court of this
    or another state.   Yes ❑ No ❑
    I know of a person who is not a party to this proceeding who has physical custody of the
    child(ren) or claims to have custody or visitation rights with respect to the child(ren).
                                                                    Yes ❑ No ❑

13   The parties are covered by the following group health plans:

Plaintiff   **Defendant**

Group Health Plan:_____   Group Health Plan:_____
Address:_____   Address:_____
Identification Number:_____   Identification Number:_____
Plan Administrator:_____   Plan Administrator:_____
Type of Coverage:_____   Type of Coverage:_____

                              OR

     ❑ Not Applicable.

14   5.   In addition to the dissolution of the marriage, I am seeking the following relief:

_____
_____
_____

                              AND
     ❑   equitable distribution of marital property;
                              OR
     ❑   marital property to be distributed pursuant to the annexed separation agreement
           / stipulation;
                              OR
     ❑   I waive equitable distribution of marital property;

           and any other relief the court deems fitting and proper.

15   6.   The grounds for dissolution of the marriage are as follows:

Cruel and Inhuman Treatment (DRL §170(1)):

❑   At the following times, none of which are earlier than (5) years prior to commencement of this
      action, the Defendant engaged in conduct that so endangered the mental and physical well-being
      of the Plaintiff, so as to render it unsafe or improper for the parties to cohabit (live together) as
      husband and wife.

      (State the facts that demonstrate cruel and inhuman conduct giving dates, places and specific acts.
      Conduct may include physical, verbal, sexual or emotional behavior.)

_____
_____
_____
_____
_____
_____
_____
_____

(Attach an additional sheet, if necessary).

(Form UD-6 - Rev. 5/99)

Abandonment (DRL 170(2)):

❑ That commencing on or about _____, and continuing for a period of more than one (1) year immediately prior to commencement of this action, the Defendant left the marital residence of the parties located at _____, and did not return. Such absence was without cause or justification, and was without Plaintiff's consent.

❑ That commencing on or about _____, and continuing for a period of more than one (1) year immediately prior to commencement of this action, the Defendant refused to have sexual relations with the Plaintiff despite Plaintiff's repeated requests to resume such relations. Defendant does not suffer from any disability which would prevent *her / him* from engaging in such sexual relations with Plaintiff. The refusal to engage in sexual relations was without good cause or justification and occurred at the marital residence located at _____ _____.

❑ That commencing on or about the _____, and continuing for a period of more than one (1) year immediately prior to commencement of this action, the Defendant willfully and without cause or justification abandoned the Plaintiff, who had been a faithful and dutiful *husband / wife* , by depriving Plaintiff of access to the marital residence located at _____. This deprivation of access was without the consent of the Plaintiff and continued for a period of greater than one year.

Confinement to Prison (DRL §170(3)):

❑ (a) That after the marriage of Plaintiff and Defendant, Defendant was confined in prison for a period of three or more consecutive years, to wit: that Defendant was confined in _____ _____ prison on _____, and has remained confined to this date; and

(b) not more that five (5) years elapsed between the end of the third year of imprisonment and the date of commencement of this action.

Adultery (DRL §170(4)):

❑ (a) That on _____, at the premises located at _____ _____, the Defendant engaged in sexual intercourse with _____, without the procurement nor the connivance of the Plaintiff, and the Plaintiff ceased to cohabit (live) with the Defendant upon the discovery of the adultery; and

(b) not more than five (5) years elapsed between the date of said adultery and the date of commencement of this action.

(Attach a corroborating affidavit of a third party witness or other additional proof).

Living Separate and Apart Pursuant to a Separation Decree or Judgment of Separation (DRL §170(5)):

❑ (a) That the _____ Court, _____ County, _____ (Country or State) rendered a decree or judgment of separation on _____ under Index Number: _____; and

(b) that the parties have lived separate and apart for a period of one year or longer after the granting of such decree; and

(c) that the Plaintiff has substantially complied with all the terms and conditions of such decree or judgment.

Living Separate and Apart Pursuant to a Separation Agreement (DRL §170(6)):

❑ (a) That the Plaintiff and Defendant entered into a written agreement of separation, which they subscribed and acknowledged on _____, in the form required to entitle a deed to be recorded; and

(b) that the *agreement / memorandum of said agreement* was filed on _____ in the Office of the Clerk of the County of _____, wherein *Plaintiff / Defendant* resided; and

(c) that the parties have lived separate and apart for a period of one year or longer after the execution of said agreement; and

(d) that the Plaintiff has substantially complied with all terms and conditions of such agreement.

16   7.   Defendant is not in the active military service of this state, or any other state or this nation.

❑ I know this because: *he/she* admitted it to *me / the process server* on _____.

❑ I have submitted with these papers an *investigator's affidavit / Defendant's affidavit* which states that Defendant is not in the active military service of this state, or any other state or this nation.

17   8.   I am *not* receiving Public Assistance. To my knowledge the Defendant is *not* receiving Public Assistance.

18   9.   No other matrimonial action is pending in this court or in any other court, and the marriage has not been terminated by any decree of any court of competent jurisdiction.

19   10.   *Annexed to the "Affidavit of Service" of Summons and Complaint / Summons With Notice is a photograph. It is a fair and accurate representation of the Defendant.*

20   11A. ❑ I am not the custodial parent of the child*(ren)* of the marriage.
OR

11B. ❑ I am the custodial parent of the unemancipated child *(ren)* entitled to receive child support pursuant to DRL §236(B)(7)(b),
AND

❑ (1) I request child support services through the Support Collection Unit which would authorize collection of the support obligation by the immediate issuance of an income execution for support enforcement.
OR

(Form UD-6 - Rev. 5/99)

❑ (2) I am in receipt of such services through the Support Collection Unit.

OR

❑ (3) I have applied for such services through the Support Collection Unit.

OR

❑ (4) I am aware of but decline such services through the Support Collection Unit at this time. I am aware that an income deduction order may be issued pursuant to CPLR §5242(c) without other child support enforcement services and that payment of an administrative fee may be required.

If (1) or (4) is selected, the following information must be included on a separate information sheet (Form UD-8a):

Name, date of birth, address and social security number of each party; date and place of marriage; names and dates of birth of the children; and name and address of employer of the payor (non-custodial parent).

21   ❑ *Plaintiff's* **OR** ❑ *Defendant's* prior surname is: _____.

WHEREFORE, I _____ (print name), respectfully request that judgment be entered for the relief sought and for such other relief as the court deems fitting and proper.

22   Subscribed and Sworn to
before me on

_____
Plaintiff's Signature

_____

_____
NOTARY PUBLIC

SUPREME COURT OF THE STATE OF NEW YORK
COUNTY OF _____

---X

Plaintiff,   Index No.:

-against-   **AFFIDAVIT OF DEFENDANT**
IN ACTION FOR DIVORCE

Defendant.

---X

STATE OF _____   }
                                                        ss:
COUNTY OF _____   }

_____being duly sworn, says:

I am the Defendant in the within action for divorce, and I am over the age of 18. I reside at
_____.

1.   I admit service of the ❑ *Summons with Notice* **OR** ❑ *Summons and Complaint* for divorce   on   _____   based   upon   the   following   grounds*: _____.

2.   I appear in this action; however, I do not intend to respond to the summons or answer the complaint, and I waive the twenty (20) or thirty (30) day period provided by law to respond to the summons or answer the complaint. I waive the forty (40) day waiting period to place this matter on the calendar, and I hereby consent to this action being placed on the uncontested divorce calendar immediately.

3. ❑ I am not a member of the military service of this state, any other state or this nation
OR
   ❑ If in the military: I am aware of my rights under the New York State Soldiers' and Sailors' Civil Relief Act; however, I consent that this matter be placed on the Uncontested Matrimonial calendar and waive any rights I may have under the Act.

4a. ❑ I waive the service of all further papers in this action except for a copy of the final Judgment of Divorce.
OR
   b. ❑ I request service of the following documents: *Note of Issue, Request for Judicial Intervention, Barriers to Remarriage Affidavit, Proposed Judgment of Divorce, Proposed Findings of Facts and Conclusions of Law, Notice of Settlement, Qualified Medical Child Support Order, and any other proposed orders.*

5.   I am not seeking equitable distribution *other than what was already agreed to in a written stipulation.*   I understand that I may be prevented from further asserting my right to equitable distribution.

6.   *I will take or have taken all steps solely within my power to remove any barriers to the Plaintiff's remarriage.*

(Form UD-7 - Rev. 5/99)

14   7a. ❑ I am not the custodial parent of the child(ren) of the marriage.

OR

b. ❑ I am the custodial parent of the unemancipated child(ren) entitled to receive child support pursuant to DRL §236(B)(7)(b),

AND

❑ (1) I request child support services through the Support Collection Unit which would authorize collection of the support obligation by the immediate issuance of an income execution for support enforcement.

OR

❑ (2) I am in receipt of such services through the Support Collection Unit.

OR

❑ (3) I have applied for such services through the Support Collection Unit.

OR

❑ (4) I am aware of but decline such services through the Support Collection Unit at this time. I am aware that an income deduction order may be issued pursuant to CPLR §5242(c) without other child support enforcement services and that payment of an administrative fee may be required.

If (1) or (4) is selected the following information must be included on a separate information sheet (Form UD-8a):

Name, date of birth, address and social security number of each party; date and place of marriage; names and dates of birth of the children; and name and address of employer of the payor (non-custodial parent).

15

_____
Defendant's Signature

Subscribed and Sworn to
before me on

_____

_____
NOTARY PUBLIC

*Insert the grounds alleged in the complaint:
DRL §170(1) cruel and inhuman treatment   DRL §170(4) adultery
DRL §170(2) abandonment   DRL §170(5) living apart one year after separation decree or judgment of separation
DRL §170(3) confinement in prison   DRL §170(6) living apart one year after execution of a separation agreement

(Form UD-7 - Rev. 5/99)

SUPREME COURT OF THE STATE OF NEW YORK
COUNTY OF _____
--X

Plaintiff,	Index/Docket No.:
-- against --	**CHILD SUPPORT** **WORKSHEET**
Defendant	

--X

Prepared by _____
This Worksheet is submitted by • Plaintiff • Defendant
(All numbers used in this worksheet are YEARLY figures. Convert weekly or monthly figures to annualized numbers.)

STEP 1 MANDATORY PARENTAL INCOME *(b)(5)*   FATHER   MOTHER

1. Gross (total) income (as reported on most recent Federal tax return, or as computed in accordance with Internal Revenue Code and regulations): *(b)(5)(i)*.. _____ _____

   The following items **MUST** *be added if not already included in Line 1:*
2. Investment income: *(b)(5)(ii)*.. _____ _____
3. Workers' compensation: *(b)(5)(iii)(A)*.. _____ _____
4. Disability benefits: *(b)(5)(iii)(B)*.. _____ _____
5. Unemployment insurance benefits: *(b)(5)(iii)(C)*............................ _____ _____
6. Social Security benefits: *(b)(5)(iii)(D)*.. _____ _____
7. Veterans benefits: *(b)(5)(iii)(E)*.. _____ _____
8. Pension/retirement income: *(b)(5)(iii)(F)*.. _____ _____
9. Fellowships and stipends: *(b)(5)(iii)(G)*.. _____ _____
10. Annuity payments: *(b)(5)(iii)(H)*.. _____ _____
11. If self-employed, depreciation greater than straight-line depreciation used in determining business income or investment credit: *(b)(5)(vi)(A)*.... _____ _____
12. If self-employed, entertainment and travel allowances deducted from business income to the extent the allowances reduce personal expenditures: *(b)(5)(vi)(B)*.. _____ _____
13. Former income voluntarily reduced to avoid child support: *(b)(5)(v)*.
14. Income voluntarily deferred: *(b)(5)(iii)*.. _____ _____

A. TOTAL MANDATORY INCOME:.. _____ _____

(Form UD-8 - Rev. 5/99)

STEP 2 NON-MANDATORY PARENTAL INCOME

These items must be disclosed here. Their inclusion in the final calculations, however, is discretionary. In contested cases, the Court determines whether or not they are included. In uncontested cases, the parents and their attorneys or mediators must determine which should be included.

15. Income attributable to non-income producing assets: *(b)(5)(iv)(A)*.............
16. Employment benefits that confer personal economic benefits: *(b)(5)(iv)(B)*
    (Such as meals, lodging, memberships, automobiles, other)....................

17. Fringe benefits of employment: *(b)(5)(iv)(C)*
18. Money, goods and services provided by relatives and friends: *(b)(5)(iv)(D)*

B. TOTAL NON-MANDATORY INCOME:..

C. TOTAL INCOME *(add Line A + Line B)*:...

STEP 3 DEDUCTIONS

19. Expenses of investment income listed on line 2: *(b)(5)(ii)*.............................
20. Unreimbursed business expenses that do not reduce personal
    expenditures: *(b)(5)(vii)(A)*...
21. Alimony or maintenance actually paid to a former spouse: *(b)(5)(vii)(B)*......
22. Alimony or maintenance paid to the other parent but only
    if child support will increase when alimony stops: *(b)(5)(vii)(C)*.................
23. Child support actually paid to other children the parent
    is legally obligated to support: *(b)(5)(vii)(D)*...
24. Public assistance: *(b)(5)(vii)(E)*..
25. Supplemental security income: *(b)(5)(vii)(F)*..
26. New York City or Yonkers income or earnings taxes actually paid:
    (b)(5)(vii)(G)...
27. Social Security taxes (FICA) actually paid: *(b)(5)(vii)(H)*................................

D. TOTAL DEDUCTIONS:...

Form reproduced by permission of Author: Steven L. Abel, Esq.

15   **E.   FATHER'S INCOME (Line C minus Line D):**... $ _____

(Form UD-8 - Rev. 5/99)
16   **F.   MOTHER'S INCOME (Line C minus Line D):**.. $ _____

17   **STEP 4** *(b)(4)*   **G.   COMBINED PARENTAL INCOME (Line E + Line F):**........... $ _____

18   **STEP 5** *(b)(3) and (c)(2)*

MULTIPLY Line G (up to $80,000) by the proper percentage *(insert in Line H):*
For 1 child.......................17%   For 3 children.................29%   For 5 or more children....... 35% (minimum)
For 2 children.................25%   For 4 children.................31%

H.   COMBINED CHILD SUPPORT:...   _____

STEP 6 *(c)(2)*

19   DIVIDE the noncustodial parent's amount on Line E or Line F:.........................   _____
20   by the amount of Line G:...   _____
       to obtain the percentage allocated
21   **I. to the noncustodial parent:**...   _____

22   **STEP 7** *(c)(2)*   **J. MULTIPLY line H by Line I:**...   _____

STEP 8 *(c)(3)*

23   **K. DECIDE the amount of child support to be paid on any combined**
       parental income exceeding $80,000 per year using the percentages
       in STEP 5 or the factors in STEP 11-C or both:...   _____

24   **L. ADD Line J and Line K:**...   _____
       This is the amount of child support to be paid by the non-custodial parent to the custodial parent for all costs of the
       children, except for child care expenses, health care expenses, and college, post-secondary, private, special or
       enriched education.

STEP 9 SPECIAL NUMERICAL FACTORS

CHILD CARE EXPENSES

25   **M. Cost of child care resulting from custodial parent's:**
       • seeking work *(c)(6)[discretionary]*   • working   • attending elementary education
       • attending secondary education   • attending higher education
       • attending vocational training leading to employment: *(c)(4)*...............................   _____

26   **N. MULTIPLY Line M by Line I:**..   _____
       This is the amount the non-custodial parent must contribute to the custodial parent
       for child care.

Form reproduced by permission of Author: Steven L. Abel, Esq.

(Form UD-8 - Rev. 5/99)

HEALTH EXPENSES *(c)(5)*

27   **O. Reasonable future health care expenses not covered by insurance**:.......... _____

28   **P. MULTIPLY Line O by Line I**:... _____
     This is the amount the non-custodial parent must contribute to the custodial parent for health care or pay directly to the health care provider.

29   **Q. EDUCATIONAL EXPENSE, if appropriate, see STEP 11(b)** *(c)(7)*................ _____

STEP 10 LOW INCOME EXEMPTIONS *(d)*

30   **R. INSERT amount of noncustodial parent's income from Line E or Line F**:... _____

31   **S. ADD amounts on Line L, Line N, Line P and Line Q**
     (This total is "basic child support"):... _____

32   **T. SUBTRACT Line S from Line R**:... _____

     If Line T is more than the self-support reserve*, then the low income exemptions do not apply and child support remains as determined in Steps 8 and 9. **If so, go to Step 11.**

     If Line T is less than the poverty level†, then

33   **U. INSERT amount of non-custodial parent's income from Line E or Line F**:.......... _____

34   **V. Self-support reserve**:... _____

35   **W. SUBTRACT Line V from Line U**:.. _____

     If Line W is more than $300 per year, then Line W is the amount of basic child support. If Line W is less than $300 per year, then basic child support must be a minimum of $300 per year.

     If Line T is less than the self-support reserve* but more than the poverty level†, then

36   **X. INSERT amount of noncustodial parent's income from Line E or Line F**:.................. _____

37   **Y. Self-support reserve**:... _____

***The self-support reserve.** This figure changes on April 1 of each year. The current self-support reserve is 135% of the office Federal poverty level for a single person household as promulgated by the U.S. Department of Health and Human Services.

†**The poverty level.** This figure changes on April 1 of each year. The current Federal poverty level for a single person household in any year is as promulgated by the U.S. Department of Health and Human Services.

(Form UD-8 - Rev. 5/99)

Z. SUBTRACT Line Y from Line X:.. ___

If Line Z is more than $600 per year, then Line Z is the amount of basic child support. If Line Z is less than $600 per year, then basic child support must be a minimum of $600 per year.

STEP 11 NON-NUMERICAL FACTORS

(a) NON-RECURRING INCOME *(e)*

A portion of non-recurring income, such as life insurance proceeds, gifts and inheritances or lottery winnings, may be allocated to child support. The law does not mention a specific percentage for such non-recurring income. Such support is not modified by the low income exemptions.

(b) EDUCATIONAL EXPENSES *(c)(7)*

New York's child support law does not contain a specific percentage method to determine how parents should share the cost of education of their children. Traditionally, the courts have considered both parents' complete financial circumstances in deciding who pays how much. The most important elements of financial circumstances are income, reasonable expenses, and financial resources such as savings and investments.

(c) ADDITIONAL FACTORS *(f)*

The child support guidelines law lists 10 factors that should be considered in deciding on the amount of child support for:

P combined incomes of more than $80,000 per year or

P to vary the numerical result of these steps because the result is "unjust or inappropriate". However, any court order deviating from the guidelines must set forth the amount of "basic child support" (Line S) resulting from the Guidelines and the reason for the deviation.

These factors are:

1. The financial resources of the parents and the child.
2. The physical and emotional health of the child and his/her special needs and aptitudes.
3. The standard of living the child would have enjoyed if the marriage or household was not dissolved.
4. The tax consequences to the parents.
5. The non-monetary contributions the parents will make toward the care and well-being of the child.
6. The educational needs of the parents.
7. The fact that the gross income of one parent is substantially less than the gross income of the other parent.
8. The needs of the other children of the non-custodial parent for whom the non-custodial parent is providing support, but only (a) if Line 23 is not deducted; (b) after considering the financial resources of any other person obligated to support the other children; and (c) if the resources available to support the other children are less then the resources available to support the children involved in this matter.
9. If a child is not on public assistance, the amount of extraordinary costs of visitation (such as out-of-state travel) or extended visits (other than the usual two to four week summer visits), but only if the custodial parent's expenses are substantially reduced by the visitation involved.
10. Any other factor the court decides is relevant.

(Form UD-8 - Rev. 5/99)

NON-JUDICIAL DETERMINATION OF CHILD SUPPORT *(h)*

Outside of court, parents are free to agree to any amount of support, so long as they sign a statement that they have been advised of the provisions of the child support guidelines law, the amount of "basic child support" (Line S) resulting from the Guidelines and the reason for any deviation. Further, the Court must approve any deviation, and the court cannot approve agreements of less than $300 per year. This minimum is not per child, meaning that the minimum for 3 children is $300 per year, not $900 per year. In addition, the courts retain discretion over child support.

_____

Plaintiff's Signature

(The name signed must be printed beneath)

Subscribed and Sworn to
before me on

_____

_____
NOTARY PUBLIC

Form reproduced by permission of Author: Steven L. Abel, Esq.

SUPREME COURT OF THE STATE OF NEW YORK
COUNTY OF _____

--x

<table>
<tr><td>Plaintiff,</td><td>Index No. _____</td></tr>
<tr><td>-against-</td><td>**SUPPORT COLLECTION UNIT**
INFORMATION SHEET</td></tr>
<tr><td>Defendant.</td><td></td></tr>
</table>

--x

The following information is required pursuant to Section 240(1) of the Domestic Relations Law:

PLAINTIFF: _____

　　　Address: _____

　　　Date of Birth _____ SS #: _____

DEFENDANT: _____

　　　Address: _____

　　　Date of Birth _____ SS #: _____

Date and Place of Marriage: _____

• _Plaintiff_ **OR** • _Defendant_ is the custodial parent and • _is_ **OR** • _is not_ receiving public assistance.

UNEMANCIPATED CHILDREN:　　　<u>Name</u>　　　<u>Date of Birth</u>

SUPPORT: Maintenance $_____ • _per week_ **OR** • _bi-weekly_ **OR** • _per month_

　　　　　Child Support $_____ • _per week_ **OR** • _bi-weekly_ **OR** • _per month_

　　　　　Total Support $_____ • _per week_ **OR** • _bi-weekly_ **OR** • _per month_

Support payments are to be made to • _Plaintiff_ **OR** • _Defendant_ **OR** • _Third Party._

If third party, list name and address: _____

Non-custodial parent's employer: _____

　　　　　Address: _____

Dated: _____

1

At the *Matrimonial/IAS* Part _____
of New York State Supreme Court at
the Courthouse, _____
County, on _____.

2

3

Present:

4   Hon.   *Justice/Referee*
--X

5

6
                                        Index No.:
                    Plaintiff,   Calendar No.:
     -against-

                                        FINDINGS OF FACT
                                        AND
                                        CONCLUSIONS OF LAW

7
                    Defendant.
--X

8   The issues of this action having   *been submitted to* **OR**   *been heard* before me
as one of the *Justices/Referees* of this Court at Part _____ hereof, held in and for the County
of _____ on _____, and having considered the allegations and proofs
of the respective parties, and due deliberation having been had thereon.

           NOW, after   *reading and considering the papers submitted*   *hearing the testimony*,
I do hereby make the following findings of essential facts which I deem established by the evidence
and reach the following conclusions of law.

                              FINDINGS OF FACT

9   **FIRST:**   Plaintiff and Defendant were both eighteen (18) years of age or over when this
action was commenced.

10   **SECOND:**

           The Plaintiff has resided in New York State for a continuous period in excess of two years
immediately preceding the commencement of this action.

                                      OR

(Form UD-10 - Rev. 5/99)

Name: Address: Identification No.:

The administrator of said plan is:
Name: Address:

The type of coverage provided is:

ORDERED that coverage shall include all plans covering the health, medical, dental, pharmaceutical and optical needs of the aforementioned Dependents named above for which the Participant is eligible.

ORDERED that said coverage shall be effective as of (give date) _____
and shall continue as available until the respective emancipation of the aforementioned dependents.

ENTER:

    DATED:_____   _____
                                          JSC/Referee

TO: [Health Insurer]

NOTICE: Pursuant to Section 5241(g)(4) of the Civil Practice Laws and Rules, if an employer, organization or group health plan fails to enroll eligible dependents or to deduct from the debtor's income the debtor's share of the premium, such employer, organization or group health plan administrator shall be jointly and severally liable for all medical expenses incurred on behalf of the debtor's dependents named in the execution while such dependents are not so enrolled to the extent of the insurance benefits that should have been provided under such execution.

The group health plan is not required to provide any type or form of benefit or option not otherwise provided under the group health plan except to the extent necessary to meet the requirements of a law relating to medical child support described in section one thousand three hundred and ninety-six g-1 of title forty-two of the United States Code.

NOTE OF ISSUE - UNCONTESTED DIVORCE

For Use of Clerk

SUPREME COURT OF THE STATE OF NEW YORK
COUNTY OF _____
---X

                                    Plaintiff,   Index No.:

        - against -   Calendar No.:

                                    Defendant.
---X

NO TRIAL

FILED BY: • *Plaintiff* **OR** • *Plaintiff's Attorney* **OR** • *Defendant* **OR**
             • *Defendant's Attorney*

DATE SUMMONS FILED: _____

DATE SUMMONS SERVED: _____

DATE ISSUE JOINED: **NOT JOINED -** • *Waiver* **OR** • *Default* **OR**
                              • *Stipulation/Separation Agreement*
NATURE OF ACTION: **UNCONTESTED DIVORCE**
RELIEF: **ABSOLUTE DIVORCE**

• *Plaintiff* **OR** • *Attorney(s) for Plaintiff*
Office and P.O. Address:

Phone No.:
Fax No.:

• *Defendant* **OR** • *Attorney(s) for Defendant*
Office and P.O. Address:

Phone No.:
Fax No.:

1

2

3

At the *Matrimonial/IAS* Part _____
of New York State Supreme Court at
the Courthouse, _____
County, on _____ .

Present:

4   Hon. _____ *Justice/Referee*

--X

5

6

Plaintiff,	Index No.:
-against-	Calendar No.:

**FINDINGS OF FACT
AND
CONCLUSIONS OF LAW**

7   Defendant.

--X

8   The issues of this action having ❑ *been submitted to* **OR** ❑ *been heard* before me as one of the *Justices/Referees* of this Court at Part _____ hereof, held in and for the County of _____ on _____, and having considered the allegations and proofs of the respective parties, and due deliberation having been had thereon.

NOW, after ❑ *reading and considering the papers submitted* ❑ *hearing the testimony*, I do hereby make the following findings of essential facts which I deem established by the evidence and reach the following conclusions of law.

FINDINGS OF FACT

9   **FIRST:**   Plaintiff and Defendant were both eighteen (18) years of age or over when this action was commenced.

10   **SECOND:**

❑ The Plaintiff has resided in New York State for a continuous period in excess of two
years immediately preceding the commencement of this action.

OR

(Form UD-10 - Rev. 5/99)

❑ The Defendant has resided in New York State for a continuous period in excess of two years immediately preceding the commencement of this action.

OR

❑ The Plaintiff has resided in New York State for a continuous period in excess of one year immediately preceding the commencement of this action, and:

    a. ❑ the parties were married in New York State.
    b. ❑ the Plaintiff has lived as husband or wife in New York State with the Defendant.
    c. ❑ the cause of action occurred in New York State.

OR

❑ The Defendant has resided in New York State for a continuous period in excess of one year immediately preceding the commencement of this action; and:

    a. ❑ the parties were married in New York State.
    b. ❑ the Defendant has lived as husband or wife in New York State with the Plaintiff.
    c. ❑ the cause of action occurred in New York State.

OR

❑ The cause of action occurred in New York State and both parties were residents thereof at the time of the commencement of this action.

11   **THIRD:** The Plaintiff and the Defendant were married on the date of _____ in the City, Town or Village of _____, County of _____, State or Country of _____; in a ❑ *civil* **OR** ❑ *religious* ceremony.

12   **FOURTH:** That no decree, judgment or order of divorce, annulment or dissolution of marriage has been granted to either party against the other in any Court of competent jurisdiction of this state or any other state, territory or country, and that there is no other action pending for divorce by either party against the other in any Court.

13   **FIFTH:** That this action was commenced by filing the ❑ *Summons With Notice* **OR** ❑ *Summons and Verified Complaint* with the County Clerk on _____. Defendant was served ❑ *personally* **OR** ❑ *pursuant to Court order dated* _____ with the above stated pleadings. Defendant ❑ *defaulted in appearance* **OR** ❑ *appeared and waived his / her right to answer* **OR** ❑ *filed an answer / amended answer withdrawing any previous pleading, and neither admitting nor denying the allegations in plaintiff's complaint, and consenting to entry of judgment.*

(Form UD-10 - Rev. 5/99)

14   **SIXTH:** ❑ That Defendant is not in the military service of the United States of America, the State of New York, or any other state. **OR** ❑ Defendant is a member of the military service of the _____ and ❑ has appeared by affidavit and does not oppose the action **OR** ❑ is in default.

15   **SEVENTH:** ❑ There are no children of the marriage. **OR** ❑ There *is/are* _____ child(ren) of the marriage. Their name(s), social security number(s), address(es) and date(s) of birth are:

Name & Social Security Number	*Date of Birth*	*Address*
_____	_____	_____
_____	_____	_____
_____	_____	_____
_____	_____	_____
_____	_____	_____

16   **EIGHTH:** The grounds for divorce that are alleged in the Verified Complaint were proved as follows:

Cruel and Inhuman Treatment (DRL §170(1)):

❑   At the following times, none of which are earlier than (5) years prior to commencement of this action, the Defendant engaged in conduct that so endangered the mental and physical well being of the Plaintiff, so as to render it unsafe or improper for the parties to cohabit (live together) as husband and wife.

(State the facts that demonstrate cruel and inhuman conduct giving dates, places and specific acts. Conduct may include physical, verbal, sexual or emotional behavior).

_____
_____
_____
_____
_____
_____
_____
_____
_____
_____

(Attach an additional sheet, if necessary).

(Form UD-10 - Rev. 5/99)

Abandonment (DRL 170(2)):

❑ That commencing on or about _____, and continuing for a period of more than one (1) year immediately prior to commencement of this action, the Defendant left the marital residence of the parties located at _____ _____, and did not return. Such absence was without cause or justification, and was without Plaintiff's consent.

❑ That commencing on or about _____, and continuing for a period of more than one (1) year immediately prior to commencement of this action, the Defendant refused to have sexual relations with the Plaintiff despite Plaintiff's repeated requests to resume such relations. Defendant does not suffer from any disability which would prevent *her / him* from engaging in such sexual relations with Plaintiff. The refusal to engage in sexual relations was without good cause or justification and occurred at the marital residence located at _____.

❑ That commencing on or about _____, and continuing for a period of more than one (1) year immediately prior to commencement of this action, the Defendant willfully and without cause or justification abandoned the Plaintiff, who had been a faithful and dutiful *husband / wife*, by depriving Plaintiff of access to the marital residence located at _____. This deprivation was without the consent of the Plaintiff and continued for a period of greater than one year.

Confinement to Prison (DRL §170(3)):

❑ (a) That after the marriage of Plaintiff and Defendant, Defendant was confined in prison for a period of three or more consecutive years, to wit: that Defendant was confined in _____ prison on _____, and has remained confined to this date; and

(b) not more that five (5) years elapsed between the end of the third year of imprisonment and the date of commencement of this action.

Adultery (DRL §170(4)):

❑ (a) That on _____, at the premises located at _____ _____, the Defendant engaged in sexual intercourse with _____, without the procurement nor the connivance of the Plaintiff and the Plaintiff ceased to cohabit (live) with the Defendant upon the discovery of the adultery.

(b) not more than five (5) years elapsed between the date of said adultery and the date of commencement of this action.

(Attach a corroborating affidavit of a third party witness or other additional proof).

Living Separate and Apart Pursuant to a Separation Decree or Judgment of Separation (DRL §170(5)):

❑ (a) That the _____ Court, _____ County, _____(Country or State) rendered a decree or judgment of separation on _____, under Index Number _____; and

(b) that the parties have lived separate and apart for a period of one year or longer after the granting of such decree; and

(c) that the Plaintiff has substantially complied with all the terms and conditions of such decree or judgment.

Living Separate and Apart Pursuant to a Separation Agreement (DRL §170(6)):

    ❑   (a)   That the Plaintiff and Defendant entered into a written agreement of separation, which they subscribed and acknowledged on _____, in the form required to entitle a deed to be recorded; and

            (b)   that the *agreement / memorandum of said agreement* was filed _____ _____ in the Office of the Clerk of the County of _____, wherein *Plaintiff / Defendant* resided; and

            (c)   that the parties have lived separate and apart for a period of one year or longer after the execution of said agreement; and

            (d)   that the Plaintiff has substantially complied with all terms and conditions of such agreement.

NINTH: ❑ A sworn statement pursuant to DRL §253 that Plaintiff has taken all steps within his or her power to remove all barriers to Defendant's remarriage following the divorce was served on the Defendant.

    ❑ A sworn statement as to the removal of barriers to remarriage is not required because the parties were married in a civil ceremony.

    ❑ A sworn statement as to the removal of barriers to remarriage is not required because Defendant waived the need for the statement in his or her affidavit.

TENTH: ❑ *The parties have agreed* **OR** ❑ *the court has determined* that ❑ *Plaintiff* **OR** ❑ *Defendant* will receive maintenance of $_____ ❑ *per week* **OR** ❑ *bi-weekly* **OR** ❑ *per month* commencing on _____ pursuant to DRL §236(B)(6)(c).

ELEVENTH: The children of the marriage now reside with ❑ *Plaintiff* **OR** ❑ *Defendant* **OR** ❑ *third party,* namely _____. The ❑ *Plaintiff* **OR** ❑ *Defendant* is entitled to visitation away from the custodial residence. The ❑ *Plaintiff* **OR** ❑ *Defendant* **OR** ❑ *Third Party, namely* _____ is entitled to custody. **OR** ❑ No award of custody due to the child(ren) of the marriage not residing in New York State. **OR** ❑ Other custody arrangement (specify): _____ _____.

TWELFTH: Equitable Distribution and ancillary issues shall be ❑ *in accordance with the settlement agreement* **OR** ❑ *pursuant to the decision of the court* **OR** ❑ *Equitable Distribution is not an issue.*

THIRTEENTH: ❑ There *is/are* no unemancipated child(ren). **OR** ❑ The award of child support is based upon the following:

(A)   The children of the marriage entitled to receive support are:

Name   *Date of Birth*

_____   _____

_____   _____

_____   _____

_____   _____

_____   _____

(B)   (1)   By order of _____ Court, _____ County, *Index/Docket No.* _____
            dated _____ the *Plaintiff/Defendant* was directed to pay   the sum of
            _____ per _____ for child support. Said Order shall continue.

                                    OR

      (2)   The adjusted gross income of the Plaintiff who is the ❑ *custodial* **OR** ❑ *non-
            custodial* parent is _____ per year and the adjusted gross income of the Defendant
            who is the ❑ *custodial* **OR** ❑ *non-custodial* parent is _____ per year
            and the combined parental annual income is _____.   The applicable
            child support percentage is *17/25/29/31/35 %*.   The combined basic child support
            obligation attributable to both parents is _____ per year on income to $80,000
            and _____ per year on income over $80,000. The Plaintiff's pro rata share of
            the combined parental income is _____% and the Defendant's pro rata share of the
            combined parental income is _____%. The non-custodial parent's pro rata share of the
            child support obligation on combined income to $80,000 is _____per year or
            _____ ❑ *per week* ❑ *bi-weekly* ❑ *per month*. The non-custodial parent's pro
            rata share of the child support obligation on combined income over $80,000 is _____
            _____ per year or _____ ❑ per week ❑ bi-weekly ❑ per month. The non-
            custodial parent's pro rata share of future health care expenses not covered by insurance,
            child care expenses, educational or other extraordinary expenses is _____%.

                                    OR

      (3)   The parties entered into a *stipulation/agreement* on _____wherein the
            ❑ *Plaintiff* **OR** ❑ *Defendant* agrees to pay _____ ❑ *per week* **OR** ❑
            bi-weekly **OR** ❑ *per month* child support ❑ *directly* **OR** ❑ *through the Support
            Collection Unit* to ❑ *Plaintiff* **OR** ❑ *Defendant* **OR** ❑ *Third Party, namely*
            _____. The parties agree to ❑ *waive* **OR** ❑ *apply* the
            Child Support Standards Act to combined income over $80,000. The parties have agreed
            that health care expenses not covered by insurance shall be paid by ❑ *Plaintiff* **OR**
            ❑ *Defendant* in the amount of _____ ❑ *per week* **OR** ❑ *bi-weekly* **OR** ❑
            per month **OR** ❑ _____% of the uncovered expenses. The parties have agreed

(Form UD-10 - Rev. 5/99)

that child care expenses shall be paid by ❑ *Plaintiff* **OR** ❑ *Defendant* to ❑ *Plaintiff* **OR** ❑ *Defendant* in the amount of _____ ❑ *per week* **OR** ❑ *bi-weekly* **OR** ❑ *per month* **OR** ❑ ____% of said child care expenses. The parties have agreed that educational and extraordinary expenses shall be paid by ❑ *Plaintiff* **OR** ❑ *Defendant* to ❑ *Plaintiff* **OR** ❑ *Defendant* in the amount of _____ _____ ❑ *per week* **OR** ❑ *bi-weekly* **OR** ❑ *per month* **OR** ❑ ____% of said educational and extraordinary expenses. Said agreement reciting in compliance with DRL §2401-b(h): The parties have been advised of the Child Support Standards Act. The basic child support obligation presumptively results in the correct amount of child support. The unrepresented party, if any, has received a copy of the Child Support Standards Chart promulgated by Commissioner of Social Services pursuant to Social Services Law Section 111-I. The presumptive amount of child support attributable to the non-custodial parent is _____ ❑ *per week* **OR** ❑ *bi-weekly* **OR** ❑ *per month*. The amount of child support agreed to ❑ *conforms with the non-custodial parent's basic child support obligation* **OR** ❑ *deviates from the non-custodial parent's basic child support obligation for the following reasons:*

_____
_____
_____

22   **FOURTEENTH:** The Plaintiff's address is _____,

and social security number is _____. The Defendant's address is _____

- _____, and social security number is _____.

23   ❑   There are no unemancipated children.   **OR**

         ❑   There are no health plans available to the parties through their employment.   **OR**

         ❑   The parties are covered by the following group health plans through their employment:

Plaintiff	**Defendant**
Group Health Plan:_____	Group Health Plan:_____
Address:_____	Address:_____
Identification Number:_____	Identification Number:_____
Plan Administrator:_____	Plan Administrator:_____
Type of Coverage:_____	Type of Coverage:_____

     ❑ *The parties have agreed or stipulated* **OR** ❑ *the court has determined* that the ❑ *Plaintiff* **OR** ❑ *Defendant* shall be the legally responsible relative and that the unemancipated child(ren) shall be enrolled in *his / her* group health plan as specified above *until the age of 21 years* **OR** *until the child(ren) is / are sooner emancipated.*

(Form UD-10 - Rev. 5/99)

24   **FIFTEENTH:** The _____ Court entered the following order(s) under Index No(s). / Docket No(s).:_____

_____

25   **SIXTEENTH:** ❑ _Plaintiff_ **OR** ❑ _Defendant_ may resume use of the prior surname:

_____.

CONCLUSIONS OF LAW

26   **FIRST:** Residency as required by DRL §230 has been satisfied.

27   **SECOND:** ❑ _Plaintiff_ **OR** ❑ _Defendant_ is entitled to a judgment of divorce on the grounds of DRL §170 subd._____ and granting the incidental relief awarded.

28   Dated:_____   _____

                                       J.S.C./Referee

1

At the *Matrimonial/IAS* Part _____
of New York State Supreme Court at
the Courthouse, _____

2

3

County, on _____.

Present:

4

Hon. _____ *Justice/Referee*

--X

5

6

Plaintiff,

-against-

Index No.:
Calendar No.:
Social Security No.:

JUDGMENT OF DIVORCE

7

Defendant.

--X

8   **THE FOLLOWING NOTICE IS ❑ *APPLICABLE*   OR   ❑   *NOT APPLICABLE***

NOTICE REQUIRED WHERE PAYMENTS THROUGH SUPPORT COLLECTION UNIT

NOTE: (1) THIS ORDER OF CHILD SUPPORT SHALL BE ADJUSTED BY THE APPLICATION OF A COST OF LIVING ADJUSTMENT AT THE DIRECTION OF THE SUPPORT COLLECTION UNIT NO EARLIER THAN TWENTY-FOUR MONTHS AFTER THIS ORDER IS ISSUED, LAST MODIFIED OR LAST ADJUSTED, UPON THE REQUEST OF ANY PARTY TO THE ORDER OR PURSUANT TO PARAGRAPH (2) BELOW. UPON APPLICATION OF A COST OF LIVING ADJUSTMENT AT THE DIRECTION OF THE SUPPORT COLLECTION UNIT, AN ADJUSTED ORDER SHALL BE SENT TO THE PARTIES WHO, IF THEY OBJECT TO THE COST OF LIVING ADJUSTMENT, SHALL HAVE THIRTY-FIVE (35) DAYS FROM THE DATE OF MAILING TO SUBMIT A WRITTEN OBJECTION TO THE COURT INDICATED ON SUCH ADJUSTED ORDER. UPON RECEIPT OF SUCH WRITTEN OBJECTION, THE COURT SHALL SCHEDULE A HEARING AT WHICH THE PARTIES MAY BE PRESENT TO OFFER EVIDENCE WHICH THE COURT WILL CONSIDER IN ADJUSTING THE CHILD SUPPORT ORDER IN ACCORDANCE WITH THE CHILD SUPPORT STANDARDS ACT.

(2) A RECIPIENT OF FAMILY ASSISTANCE SHALL HAVE THE CHILD SUPPORT ORDER REVIEWED AND ADJUSTED AT THE DIRECTION OF THE SUPPORT COLLECTION UNIT NO EARLIER THAN TWENTY-FOUR MONTHS AFTER SUCH ORDER IS ISSUED, LAST MODIFIED OR LAST ADJUSTED WITHOUT FURTHER APPLICATION BY ANY PARTY. ALL PARTIES WILL RECEIVE A COPY OF THE ADJUSTED ORDER.

(3) WHERE ANY PARTY FAILS TO PROVIDE, AND UPDATE UPON ANY CHANGE, THE SUPPORT COLLECTION UNIT WITH A CURRENT ADDRESS, AS REQUIRED BY SECTION TWO HUNDRED FORTY-B OF THE DOMESTIC RELATIONS LAW, TO WHICH AN ADJUSTED ORDER CAN BE SENT, THE SUPPORT OBLIGATION AMOUNT CONTAINED THEREIN SHALL BECOME DUE AND OWING ON THE DATE THE FIRST PAYMENT IS DUE UNDER THE TERMS OF THE ORDER OF SUPPORT WHICH WAS REVIEWED AND ADJUSTED OCCURRING ON OR AFTER THE EFFECTIVE DATE OF THE ADJUSTED ORDER, REGARDLESS OF WHETHER OR NOT THE PARTY HAS RECEIVED A COPY OF THE ADJUSTED ORDER.

9 This action was submitted to ❑ *the referee* **OR** ❑ *this court* for ❑ *consideration*

this ____ day of _____ **OR** for ❑ *inquest* on this ____ day of _____

10 The Defendant was served ❑ *personally* **OR** ❑ *pursuant to court order dated*

_____ ❑ *within* **OR** ❑ *outside* the State of New York.

11 Plaintiff presented a ❑ *Verified Complaint and Affidavit of Plaintiff constituting the facts of the matter* **OR** ❑ *Summons With Notice and Affidavit of Plaintiff constituting the facts of the matter.*

12 The Defendant has ❑ *not appeared and is in default* **OR** ❑ *appeared and waived his or her right to answer* **OR** ❑ *filed an answer or amended answer withdrawing any prior pleadings and neither admitting nor denying the allegations in the complaint and consenting to the entry of judgment* **OR** ❑ *the parties settled the ancillary issues by* ❑ *written stipulation* **OR** ❑ *oral stipulation on the record dated* _____

_____.

13 The Court accepted ❑ *written* **OR** ❑ *oral* proof of non-military status.

14 The Plaintiff's address is _____, and social

security number is _____. The Defendant's address is _____

_____, and social security number is _____.

(Form UD-11 - Rev. 5/99)

15   Now on motion of _____, the ❑ *attorney for Plaintiff* **OR**

❑ *Plaintiff*, it is:

16   **ORDERED AND ADJUDGED** that the Referee's Report, if any, is hereby

confirmed; and it is further

17   **ORDERED, ADJUDGED AND DECREED** that the marriage between_____

_____, plaintiff, and _____, defendant, is hereby dissolved by

reason of:

❑ (a)   the cruel and inhuman treatment of ❑ *Plaintiff by Defendant* **OR** ❑

Defendant by Plaintiff pursuant to DRL §170(1); and/or

❑ (b)   the abandonment of ❑ *Plaintiff* **OR** ❑ *Defendant* by ❑ *Plaintiff* **OR**

❑ *Defendant,* for a period of one or more years, pursuant to DRL §170(2);

and/or

❑ (c)   the confinement of ❑ *Plaintiff* **OR** ❑ *Defendant* in prison for a

period of three or more consecutive years after the marriage of Plaintiff and

Defendant, pursuant to DRL §170(3); and/or

❑ (d)   the commission of an act of adultery by ❑ *Plaintiff* **OR** ❑ *Defendant,*

pursuant to DRL §170(4); and/or

❑ (e)   the parties having lived separate and apart pursuant to a decree or judgment

of separation dated _____ for a period of one or more years

after the granting of such decree or judgment, pursuant to DRL §170(5);

and/or

❑ (f)   the parties having lived separate and apart pursuant to a Separation

Agreement dated _____ in compliance with the provisions of

DRL §170(6); and it is further

18   **ORDERED AND ADJUDGED** that ❑ *Plaintiff* **OR** ❑ *Defendant* **OR**

❑ *third party, namely:* _____ shall have custody of the minor

child(ren) of the marriage, i.e.:

19

Name	Date of Birth	Social Security No.
_____	_____	_____
_____	_____	_____
_____	_____	_____
_____	_____	_____

OR ❑ *There are no minor children of the marriage*; and it is further

20   **ORDERED AND ADJUDGED** that ❑ *Plaintiff* **OR** ❑ *Defendant* shall have

visitation with the minor child(ren) of the marriage ❑ *in accordance with the parties'*

settlement agreement **OR** ❑ *according to the following schedule:* _____

_____

_____

_____

_____ ;

OR ❑ *Visitation is not applicable*; and it is further;

21   **ORDERED AND ADJUDGED** that the existing _____ County, _____

Court order(s) under ❑ *Index No..*_____ **OR** ❑ *Docket No.*_____

as to ❑ *custody* **OR** ❑ *visitation* **OR** ❑ *maintenance* shall continue, and a copy of

this judgment shall be served by ❑ *Plaintiff* **OR** ❑ *Defendant* upon the Clerk of the

_____ County _____ Court within _____ days of its entry;

OR ❑ *There are no court orders with regard to custody, visitation or maintenance to be*

continued; and it is further

(Form UD-11 - Rev. 5/99)

22   **ORDERED AND ADJUDGED** that ❑ *Plaintiff* **OR** ❑ *Defendant*   shall pay to ❑ *Plaintiff* **OR** ❑ *Defendant* **OR** ❑ *third party, namely:*_____, as and for the support of the parties' unemancipated children, the sum of $_____ per _____, pursuant to an existing order issued by the _____ County, _____ Court, under ❑ *Index* **OR** ❑ *Docket* Number _____, the terms of which are hereby continued. ❑ *Plaintiff* **OR** ❑ *Defendant*   shall serve a copy of this Judgment upon the Clerk of the _____ County, _____ Court within _____ days of its entry; **OR** ❑ *There are no orders from other courts to be continued*; and it is further

23   **ORDERED AND** ADJUDGED that ❑ *Plaintiff* **OR** ❑ *Defendant* shall pay to ❑ *Plaintiff* **OR** ❑ *Defendant*   the sum of $_____ ❑ *per week* **OR** ❑ *bi-weekly* **OR** ❑ *per month* as and for maintenance commencing on _____ and thereafter on the _____ day of each ❑ *week* **OR** ❑ *bi-week* **OR** ❑ *month* until _____; **OR** ❑ *That there is no award of maintenance*; and it is further

24   **ORDERED AND ADJUDGED** that ❑ *Plaintiff* **OR** ❑ *Defendant* shall pay to ❑ *Plaintiff* **OR** ❑ *Defendant* **OR** ❑ *third party, namely:* _____, as and for the support of the parties' unemancipated child(ren), namely:

<u>Name</u>   <u>Date of Birth</u>

_____   _____

_____   _____

_____   _____

_____   _____

the sum of $_____ ❑ *per week* **OR** ❑ *bi-weekly* **OR** ❑ *per month*, commencing on _____, and to be paid ❑ *directly to* ❑ *Plaintiff* **OR** ❑ *Defendant* **OR** ❑ *third party, namely:*_____, **OR** ❑ *through the New York State Child Support Processing Center, PO Box 15363, Albany, NY 12212-5363*, together with such dollar amounts or percentages for ❑ *child care* **OR** ❑ *education* **OR** ❑ *health care* as set forth below in accordance with ❑ *the Court's decision* **OR** ❑ *the parties' Settlement Agreement.* Such Agreement is in compliance with DRL §240(1-b)(h) because:

The parties have been advised of the provisions of DRL Sec. 240(1-b); the unrepresented party, if any, has received a copy of the Child Support Standards Chart promulgated by the Commissioner of Social Services pursuant to Social Services Law Sec. 111-I;
the basic child support obligation, as defined in DRL Sec. 240(1-b), presumptively results in the correct amount of child support to be awarded, and the agreed upon amount substantially conforms to the basic support obligation attributable to the non-custodial parent;
the amount awarded is neither unjust nor inappropriate, and the Court has approved such award through the Findings of Fact and Conclusions of Law;

OR

The basic support obligation, as defined in DRL Sec. 240 (1-b), presumptively results in the correct amount of child support to be awarded, and the amount attributable to the non-custodial parent is $_____ per _____;
the amount of child support agreed to in this action deviates from the amount attributable to the non-custodial parent, and the Court has approved of such agreed-upon amount based upon the reasons set

forth in the Findings of Fact and Conclusions of Law, which are incorporated herein by reference; and it is further

OR ❑ *This provision is not applicable.*

25   **ORDERED AND ADJUDGED** that ❑ *Plaintiff* **OR** ❑ *Defendant* shall pay to ❑ *Plaintiff* **OR** ❑ *Defendant* **OR** ❑ *third party, namely:* _____, the sum of $ _____ ❑ *per week* **OR** ❑ *bi-weekly* **OR** ❑ *per month* as and for child care expenses, **OR** ❑ as follows: _____

_____

_____,

OR ❑ *Not applicable*; and it is further

26   **ORDERED AND ADJUDGED** that ❑ *Plaintiff* **OR** ❑ *Defendant* shall pay to ❑ *Plaintiff* **OR** ❑ *Defendant* **OR** ❑ *third party, namely:* _____, the sum of $ _____ ❑ *per week* **OR** ❑ *bi-weekly* **OR** ❑ *per month* as and for future reasonable health care, **OR** ❑ as follows:

_____

_____

_____;

OR ❑ *Not applicable*; and it is further

27   **ORDERED AND ADJUDGED** that ❑ *Plaintiff* **OR** ❑ *Defendant* shall pay to ❑ *Plaintiff* **OR** ❑ *Defendant* **OR** ❑ *third party, namely:* _____; the sum of $ _____ ❑ *per week* **OR** ❑ *bi-weekly* **OR** ❑ *per month* as and for ❑ *present* **OR** ❑ *future* **AND** ❑ *post-secondary* **OR** ❑ *private* **OR** ❑ *special* **OR** ❑ *enriched* education for the children, **OR** ❑ as follows:

_____

_____ ;

OR ❑ *Not applicable*; and it is further

28   **ORDERED AND ADJUDGED** that ❑ *Plaintiff* **OR** ❑ *Defendant* is hereby

awarded exclusive occupancy of the marital residence located at_____

_____ , together with its contents until further order of the

court, **OR** ❑ as follows: _____

_____

_____

_____ ; **OR** ❑ *Not applicable*; and it is further

29   **ORDERED AND ADJUDGED** that the Settlement Agreement entered into between

the parties on the_____day of_____ , a   ❑ *copy* **OR** ❑ *transcript* of

which is on file with this Court and incorporated herein by reference, shall survive and shall

not be merged into this judgment, and the parties are hereby directed to comply with all

legally enforceable terms and conditions of said agreement as if such terms and conditions

were set forth in their entirety herein, and this Court retains jurisdiction of this matter

concurrently with the Family Court for the purposes of specifically enforcing such of the

provisions of said Agreement as are capable of specific enforcement to the extent permitted

by law with regard to maintenance, child support, custody and/or visitation, and of making

such further judgment as it finds appropriate under the circumstances existing at the time

application for that purpose is made to it, or both; and it is further

30   **ORDERED AND ADJUDGED** that a separate Qualified Medical Child Support

Order shall be issued simultaneously herewith   **OR** ❑ Not applicable; and it is further

31   **ORDERED AND ADJUDGED** that, pursuant to the ❑ *parties' Settlement Agreement* **OR** ❑ *the court's decision*, a separate Qualified Domestic Relations Order shall be issued simultaneously herewith or as soon as practicable **OR** ❑ *Not applicable*; and it is further

32   **ORDERED AND ADJUDGED** that, ❑ *pursuant to this Court's direction* **OR** ❑ *pursuant to the parties' agreement*, this Court shall issue an income deduction order simultaneously herewith **OR** ❑ *Not applicable*; and it is further

33   **ORDERED AND ADJUDGED** that both parties are authorized to resume the use of any former surname, and it is further

34   **ORDERED AND ADJUDGED** that ❑ *Plaintiff* **OR** ❑ *Defendant* is authorized to resume use of the prior surname _____.

35   **ORDERED AND ADJUDGED** that ❑ *Plaintiff* **OR** ❑ *Defendant* shall be served with a copy of this judgment, with notice of entry, by the ❑ *Plaintiff* **OR** ❑ *Defendant*, within _____ days of such entry.

36   Dated:

ENTER:

_____
J.S.C./Referee

_____
CLERK

(Form UD-11 - Rev. 5/99)

SUPREME COURT OF THE STATE OF NEW YORK
COUNTY OF _____
---x

Plaintiff,	Index No. _____
-against-	
	PART 130
	CERTIFICATION
Defendant.	

---x

CERTIFICATION: I hereby certify that all of the papers that I have served, filed or submitted to the court in this divorce action are not frivolous as defined in subsection (c) of Section 130-1.1 of the Rules of the Chief Administrator of the Courts.

Dated: _____   _____
                                       SIGNATURE
                                       Print or type name below signature

REQUEST FOR JUDICIAL INTERVENTION

UNCONTESTED DIVORCE

SUPREME COURT, _____ COUNTY

INDEX #:_____ DATE PURCHASED:_____

--X

Plaintiff,

-against-

Defendant.

--X

FOR CLERK USE ONLY
_____
IAS ENTRY DATE
_____
JUDGE ASSIGNED
_____
RJI DATE
_____
RJI NUMBER

. . . .

<u>NATURE OF JUDICIAL INTERVENTION</u> - **EX PARTE APPLICATION FOR THE DISSOLUTION OF MARRIAGE.**

<u>ATTORNEY(S) FOR PLAINTIFF:</u>

Name   Address   Phone No.

<u>ATTORNEY(S) FOR DEFENDANT:</u>

Name   Address   Phone No.

Parties appearing without an attorney should enter information in the space provided above for attorneys.

<u>RELATED CASES:</u> (If none, write "NONE" below)

<u>Title</u>   <u>Index #</u>   <u>Court</u>   <u>Nature of Relationship</u>

I affirm under penalty of perjury that, to my knowledge, other than as noted above, there are and have been no related actions or proceedings, nor has a request for judicial intervention previously been filed in this action or proceeding.

Dated:

_____
(Signature)

_____
(Print or type name)

_____
Attorney for

(Form UD-13 - Rev. 5/99)

SUPREME COURT OF THE STATE OF NEW YORK
COUNTY OF _____
--X

                                    Plaintiff.   Index No.:_____

     -against-

                                                                 NOTICE OF ENTRY

                                    Defendant.
--X

        PLEASE TAKE NOTICE that the attached is a true copy of a judgment of divorce in

this matter that was entered in the Office of the County Clerk of _____ County, on the

_____ day of _____.

Dated:_____

                                                    _____
                                                    • *Plaintiff* **OR** • *Attorney(s) for Plaintiff*

                                                    _____
                                                    _____
                                                    _____

                                                    Address

TO:

_____
• Defendant **OR** • Attorney *for Defendant*

_____
_____
_____

        Address

SUPREME COURT OF THE STATE OF NEW YORK
COUNTY OF _____
---X

                            Plaintiff.   Index No.:_____

-vs-   **NOTICE OF MOTION FOR
                                                           PERMISSION TO PROCEED
                                                           AS A POOR PERSON**

                            Defendant.
---X

Please take notice that the undersigned Plaintiff will move this court at a term to be held on _____, _____, at _____a.m./p.m. upon the attached affidavits for an order allowing Plaintiff permission to prosecute an Action for Divorce as a Poor Person.

                              _____

                              _____

                              _____

To: _____

SUPREME COURT OF THE STATE OF NEW YORK

COUNTY OF _____

---X

In the Matter of the Application of

_____,

Plaintiff.

For Permission to Prosecute as a Poor Person

- against -

_____,

Defendant.

---X

Index No.:_____

AFFIDAVIT IN SUPPORT OF APPLICATION TO PROCEED AS A POOR PERSON

STATE OF NEW YORK   }

                           ss:

COUNTY OF_____   }

_____ _____, being duly sworn, says:

1. I reside at _____ in the City, Town or Village of_____, County of _____, State of New York, and I have resided in the State of New York for the past _____ years.

2. I am about to commence a lawsuit for divorce. This lawsuit is based upon **DRL §170 _____ - _____.

3. My sole source of income is:_____

   _____

   _____

   I earn $_____ per _____.

4. My property and its value are as follows:

   _____

   _____

   _____

   _____

5. I make this application pursuant to Section 1101 of the Civil Practice Law and Rules upon the ground that I am unable to pay costs, fees and expenses necessary to pursue my case and am unable to obtain the funds to do so, and unless an order is entered relieving me from the obligation to pay, I will be unable to prosecute my case.

12   6.   No other person is beneficially interested in the recovery sought herein.

13   7.   No previous application for the same or similar relief has been made by me in this case except: _____

_____ .

        WHEREFORE, I respectfully ask for an order permitting me to prosecute an action as a poor person.

        The foregoing statements have been carefully read by the undersigned who states that they are true and correct.

14

                                          _____
                                               Plaintiff

Subscribed and sworn to
before me on

_____

_____
      NOTARY PUBLIC

**Insert the grounds for the divorce:

DRL §170(1) - cruel and inhuman treatment	DRL §170(4) - adultery
DRL §170(2) - abandonment	DRL §170(5) - living apart one year after separation decree or judgment of separation
DRL §170(3) - confinement in prison	DRL §170(6) - living apart one year after execution of a separation agreement

At the Supreme Court of the State of
New York, held in and for the County
of _____ at the County
Courthouse at _____, New
York, on the ____ day of _____

PRESENT: HON._____
        Justice of the Supreme Court

--X

In the Matter of the Application of   Index No.:_____

_____,
                Plaintiff,

For Permission to Prosecute an Action as a Poor Person
        -against-   **POOR PERSON ORDER**

_____,
                Defendant.

--X

Upon the annexed affidavit of _____,

And it being alleged that said Plaintiff _____ has a good cause of

action or claim based upon **DRL § 170 subd._____ - _____, and that

he/she is unable to pay the costs, fees and expenses to prosecute this action, and that there is no other

person beneficially interested in the action, thereof

NOW on motion of _____, Plaintiff, it is hereby

ORDERED that _____ is permitted to prosecute this action as a poor

person against _____ and it is further

ORDERED that any recovery by Judgment or Settlement in favor of Plaintiff shall be paid to

the Clerk of the Court to await distribution pursuant to court order, and it is further

ORDERED that the Clerk of this Court is directed to make no charge for costs or fees in

connection with the prosecution of this action, including one (1) certified copy of the judgment.

E N T E R:

_____
                J.S.C.

**Insert the grounds for the divorce:
        DRL §170(1) - cruel and inhuman treatment   DRL §170(4) - adultery
        DRL §170(2) - abandonment   DRL §170(5)   living apart one year after separation decree or judgment of separation
        DRL §170(3) - confinement in prison   DRL §170(6) - living apart one year after execution of a separation agreement

Postcard—Matrimonial Action

SUPREME COURT :   COUNTY OF _____

_____VS. _____   Index No. _____

- Submitted divorce papers insufficient. Please go to the Court Clerk's Office to review papers for corrections and bring _new_ self-addressed stamped post card.

- Judgment of Divorce signed _____. You may go to the County Clerk's Office to obtain a certified copy of the judgment.

- Judgment of Divorce signed. Please call _____ for instructions on how to retrieve your papers for filing with the County Clerk's Office.

Instructions: Complete, affix postage and give to Matrimonial Clerk with divorce papers.
Be sure to indicate your name and address on the reverse side of the post card.

LOCAL INDEX NUMBER

TYPE, OR PRINT IN PERMANENT BLACK INK

New York State
Department of Health
CERTIFICATE OF DISSOLUTION OF MARRIAGE

STATE FILE NUMBER

HUSBAND

1. HUSBAND - NAME: FIRST MIDDLE LAST	1A. SOCIAL SECURITY NUMBER

2. DATE OF BIRTH Month Day Year	3. STATE OF BIRTH (COUNTRY IF NOT USA)	4.A RESIDENCE: STATE	4B. COUNTY	4C. LOCALITY (CHECK ONE AND SPECIFY) ☐ CITY OF ☐ TOWN OF ☐ VILLAGE OF

4 —

4D. STREET AND NUMBER OF RESIDENCE (INCLUDE ZIP CODE)	4E. IF CITY OR VILLAGE, IS RESIDENCE WITHIN CITY OR VILLAGE LIMITS? YES ☐ NO ☐ IF NO, SPECIFY TOWN:

5A. ATTORNEY - NAME	5B. ADDRESS (INCLUDE ZIP CODE)

WIFE

6A. WIFE - NAME FIRST MIDDLE LAST	6B. MAIDEN	6C. SOCIAL SECURITY NUMBER

9 —

7. DATE OF BIRTH Month Day Year	8. STATE OF BIRTH (COUNTRY IF NOT USA)	9.A RESIDENCE: STATE	9B. COUNTY	9C. LOCALITY (CHECK ONE AND SPECIFY) ☐ CITY OF ☐ TOWN OF ☐ VILLAGE OF

9D. STREET AND NUMBER OF RESIDENCE (INCLUDE ZIP CODE)	9E. IF CITY OR VILLAGE, IS RESIDENCE WITHIN CITY OR VILLAGE LIMITS? YES ☐ NO ☐ IF NO, SPECIFY TOWN:

10A. ATTORNEY - NAME	10B. ADDRESS (INCLUDE ZIP CODE)

11 —

11A. PLACE OF THIS MARRIAGE - CITY, TOWN OR VILLAGE	11B. COUNTY	11C. STATE (COUNTRY IF NOT USA)

12A. DATE OF THIS MARRIAGE Month Day Year	12B. APPROXIMATE DATE COUPLE SEPARATED Month Year	13A. NUMBER OF CHILDREN EVER BORN ALIVE OF THIS MARRIAGE (SPECIFY)	13B. NUMBER OF CHILDREN UNDER 18 IN THIS FAMILY (SPECIFY)

DECREE

15 —

14A. I CERTIFY THAT A DECREE OF DISSOLUTION OF THE ABOVE MARRIAGE WAS RENDERED ON Month Day Year	14B. DATE OF ENTRY: Month Day Year	14C. TYPE OF DECREE - DIVORCE, ANNULMENT, OTHER DISSOLUTION (SPECIFY)

14D. COUNTY OF DECREE	14E. TITLE OF COURT

23 —

14F. SIGNATURE OF COUNTY CLERK   >

CONFIDENTIAL INFORMATION

HUSBAND

24 —

15. RACE: WHITE, BLACK, AMERICAN INDIAN, OTHER (SPECIFY)	16. NUMBER OF THIS MARRIAGE - FIRST, SECOND, ETC. (SPECIFY)	17. IF PREVIOUSLY MARRIED HOW MANY ENDED BY		18. EDUCATION: INDICATE HIGHEST GRADE COMPLETED ONLY
		A. DEATH NUMBER——— NONE ☐	B. DIVORCE OR ANNULMENT NUMBER——— NONE ☐	ELEMENTARY 0 1 2 3 4 5 6 7 8 (00 01 02 03 04 05 06 07 08) HIGH SCHOOL 1 2 3 4 (09 10 11 12) COLLEGE 1 2 3 4 5+ (13 14 15 16 17)

WIFE

25 —

19. RACE: WHITE, BLACK, AMERICAN INDIAN, OTHER (SPECIFY)	20. NUMBER OF THIS MARRIAGE - FIRST, SECOND, ETC. (SPECIFY)	21. IF PREVIOUSLY MARRIED HOW MANY ENDED BY		22. EDUCATION: INDICATE HIGHEST GRADE COMPLETED ONLY
		A. DEATH NUMBER——— NONE ☐	B. DIVORCE OR ANNULMENT NUMBER——— NONE ☐	ELEMENTARY 0 1 2 3 4 5 6 7 8 (00 01 02 03 04 05 06 07 08) HIGH SCHOOL 1 2 3 4 (09 10 11 12) COLLEGE 1 2 3 4 5+ (13 14 15 16 17)

QR —

23. PLAINTIFF - HUSBAND, WIFE, OTHER (SPECIFY)	24. DECREE GRANTED TO HUSBAND, WIFE, OTHER (SPECIFY)	25. LEGAL GROUNDS FOR DECREE (SPECIFY)

QS —

26. SIGNATURE OF PERSON PREPARING CERTIFICATE   >   ATTORNEY AT LAW

NOTE: Social Security Numbers of the husband and wife are mandatory. They are required by New York State Public Health Law Section 4139 and 42 U.S.C. 666(a). They may be used for child support enforcement purposes.

DOH-2168 (5/2000)

1 **SUPREME COURT OF THE STATE OF NEW YORK**
COUNTY OF _____

2 --x

3   Plaintiff,   **Index No.** _____

                    -against-   **NOTICE OF**
4   **SETTLEMENT**
                              Defendant.
     --x

5   **PLEASE TAKE NOTICE** that the annexed ❑ *Proposed Judgment of Divorce,*

OR ❑ *Qualified Medical Child Support Order,* **OR** ❑ *Order:* _____

6 of which the within is a true copy, will be presented for signature to the Supreme Court

Clerk's Office, at _____, on

_____.

7 Dated: _____

                                        Yours, etc.

8   _____
                                        ❑ *Plaintiff;*   ❑ *Attorney(s) for Plaintiff*
                                        ❑ *Defendant;* ❑ *Attorney(s) for Defendant*
                                        Address:_____

                                                _____
                                                _____

                                        Tel No. _____

9 TO: _____
       ❑ *Plaintiff;*   ❑ *Attorney(s) for Plaintiff*
       ❑ *Defendant;* ❑ *Attorney(s) for Defendant*
       Address:_____

               _____
               _____

       Tel No. _____

(Appendix - Rev. 5/99)

SUPREME COURT OF THE STATE OF NEW YORK
COUNTY OF _____
---x

Plaintiff,

Index No. _____

-against-

INCOME DEDUCTION
ORDER

Defendant.

---x

ORDERED that the payments required by the support order issued simultaneously herewith shall be withheld by the debtor's employer from the debtor's compensation, made payable to the creditor identified below and sent to:

•   *Direct Payment*   **OR**   •   *Forwarded Payment*

Address: _____
_____
_____

Debtor: Name: _____
Address: _____
_____
Social Security No.: _____

Creditor: Name: _____
Address: _____
_____
Social Security No.: _____

Debtor's Employer: _____
_____
_____

Amount to be withheld: $_____ per _____

Date of Termination of Payments: _____

Dated: _____

SO ORDERED:

_____
Justice

Supreme Court

New York State Case Registry Filing Form *
For Use With Child Support Orders and Combined Child and Spousal Support Orders Payable To Other Than A Child Support Collection Unit

*Social Services Law §111-b(4)(a) and Domestic Relations Law §240(5) direct that such orders must be filed with the State Case Registry

Name of Court: _____   County Name: _____   Index Number: _____

Child Support
Payor: _____
    (first)   (last)   (middle initial)

Social Security #: _____
    (Payor)

Date of Birth: _____
    (Payor)

Child Support
Payee: _____
    (first)   (last)   (middle initial)

Social Security #: _____
    (Payee)

Date of Birth: _____
    (Payee)

Child #1 Name: _____
    (first)   (last)   (middle initial)

Social Security #: _____
    (Child #1)

Date of Birth: _____
    (Child #1)

Child #2 Name: _____
    (first)   (last)   (middle initial)

Social Security #: _____
    (Child #2)

Date of Birth: _____
    (Child #2)

Child #3 Name: _____
    (first)   (last)   (middle initial)

Social Security #: _____
    (Child #3)

Date of Birth: _____
    (Child #3)

(If more children, please use additional form.)

FAMILY VIOLENCE INQUIRY

Has a Temporary or Final Order of Protection been granted on behalf of either party?   ☐ yes   ☐ no   ☐ do not know

If yes, which party - ☐ Payor ☐ Payee

Has a request for confidentiality of address been granted on behalf of either party?   ☐ yes   ☐ no

If yes, which party - ☐ Payor ☐ Payee

SupremeCourt.doc

UCS-111 (rev: 12/01)

CHILD SUPPORT SUMMARY FORM
SUPREME AND FAMILY COURT

COMPLETE FORM FOR EACH BASIC CHILD SUPPORT OBLIGATION ORDER[1]

A. Court: ☐ Supreme   ☐ Family

B. County: _____

C. Index #/Docket #: _____

D. Date Action Commenced:

_____/_____/_____

E. Date Judgment/Order Submitted or Signed:

_____/_____/_____

F. # Of Children Subject to Child Support Order:

_____

G. Annual Gross Income:

1. Father: $ _____   Mother: $ _____

H. Amount of Child Support Payment:

1. By Father: $ _____   2. By Mother: $ _____
   annually   annually

I. Additional Child Support:
(Circle as many as appropriate)

By Father:	By Mother:
1. Medical/Med. Ins.	1. Medical/Med. Ins.
2. Child Care	2. Child Care
3. Education	3. Education
4. Other	4. Other

J. Did the court make a finding that the child support award varied from the Child Support Standards Act amount?   (Circle one)

   1. Yes   2. No

K. If answer to "J" was yes, circle court's reason(s):

1. Financial resources of parents/child.

2. Physical/emotional health of child: special needs or aptitudes.

3. Child's expected standard of living had household remained intact.

4. Tax consequences.

5. Non-monetary contribution toward care and well-being of child.

6. Educational needs of either parent.

7. Substantial differences in gross income of parents.

8. Needs of other children of non-custodial parent.

9. Extraordinary visitation expenses of non-custodial parent.

10. Other (specify):

_____

_____

_____

L. Maintenance/Spousal Support: (Circle one)

   1. None   2. By Father   3. By Mother

M. Value of Maintenance/Spousal Support:

   $_____ annually

SUPREME COURT ONLY

N. Allocation of Property:

   _____% To Father   _____% To Mother

---

[1] Defined by FCA 413(2) and DRL §240(1-b)(b)(2): "Child Support" shall mean a sum to be paid pursuant to court order or decree by either or both parents or pursuant to a valid agreement between the parties for care, maintenance and education of any unemancipated child under the age of twenty-one years.

UCS-111 (rev:12/01)

NEW YORK STATE UNIFIED COURT SYSTEM
SUPPORT SUMMARY FORM: FAMILY & SUPREME COURT

INSTRUCTION SHEET

Prepare one report for each proposed judgment or <u>final</u> order granted pursuant to Article 4 or 5 of the Family Court Act and DRL §240 and §236 B(9)(b) which includes a provision for child support (including modification of order).

SUBMIT COMPLETED FORM TO:

Office of Court Administration
Office of Court Research
25 Beaver Street, Room 975
New York, New York 10004

GENERAL INSTRUCTIONS: → **ALL ITEMS MUST BE ANSWERED**

- If a number or amount in dollars is required and the answer is none, write 0.
- If a certain item is not applicable, write NA.
- If the information is unknown or not known to the party filling out the form, write UK.
- "mm/dd/yy" means "month/day/year".

SPECIAL INSTRUCTIONS FOR PARTICULAR ITEMS:

G.   Use gross income figures from the last complete calendar year. <u>Do not include maintenance or child support as income.</u>

H.   If the child support award is calculated weekly, multiply it by 52 for the annual amount; if biweekly, multiply it by 26, if monthly, multiply it by 12.

M.   If the maintenance award is calculated weekly, multiply it by 52 for the annual amount; if biweekly, multiply it by 26; if monthly, multiply it by 12. If the maintenance award calls for decreasing or increasing amounts (for example, a certain amount for five years and half that amount for another three years), then provide the average of the awards (total amount for all years divided by the number of years).

NOTE: THIS INFORMATION IS CONFIDENTIAL AND WILL BE USED FOR STATISTICAL PURPOSES ONLY. IT WILL NOT BE RETAINED IN THE CASE FILE.

UNIFIED COURT SYSTEM DIVORCE AND CHILD SUPPORT SUMMARY FORM: SUPREME COURT   **UCS-113**
(10/94)

1. County _____

2. Case Number _____

3. Date Action Commenced: ___/___/___

4. Party filling out form (circle one):

    a. Husband or Husband;s Attorney

    b. Wife or Wife's Attorney

5. Husband's Date of Birth: ___/___/___
    mm dd yy

6. Wife's Date of Birth: ___/___/___
    mm dd yy

7. Date of marriage: ___/___/___
    mm dd yy

8. Children of the Marriage:

    [For each living child of the marriage indicate date of birth and who has physical custody (F=Father, M–Mother, J=Joint, T=Third Party)]

Child	Date of Birth	Custody
1	___/___/___ mm dd yy	_____
2	___/___/___ mm dd yy	_____
3	___/___/___ mm dd yy	_____
4	___/___/___ mm dd yy	_____
5	___/___/___ mm dd yy	_____

9. Was Husband represented by an attorney? (circle one)
    YES   NO

10. Was Wife represented by an attorney? (circle one)
    YES   NO

11. Financial arrangements (circle one):

    a. By Judge, Referee or Appellate Court

    b. By Written Agreement of Parties or Stipulation on the Record

    c. Both

    d. Other

12. Husband's Annual Gross Income:
    $ _____

13. Wife's Annual Gross Income:
    $ _____

14. Basic Child Support Award Paid to

(circle one)

    a. Wife b. Husband c. Third Party

15. Value of Basic Child Support Payment:

    By Husband: $ _____ Annually

    By Wife: $ _____ Annually

16. Additional Child Support:

    (circle as many as appropriate)

By Husband:	By Wife:
a. Medical/Med. Ins.	a. Medical/Med. Ins.
b. Child Care	b. Child care
c. Education	c. Education
d. Other	d. Other

17. Did court make a finding that the child support award varied from the Child Support Standards Act amount? (circle one)
    YES   NO

18. If answer to #17 was yes, was the child support award higher or lower than the Child Support Standards Act amount? (circle one)

    a. Higher   b. Lower

19. If answer to #17 was yes, circle court's reason(s)

    a. Financial resources of parents/child

    b. Physical/emotional health of child: special needs or aptitudes.

    c. Child's expected standard of living had household remained intact.

    d. Tax consequences.

    e. Non-monetary contribution toward care and well-being of child.

    f. Educational needs of either parent.

    g. Substantial differences in gross income of parents.

    h. Needs of other children of non-custodial parent.

    i. Extraordinary visitation expenses of non-custodial parent.

    j. Other (specify): _____
    _____

20. Spousal Maintenance: (circle one)

    a. None b. To Husband c. To Wife

21. Value of Maintenance:
    $_____ Annually

22. Duration of Maintenance (circle one and provide date if appropriate):

    a. Until a specific date ___/___/___
    mm dd yy

    b. Until death or remarriage.

    c. Other

23. Marital Home (circle one):

    a. Owned b. Rented c. Other

24. Marital Home Value (if owned):

    a. Value $_____

    b. Outstanding Mortgage $_____

25. Marital Home — Division:

    _____% to husband _____% to wife

26. Post divorce occupancy of marital home (circle one):

    a. By husband b. By wife c. Neither

27. Other Marital Assets Not Including Marital Home:

    $_____

28. Division of Other Marital Assets

    a. Amount to Husband $_____

    b. Amount to Wife $_____

29. Other Awards:

To Husband	To Wife	
$_____	$_____	Attorney Fees
$_____	$_____	Expert Fees
$_____	$_____	Arrears
$_____	$_____	Other

Prepared by (Attorney or Party):

_____

Print Name   Signature   Date

FOR COURT USE ONLY:
TO BE FILLED OUT BY COURT CLERK: DATE OF DECREE; ORDER; OR MODIFICATION___/___/___

SEPARATION AND PROPERTY SETTLEMENT AGREEMENT

By and Between

_____

and

_____

SEPARATION AND PROPERTY SETTLEMENT AGREEMENT

THIS AGREEMENT is made the _____ day of_____, _____, by and between,_____. (hereinafter referred to as "Husband"), and. _____(hereinafter referred to as "Wife").

RECITALS

A. The parties were married on _____, _____, in the city/town/village of _____, County of_____, State of New York.

There are _____minor children born of this marriage, to wit:

Name	Date of Birth
_____	_____
_____	_____
_____	_____
_____	_____
_____	_____
_____	_____

B. Irreconcilable differences have arisen between the parties as a result of which the parties desire to live separate and apart from each other.

C. The parties desire that this Agreement constitutes a separation and property settlement agreement between them, with respect to all assets, real and personal, now owned by the parties or either of them, including any and all property acquired prior to the marriage of the parties, during the marriage, and hereafter acquired by either the Husband or the Wife; and settles any and all questions, issues, and other matters relative to the estates of the parties, and all other issues arising out of, or incidental to, the marital relationship.

D. The parties and each of them [have conferred with their respective attorneys regarding all aspects of this Agreement and the effect thereof, and said attorneys have fully and completely explained all terms and provisions of the Agreement and the applicable laws] [are aware of their right to legal counsel and do hereby waive that right], and both parties have relied upon the accuracy and completeness of the materials exchanged. The parties have also exchanged sworn 236(B) Financial Disclosure Affidavits (Statements of Net Worth), and. other financial data including, but not limited to, joint Federal and State Income Tax Returns, W-2 Wage and Tax Statements, data regarding the benefits from employment, pension information, bank statements, checking account statements, and credit card bills, as well as other miscellaneous business and personal financial data.

E. Both Husband and Wife acknowledge that this Agreement is freely and voluntarily entered into by and between them, and with full and complete understanding of all of the terms and conditions thereof, and further that there has been disclosure by each of the parties to the other as to their respective assets and earnings by means of the production of certain documents and records, and the parties are satisfied that there has been a complete good faith financial disclosure which each party has relied upon in entering into this Agreement.

F. The parties acknowledge that this Agreement shall in no respect alter, impair, modify, or constitute a waiver of either party's right to proceed with the action for divorce initiated by the Husband/Wife against the Husband/Wife, or the Husband's/Wife's right to defend said action for divorce.

G. If a divorce or separation is eventually granted at any time to either party against the other in this State or any other State having jurisdiction over the parties, it is agreed that the terms and provisions of this Agreement shall be incorporated in and become part of any such final judgment or decree of divorce or separation, but shall not merge therein (except as specifically provided for hereinafter). It is further agreed that all of the provisions of this Agreement shall survive such incorporation into any decree of divorce or separation and shall continue to be binding upon the parties hereto.

H. Each party, prior to the entry of a final Judgment of Divorce between them, shall take all steps within his or her power to remove any barriers to the remarriage of the other following a divorce and shall, in all respects, comply with the provisions of Section 253 of the Domestic Relations Law of the State of New York.

I. This Agreement, or a memorandum of this Agreement, shall be filed in the Office of the _____ County Clerk and recorded in the same manner required of a deed.

J. The parties understand that instead of entering into this Agreement they have a right to proceed with litigation and to seek a judicial determination of the issues covered by this Agreement, but notwithstanding such right, the parties desire to avoid the delay, expense, and risk of litigation, and they believe that their rights will be better served by the terms and provisions of this Agreement.

K. In negotiating, determining, and agreeing upon the provisions of this Agreement relating to maintenance, the Husband and Wife each specifically represent, warrant, and acknowledge that they have agreed upon all of the terms and conditions hereinabove set forth based in all respects upon due, deliberate, and informed consideration as to their respective property, the standard of living enjoyed by the parties during the marriage, income means and needs, as well as the ability and means of both the Husband and Wife, both at present and in the future. The parties further acknowledge that they have specifically considered the amount and duration of the payments to be made pursuant to all of the terms and provisions of this Agreement, and have further considered in all respects any and all items, questions, and other matters relating to this Agreement and each and every provision thereof, including, but not limited to, the following factors:

1. The income and property of the respective parties, including marital property distributed.

2. The duration of the marriage and the age and health of both parties.

3. The present and future earning capacity of both parties.

4. The ability of the party seeking maintenance to become self-supporting and, if applicable, the period of time and training necessary therefore.

5. The reduced or lost lifetime earning capacity of the party seeking maintenance as a result of having foregone or delayed education, training, employment or career opportunities during the marriage.

6. The presence of children of the marriage, and the respective homes of the parties.

7. The tax consequences to each party.

8. Contributions and services of the party seeking maintenance as a spouse, parent, wage earner and homemaker and to the career or career potential of the other party.

9. The wasteful dissipation of marital property by either spouse.

10. Any transfer or encumbrance of marital assets made in contemplation of a matrimonial action without fair compensation.

11. Any other factor which the Court shall expressly find to be just and proper.

L. In negotiating, determining and agreeing upon the provisions of this Agreement with respect to the distribution of any and all marital property of every form and description and wheresoever situate, whether real, personal, or mixed, the Husband and Wife specifically represent, warrant and acknowledge that they have agreed upon such distribution as is provided for in this Agreement, based upon satisfactory (formal and) informal disclosure by and between the parties, and after due deliberation of all matters pertaining thereto, including, but not limited to, the mutual waiver of verification of both the financial information and the interpretation and effect of said information, and have resolved the issues with respect to such distribution; and the parties further acknowledge that they have considered all issues and factors relating to the distribution of all marital property, including, but not limited to, the following factors:

1. The income and property of each party at the time of the marriage and at the time of commencement of this action.

2. The duration of the marriage and the age and health of both parties.

3. The need of a custodial parent to occupy or own the marital residence and to use or own its household effects.

4. The loss of inheritance and pension rights upon dissolution of the marriage as of the date of dissolution.

5. Any award of maintenance.

6. Any equitable claim or interest in a direct or indirect contribution made to the acquisition of such marital property by the party not having title, including joint efforts or expenditures and contributions and services as a spouse, parent, wage earner and homemaker and to the career or career potential of the other party.

7. The liquid or non-liquid character of all marital property.

8. The probable future financial circumstances of each party.

9. The impossibility or difficulty in evaluating any component assets or any interest in a business, corporation or profession, and the economic desirability of retaining such asset or interest intact and free from any claim or interference by the other party.

10. The tax consequences to each party.

11. The wasteful dissipation of assets by either spouse.

12. Any transfer or encumbrance of any marital action without fair compensation.

13. Any other factor which the court shall expressly find to be just and proper.

The Husband and Wife and each of them do hereby unequivocally and without any reservation whatsoever covenant and agree and specifically express as their mutual intent that all property, whether real, personal or mixed and of every sort and description, and whatsoever situated, and whether characterized as separate property or marital property, pursuant to the laws of the State of New York (as the same now exists or in the future may be amended or enacted) now in the possession or under the control of either of them or hereafter acquired in any manner by either of them, whether prior or subsequent to the execution of this

Agreement, including but not limited to any appreciation of any such property, shall except as is specifically provided for to the contrary in this agreement, be and remain the sole, separate and exclusive property of such party, free of any claim by the other, made pursuant to any provision of the law of the State of New York, including but not limited to Section 236(B) of the Domestic Relations Law.

M. The parties do hereby ratify, confirm, and adopt each and every recital hereinabove set forth and agree to be bound by all the terms, covenants, and conditions of this Agreement

ARTICLE I: SEPARATION

A. The Husband and Wife agree to live separate and apart from each other, except as limited specifically by this Agreement, free of all control, restraint, or interference, direct or indirect, by the other.

B. Neither party shall in any way harass, disturb, trouble, or annoy the other, or interfere with the peace and comfort of the other, or compel or seek to compel the other to associate, cohabit, or dwell with him or her by any means whatsoever, nor shall either of the parties commence any action or proceeding of any form or nature for the restoration of conjugal rights.

ARTICLE II: MARITAL RESIDENCE

❑ A. The parties are tenants by the entirety of the marital residence located at _____ _____, New York, County of _____. The parties agree the home was purchased by both of them during the course of the marriage in _____for a purchase price of $_____, and agree that said property can be currently valued between $_____ and $_____.

❑ B. The parties agree that the home shall become the sole and separate property of the Husband/Wife and he/she shall be solely responsible for the mortgage, taxes, insurance, repairs, and all other expenses relating to the home.

Upon the execution of this Agreement, the premises shall be conveyed to him/her by bargain and sale deed with covenant, duly executed and acknowledged, and recorded at his/her expense, conveying all of his/her right, title, and interest in and to said premises, subject only to the mortgage held by _____ _____, in the approximate amount of $_____. There shall be no adjustment for taxes or mortgage payments. From the execution of the deed, the Husband/Wife shall have no right or claim to said premises. He/She agrees to take all steps possible to remove the other party's name from the mortgage note and indemnifies and holds the other harmless with regard to any current or future debt regarding the residence.

❑ C. The parties agree that the Husband/Wife shall purchase the Husband's/Wife's interest in the marital residence by refinancing the existing mortgage in his/her own name and paying Husband/Wife a sum of $_____ at the time of the refinance by bargain and sale deed with covenant, duly executed and acknowledged, and recorded at his/her expense, subject only to the refinanced mortgage.

❑ D. The parties agree that the home shall be placed up for sale no later than _____, _____. The parties shall agree at the time as to the real estate agent utilized and the listing price. Both parties must agree to accept a purchase price before it can be accepted, and the parties agree to cooperate in making these decisions and to act in a reasonable manner.

❑ 1. Commencing _____, _____, the Wife/Husband shall have exclusive use and occupancy, and shall pay the mortgage payment of $_____ per month until the time of sale. The Husband/Wife agrees to permit real estate agents and potential buyers into the home at reasonable times.

❑ 2.. The parties shall continue to reside together in the marital residence until _____, _____, at which time the Husband/Wife shall have exclusive use and occupancy until the time of sale. The Husband/Wife agrees to permit the real estate agents and potential buyers into the home at reasonable times.

❑ E. The parties shall continue to reside together in the marital residence until _____ _____, _____, at which time _____.

❑ F. Upon sale of the home, the parties shall first pay any unpaid taxes due and owing upon the home, the balance of the mortgage, and all closing costs, real estate agent commissions, and other costs of sale out of the proceeds. The remainder of the proceeds of the home shall then be shared equally by the parties.

❑ G. The Husband/Wife shall be responsible for the cost of home repairs up to the date of sale of the home.

❑ H. Each party warrants that he or she has not encumbered the title to the property other than the first mortgage and will not encumber the title before the sale.

❑ I. The parties no longer share a marital residence and each shall keep possession of his or her own residence.

❑ J. The Husband/Wife shall continue to have possession of the rented marital residence located at _____.

❑ K. Other: _____
_____
_____

ARTICLE III: SEPARATE PROPERTY

The parties agree that the following is and shall remain the sole and separate property of the Wife:

_____
_____
_____
_____
_____

The parties agree that the following is and shall remain the sole and separate property of the Husband:

_____
_____
_____
_____
_____

ARTICLE IV: AUTOMOBILES AND VEHICLES

❑ A.   The Wife shall have possession and ownership of _____
_____ .

The Husband shall have possession and ownership of _____
_____ .

Each party waives any right, title, or interest in and to the automobile or vehicle owned by the other, and shall hereafter consider such vehicle to be the sole and separate property of its owner. This shall be effective as of the date of this Agreement and the parties shall execute any necessary documents to effectuate this.

❑ B.   Each party will pay for the respective license renewal, upkeep, insurance, registration, and maintenance of their respective vehicles.

C.   Each party assumes all liabilities associated with his or her own vehicle and shall indemnify and hold the other party harmless from any and all such liabilities.

ARTICLE V: BANK AND FINANCIAL ACCOUNTS

❑ A.   Each party shall remain the sole and separate owner of his or her bank and financial accounts held in his or her name.

❑ B.   The following joint accounts shall be divided as follows:

Name of Bank, Stock, Fund, etc.	Balance	New Owner
_____	_____	_____
_____	_____	_____
_____	_____	_____
_____	_____	_____
_____	_____	_____
_____	_____	_____
_____	_____	_____
_____	_____	_____
_____	_____	_____
_____	_____	_____

ARTICLE VI: INTERESTS IN BUSINESS

_____
_____
_____ .

ARTICLE VII: LIFE AND DISABILITY INSURANCE

A. The Wife shall maintain and be the sole owner of _____.

B. The Husband shall maintain and be the sole owner of _____.

C. The parties agree that each party is to name and maintain the other party / the child(ren) as beneficiary on his or her life insurance policy.

D. Each party shall be solely responsible for any loan against his or her life insurance policies.

ARTICLE VIII: PENSION AND RETIREMENT RIGHTS

Each party waives his or her rights to receive any payment from the other party's pension or retirement plan. The parties have disclosed to each other information regarding both pensions or retirement rights, and both parties have freely chosen not to have either valued.

ARTICLE IX: DISTRIBUTION OF PERSONALTY AND OTHER PROPERTY

❑ A. In order to effectuate a complete distribution of the parties' marital property, the parties have mutually agreed to a division of furniture, furnishings, jewelry, and clothing, as well as other items of personal property. The parties have previously divided all of these items and all items now in the possession of the Husband shall now become his sole and separate property. All items now in the possession of the Wife shall now become her sole and separate property.

❑ B. The parties agree that the marital personal property items listed on Schedule A shall be distributed according to Schedule A and shall become the sole and separate property of the party named as owner therein.

❑ C. Other marital property that is not personalty shall be divided according to Schedule B.

ARTICLE X: DEBTS

❑ A. Each party shall be solely responsible for debts held in his or her individual name.

❑ B. The parties agree that the marital debts shall be divided as described on Schedule C.

❑ C. Except as otherwise provided in this Agreement, the parties represent that neither has incurred, and will not at any time in the future incur, any debt, charge, or liability for which the other is now or may become liable. Each party further agrees at all times to indemnify the other party from, and hold that party free and harmless against, any and all debts, charges, contracts, and liabilities contracted by such party.

❑ D. The parties agree that they hold other joint credit cards including _____ _____ _____ _____ _____ _____, and agree that said accounts have no balance and agree to close said accounts or convert them to individual accounts.

ARTICLE XI: MAINTENANCE

❑ A. Based on the fact that both parties are self-supporting and based on the division of property and all the facts and circumstances, no maintenance shall be due to either party.

❑ B. Husband/Wife shall pay $_____ as a lump sum maintenance payment to the Husband/Wife. Such payment shall be due _____.

❑ C. The parties have agreed that the Husband/Wife shall pay to the Husband/Wife $_____ per _____ as maintenance and that such payments are to be made each _____by personal check or as otherwise agreed, commencing _____. The parties acknowledge that said maintenance is due to the fact that the Husband/Wife _____ _____ _____ _____ _____.

❑ D. Such maintenance payments shall cease upon the occurrence of whichever of the following shall first occur:

1. Upon reaching _____ full years. Unless another termination event occurs, maintenance shall be paid up to and through _____.

2. The death of either party.

3. The remarriage of the Husband/Wife (party receiving maintenance) as herein defined. For purposes of this agreement, the term remarriage shall mean and include entering into a marriage contract or marriage ceremony, whether civil or religious, and whether or not such marriage be void or voidable and later annulled or avoided. Such remarriage shall also mean

cohabitating with an unrelated adult person, whether or not they hold themselves out as Husband and Wife for a consecutive period of_____; however, should such cohabitation end during the period of maintenance under this Agreement, maintenance shall resume for the balance of the payment period. In the event of such a resumption, maintenance shall not be owed for the duration of the cohabitation.

ARTICLE XII: HEALTH CARE INSURANCE AND EXPENSES

❏ A. The parties agree that the Husband/Wife shall continue to maintain health insurance for the minor child(ren) of the marriage as long as it is available to him/her and shall also continue to carry the Husband/Wife on said insurance until the date of divorce. The Husband/Wife shall be solely responsible for all payments of premiums. The parties acknowledge and agree that the insurance policy continues to carry the Husband/Wife even if the parties are legally separated.

❏ B. The parties agree that the Husband/Wife shall be permitted to pay for his/her health insurance, as permitted by COBRA, through the Husband's/Wife's insurance after the date of divorce if he/she so chooses, as long as it is available. This expense shall be the sole responsibility of the Husband/Wife.

❏ C. The Husband/Wife shall be responsible for his/her own co-pays, prescriptions, and uncovered medical, dental, optical, and mental health expenses up until the date of divorce and also afterwards if COBRA is elected.

❏ D. The parties agree that should health insurance no longer be available to the Husband/Wife or should the Husband/Wife have health insurance become available to him/her, the parties will renegotiate this portion of this agreement at that time. The parties agree that neither shall take any action causing the termination of the family's eligibility.

❏ E. The parties agree the Husband/Wife shall pay all of the child(ren)'s co-pays, prescriptions, and uncovered medical, dental, optical, and orthodontic expenses. The parties agree to renegotiate this clause should either party remarry (remarriage for this section is defined as a marriage recognized by the laws of New York State).

❏ F. The parties agree that the child(ren)'s co-pays and other uncovered medical, dental, optical, and orthodontic expenses shall be divided between the parties as follows:

_____

_____.

ARTICLE XIII: PARENTING

A. Custody and visitation shall be as follows:

_____
_____
_____
_____
_____
_____
_____
_____
_____
_____
_____
_____
_____
_____
_____
_____
_____
_____
_____
_____
_____.

B. The visitation and holiday schedule shall be as follows:

_____
_____
_____
_____
_____
_____
_____
_____
_____
_____
_____
_____
_____
_____
_____
_____
_____
_____
_____
_____.

❑ C. Each party agrees to notify the other of any change in address or telephone number.

❑ D. The parties agree to consult with and consider the opinion of their child in making living and visitation arrangements.

❑ E. The parties agree to exercise reasonable judgment regarding the introduction of and involvement with new partners as it impacts the child.

❑ F. Once a year, on the anniversary of this agreement, the parties agree to review the custody and visitation agreement and make any modifications mutually agreed upon.

❑ G. The parties agree that should the issue of relocation ever arise, they will discuss it and make good faith efforts to resolve it themselves.

❑ H. The parties agree that the Husband/Wife shall not relocate beyond a 50 mile radius of the current residence without the express written consent of the Husband/Wife or permission of the court.

❑ I. The parties agree to discuss any gift of over $100 for either of the children by either party before the purchase is made.

❑ J. The parties agree they shall have equal access to the children's school and medical records.

❑ K. Other: _____
_____
_____
_____.

ARTICLE XIV: CHILD SUPPORT

❑ A. With knowledge and understanding of the Child Support Standards Act, the parties have voluntarily entered into this Agreement, containing the provisions for child support as set forth herein. More particularly, the parties acknowledge that the Act presumptively sets the needs of the _____ child(ren) of the parties at _____% of the combined parental income up to $80,000 per year and said percentage and/or additional discretionary sum for combined parental income over $80,000 per year. Because the Husband claims an income of $_____ per year and the Wife claims an income of $_____ per year, their combined parental income exceeds/is less than $80,000 per year.

❑ **[Income is less than $80,000]**
Based upon combined parental income of $_____, the Act requires that the Husband/Wife pay to the Husband/Wife as child support the sum of $_____ per _____, which obligation is (consistent with/less than/more than) the sums provided for for in this agreement. If it is more than or less than the reasons are:

❑ **[Income is more than $80,000]**
Based upon the combined annual parental income of $_____, the child support payments required under the Act to be paid by the Husband/Wife to the Husband/Wife based upon percentage is $_____ per _____. Under the provisions of this agreement, the Husband's/Wife's obligation to the Husband/Wife is the sum of $_____ per _____ plus the obligation to pay or contribute to:

By reason of the foregoing and discretionary factors, including but not limited to transfers of property and payment of a distributive award to the Husband/Wife, for which some benefit will enure to the benefit of the children, the obligations of the Husband/Wife under this agreement comply with the requirements of the Act.

❑ B.   Having considered the above factors, the parties wish to opt-out of the Child Support Standards Act for the following reasons: _____

_____

_____.

And the parties agree that based on the above reasons, child support shall be set at $_____ to be paid each _____ by the Husband/Wife to the Husband/Wife and shall be paid as follows: _____

_____.

❑ C.   The Husband/Wife shall also be responsible for the following child(ren)'s expenses:

_____

_____.

❑ D.   The parties agree to assist their child(ren) with college expenses at a ratio to be determined at that time as they shall agree.

❑ E.   The parties agree that child support shall be reduced each time a child reaches 18 or becomes emancipated and shall completely terminate when all of the children are 18 or older or are all emancipated.

ARTICLE XV: INCOME TAX RETURNS

❑ A.   The parties agree to file as married filing jointly for the year _____. They shall share any refund on a pro rata basis based on their incomes.

❑ B.   The parties agree to file as married filing separately for the year _____ and to each be solely responsible for his or her tax owed or refund received.

❑ C.   The children shall be claimed as exemptions as follows: _____

_____

_____.

ARTICLE XVI: BANKRUPTCY

The Parties have consented to the terms of this Agreement upon their reliance on the express representations made to each other that all of its terms, particularly those with respect to the maintenance payments of debts, property division, and distributive award, or any other transfers or payments to implement equitable distribution, which are to be made pursuant to the terms and provisions of this Agreement, shall not be discharged, canceled, terminated, diminished, or in any way affected by the filing of a petition in bankruptcy, or by the making of an assignment for the benefit of creditors.

Accordingly, in the event that the either party files a petition in bankruptcy or makes an assignment for the benefit of creditors, all transfers or payments provided for in this Agreement are intended to be maintenance. The party who files such petition in bankruptcy or makes such assignment for the benefit of creditors shall be liable for any resulting tax consequences.

To the extent that any obligation arising under this Agreement may be discharged, canceled, terminated, diminished, or in any way affected by the filing of a petition in bankruptcy, or by the making of an assignment for the benefit of creditors, the party adversely affected by such action shall be entitled to apply to any court of competent and appropriate jurisdiction for modification of this Agreement and any order or decree into which it may hereafter be incorporated. The party who files such petition in bankruptcy or who makes an assignment for the benefit of creditors hereby consents that in any proceeding brought by the other party pursuant to this provision, the court hearing the same may grant economic relief of any kind or nature to relieve the other party of the adverse impact of the bankruptcy or assignment, irrespective of the otherwise applicable standards for such relief, including, but not limited to, the granting of maintenance to a party who would otherwise not qualify for such relief under the criteria of the particular jurisdiction.

ARTICLE XVII: RELEASES

A. Both parties completely waive all their rights against the other's will or estate as beneficiary, distributee, administrator or executor, including the right of set-off and all rights of election in any jurisdiction. This does not constitute a bar to a cause of action against an estate arising out of a breach of the terms of this Agreement.

B. Both parties accept the terms of this Agreement as settlement in full of any and all rights under the equitable distribution law or community property law of any state, as well as all rights against pensions, retirements, stock options, Keoghs, IRAs, or other similar items. All other obligations or liabilities of the parties to each other, except those set forth herein, are forever terminated.

C. The Husband and Wife, in consideration of the terms of this Agreement, release each other from liabilities arising from any cause of action, contract, agreement, or any claim made by the other party or his or her executor, administrator, beneficiary, distributee, or legal representative, including any claim for maintenance, support, or equitable distribution, except as specifically provided in this Agreement.

D. The releases given above do not bar the parties from bringing an action as a result of a breach of the terms of this Agreement.

E. Nothing contained in this Agreement shall operate as a release or waiver of any cause or causes of action either party may have against the other for divorce, annulment, or separation, and any defenses thereto in any pending or future action.

F. Husband and Wife hereby expressly revoke their respective existing wills concerning any disposition made therein for the other and further revoke any nomination of the other party as an estate representative therefore, it being the intent of the parties that all wills made by either of them, executed prior to the acknowledgment of this Agreement, shall be read as if the other party had predeceased them for purposes of distribution of their respective estates. The same shall further apply to any testamentary substitutes not passing under a will. Each of the parties expressly renounces, covenants, and warrants to renounce, any right of administration upon the estate of the other or nomination by the other as estate representative, as required by the laws or practices of any jurisdiction whatsoever. Any disposition to the other party and/or the other party being nominated as an estate representative in a will executed after the acknowledgment of this Agreement is specifically not revoked by this Agreement.

ARTICLE XVIII: GENERAL PROVISIONS

A. This Agreement shall be construed in accordance with the laws of the State of New York, independent of any forum where this Agreement or any terms or provisions thereof may be subjected to construction and/or enforcement.

B. Except as otherwise specifically provided for to the contrary in this Agreement, each of the parties' respective rights and obligations hereunder shall be deemed independent and may be enforced independently irrespective of any of the other rights and obligations set forth herein.

C. This Agreement and all the obligations and covenants hereunder shall bind the parties, their heirs, executors, legal representatives, administrators, and assigns.

D. No modification, recision, or amendment to this Agreement shall be effective unless in writing signed by the parties with the same formality as this Agreement.

E. This Agreement and its provisions merge prior agreements, if any, of the parties and is the complete and entire agreement of the parties, and no oral statements or prior written materials extrinsic to this Agreement shall have any force and effect whatsoever.

F. In the event that any term, provision, paragraph, or Article of this Agreement is declared illegal, void, or unenforceable, such determination shall not affect or impair the other terms, provisions, paragraphs, or Articles in this Agreement. The Doctrine of Severability shall be applied. The parties do not intend by this statement to imply the illegality or unenforceability of any term, provision, paragraph, or Article of this Agreement.

G. Each of the parties hereto, without cost to the other shall at any time and from time to time hereafter, execute and deliver any and all further instruments and assurances and perform any acts that the other party may reasonably request for the purposes of giving full force and effect to the provisions of this Agreement.

H. No representation or warranties have been made by either party to the other or by anyone else except as expressly set forth in this Agreement, and this Agreement is not being executed in reliance upon any representation or warranty not expressly set forth herein.

I. The Husband and Wife each acknowledge that they have read the foregoing Agreement prior to the signing thereof.

J. The failure of either the Husband or Wife in any one or more instances to insist or require strict performances of any of the terms or conditions of this Agreement shall not be construed as a waiver of any subsequent default of the same or similar nature, nor shall the failure by either party to exercise any option or make any election herein provided for be construed as a waiver or relinquishment for the future of any such term, option, or election and all of the terms and conditions of this Agreement shall continue in full force and effect. No waiver or relinquishment shall be deemed to have been made by either party unless in writing duly signed and acknowledged by such party.

K. The descriptive Article headings contained herein are for convenience and identification only and are not intended to limit or conclusively define all the subject matter in the paragraphs accompanying such headings, and, accordingly, such headings should not be resorted to for purposes of interpretation of this Agreement.

L. This Agreement has been executed in _____ duplicate original counterparts, each of which is deemed by the parties to be an original.

M. This Agreement shall not be invalidated, terminated, canceled, otherwise affected by a reconciliation between the parties or by resumption of cohabitation or marital relations between them, unless such reconciliation or such resumption is conformed by a written document which expressly invalidates, terminates, cancels or otherwise alters this Agreement and which is executed and acknowledges with the same degree of formality as this Agreement or unless stipulated to by the parties upon the record of a court of competent jurisdiction.

N. In addition to any other grounds for divorce which either party may presently have or may hereafter acquire, the parties agree that the execution of this agreement and the filing of it, or a memorandum of it, in the Office of the County Clerk, in the county where either party resides, may give rise to a grounds for divorce which may be asserted by either party if they live separate and apart for a period of one or more years and if the party who seeks such divorce has substantially performed his or her obligations under this agreement.

ARTICLE XIX: AGREEMENT TO MEDIATE

The parties agree that should any questions, disputes, or disagreements develop with regard to the terms of this Agreement, the parties will mediate and make a good faith attempt at resolving any issues through mediation before litigating the issue. The cost of such mediation shall be paid one-half by each party.

ARTICLE XX: ATTORNEY FEES AND COURT AND RELATED COSTS

❑ A. Each party agrees to be solely responsible for paying his or her own attorney fees.

❑ B. It is the intent of the parties that the Husband/Wife shall initiate an action for divorce and the parties agree that all costs and attorney's fees incurred by the Husband/Wife associated with the action shall be the sole responsibility of the Husband/Wife.

❑ C. The Husband/Wife shall pay to the Husband/Wife the sum of $_____ for his/her attorney's fees.

ARTICLE XXI: OTHER AGREEMENTS

❑ Additional agreements of the parties are included on _____ pages attached hereto.

IN WITNESS WHEREOF, the parties have hereunto set their signatures on the day and year first above written. EACH OF THE PARTIES REPRESENTS AND WARRANTS THAT THEY HAVE CARE-FULLY READ THIS AGREEMENT AND EACH AND EVERY PAGE THEREOF (INCLUDING THE TITLE PAGE, SCHEDULES, EXHIBITS, ATTACHMENTS, AND ADDENDA, IF ANY) PRIOR TO SIGNING.

_____
Husband

_____
Wife

STATE OF NEW YORK

                                 SS.:

COUNTY OF _____

On _____, before me, the undersigned, a Notary Public, in and for the said State, personally appeared _____, personally known to me or proved to me on the basis of satisfactory evidence to be the individual whose name is subscribed to the within instrument and acknowl-edged to me that he/she executed the same in his/her capacity and that by his/her signature on the instrument, the individual, or the person upon behalf of which the individual acted, executed the instrument.

_____
NOTARY PUBLIC

STATE OF NEW YORK

                                 SS.:

COUNTY OF _____

On _____, before me, the undersigned, a Notary Public, in and for the said State, personally appeared _____, personally known to me or proved to me on the basis of satisfactory evidence to be the individual whose name is subscribed to the within instrument and acknowl-edged to me that he/she executed the same in his/her capacity and that by his/her signature on the instrument, the individual, or the person upon behalf of which the individual acted, executed the instrument.

_____
NOTARY PUBLIC

STATE OF NEW YORK
COUNTY OF_____

--X

_____, Husband,

and

_____, Wife.

--X

MEMORANDUM OF SEPARATION AGREEMENT

A. Names and Addresses of Parties:

Husband: _____   Wife: _____

_____   _____

_____   _____

B. Date of Marriage: _____

C. Date of Separation Agreement: _____

D. Date of Subscription to Agreement: Husband:_____ Wife:_____

_____   _____

Husband's Signature   Wife's Signature

STATE OF NEW YORK   )
COUNTY OF   ) ss.:
TOWN OF   )

On this _____ day of _____, _____, before me personally appeared
_____, to me personally known and known to me to be the same person described in and who executed the foregoing instrument, and he/she duly acknowledged to me that he/she executed the same.

_____
Notary Public

STATE OF NEW YORK   )
COUNTY OF   ) ss.:
TOWN OF   )

On this _____ day of _____, _____, before me personally appeared
_____, to me personally known and known to me to be the same person described in and who executed the foregoing instrument, and he/she duly acknowledged to me that he/she executed the same.

_____
Notary Public

SUPREME COURT OF THE STATE OF NEW YORK
COUNTY OF _____   Index No.:

--X

_____ ,

Plaintiff,   **STATEMENT OF**
-against-   **NET WORTH, FINANCIAL**
                                                              AFFIDAVIT
                                                              (Section 236 DRL)

_____ ,

Defendant.

--X   **Action Commencement**

                                                              Date:_____

STATE OF NEW YORK   COUNTY OF _____**ss.:**

_____ , the Plaintiff herein, being duly sworn, deposes and says that the following is an accurate statement as of_____ , of my net worth (assets of whatsoever kind and
nature and wherever situated minus liabilities), statement of income from all sources, and statement of assets transferred
of whatsoever kind and nature and wherever situated:

1. FAMILY DATA

(a)	**Husband's Age:**	**Wife's Age:**
(b)	**Husband's Place of Birth:**	**Wife's Place of Birth:**
(c)	**Date Married:**	
(d)	**Date of Separation:**	
(e)	**Number of dependent children under 21 Years:**	
(f)	**Names, Ages and Dates of Birth of Children:**	
(g)	**Custody of Children is with (H/W/J):**	
(h)	**Minor Children of Prior Marriage:** Husband: Wife:	
(i)	**Support for children of Prior Marriage** (amount and to whom paid or paid by)**:**	
(j)	**Custody of Children of Prior Marriage:** (Name and Address of Custodial Parent)	
(k)	**The marital residence is occupied by** (H/W/Both)**:**	
(l)	**Husband's present Address:**	
	Wife's present Address:	
(m)	**Occupation of Husband:**	
	Occupation of Wife:	
(n)	**Husband's Employer:**	
(o)	**Wife's Employer:**	
(p)	**Education, training & skills:** (Include dates of attainment of degree, etc.)	
	Husband:	
	Wife:	
(q)	**Husband's Health:**	
(r)	**Wife's Health:**	
(s)	**Children's Health:**	

II. EXPENSES

(a) **Housing:**
1. Rent
2. Mortgage and
   amortization
3. Real estate taxes

4. Condominium charges
5. Cooperative Apartment
   Maintenance

Total: Housing - $

(b) **Utilities:**
1. Fuel oil
2. Gas
3. Electricity

4. Telephone
5. Water

Total: Utilities - $

(c) **Food:**
1. Groceries
2. School Lunches
3. Lunches at work

4. Liquor/alcohol
5. Home entertainment
6. Other

Total: Food - $

(d) **Clothing:**
1. Husband
2. Wife

3. Children
4. Other

Total: Clothing - $

(e) **Laundry:**
1. Laundry at home
2. Dry cleaning

3. Other

Total: Laundry - $

(f) **Insurance:**
1. Life
2. Homeowner's/tenant's
3. Fire, theft, and
   liability
4. Automotive
5. Umbrella policy

6. Medical plan
7. Dental plan
8. Optical plan
9. Disability
10. Worker's Comp.
11. Other

Total: Insurance - $

(g) **Unreimbursed medical:**
1. Medical
2. Dental
3. Optical
4. Pharmaceutical

5. Surgical, nursing, hospital
6. Other

Total: Unreimbursed medical - $

(h) **Household maintenance**
1. Repairs
2. Furniture, furnishings
   housewares
3. Cleaning Supplies
4. Appliances including
   maintenance

5. Painting
6. Sanitation/carting
7. Gardening/landscape
8. Snow removal
9. Extermination
10. Other

Total: Household maintenance - $

(i)   **Household Help**
1. Baby-sitter
2. Domestic (Maid, etc.)
3. Nurse
4. Other

Total: Household Help - $

(j)   **Automotive**
1. Year: Make: Model:
    Personal (Y/N):   Business: (Y/N)

1. Payments
2. Gas and Oil
3. Repairs
4. Car Wash
5. Registration/license
6. Parking and Tolls
7. Other

Total: Automotive - $

(k)   **Educational**
1. Pre-school: Daycare:
2. Primary and secondary
3. College
4. Post-graduate
5. Religious Instruction
6. School trans.
7. School supp./books
8. Tutoring
9. School events
10. Other

Total: Educational - $

(l)   **Recreational**
1. Summer camp
2. Vacations
3. Movies
4. Theatre, ballet, etc.
5. Video rentals
6. Tapes, CD's, etc.
7. Cable Television
8. Team Sports
9. Country/pool club
10. Health club
11. Sporting goods
12. Hobbies
13. Music/dance lessons
14. Sports lessons
15. Birthday parties
16. Other

Total: Recreational - $

(m)   **Income Taxes**
1. Federal
2. State
3. City
4. Social Security and Medicare

Total: Taxes - $

(n)   **Miscellaneous**
1. Beauty Parlor/Barber
2. Beauty aids/cosmetics, drug items
3. Cigarettes/tobacco
4. Books, magazines, newspapers
5. Children's allowances
6. Gifts
7. Charitable contribution
8. Religious organizations dues
9. Union and organization dues
10. Commutation and transportation
11. Veterinarian/pet exp.
12. Child support payments (prior marriage)
13. Alimony & maintenance payments
14. Loan Payments
15. Unreimbursed business expenses

Total: Miscellaneous - $

(o)   **Other**
1.
2.
3.
4.

Total: Other

TOTAL MONTHLY EXPENSES: $

TOTAL ANNUAL EXPENSES: $

III.   GROSS INCOME (Monthly Amounts):

(a)   Salary or Wages:
1. Salary   (+)

(b)   Monthly Deductions:
Employer 1:
1. Federal Tax   (-)
2. New York State Tax   (-)
3. Local Tax   (-)
4. Social Security   (-)
5. Medicare   (-)
6. Other Payroll Deduction (Specify)savings   (-)
7. Life insurance   (-)

(c)   Social Security Number:
(d)   Number and Names of Dependents:
(e)   Bonus, Commissions, Fringe Benefits (use of auto,
memberships, etc.)   (+)
(f)   Partnerships, Royalties, Sale of Assets:
(income and installment payments)   (+)
(g)   Dividends and Interest:
1. Taxable   (+)
2. Nontaxable   (+)
(h)   Real Estate (income only)   (+)
(i)   Trust, profit sharing, and annuity   (+)
(principal distribution and income)
(j)   Pension (income only)   (+)
(k)   Awards, Prizes, Grants:
1. Taxable   (+)
2. Nontaxable   (+)
(l)   Income from bequests, legacies and gifts: (+)
(m)   Income from all other sources: (+)
(Including alimony, maintenance, or child support
from prior marriage)
(n)   Tax preference items:
1. Long term capital gain deduction: (-)
2. Depreciation amortization or depletion: (-)
3. Stock options—Excess fair market
value over amount paid: (-)
(o)   Other Household Member's Income:
(p)   Social Security: (+)
(q)   Disability Benefits: (+)
(r)   Public Assistance: (+)
(s)   Other: (+)

TOTAL MONTHLY INCOME: $

TOTAL ANNUAL INCOME: $

IV. ASSETS (If any asset is held jointly with spouse or another, so state, and set forth your respective shares. Attach additional sheets if needed.)

A. Cash Accounts

<u>Cash</u>

1.1   a.   Location: _____
         b.   Source of funds: _____
         c.   Other information: _____
         d.   Amount: _____

<u>Checking</u>

2.1   a.   Financial Institution: _____
         b.   Account number: _____
         c.   Title holder: _____
         d.   Date opened: _____
         e.   Source of funds: _____
         f.   Other information: _____
         g.   Balance: _____

2.2   a.   Financial Institution: _____
         b.   Account number: _____
         c.   Title holder: _____
         d.   Date opened: _____
         e.   Source of funds: _____
         f.   Other information: _____
         g.   Balance: _____

2.3   a.   Financial Institution: _____
         b.   Account number: _____
         c.   Title holder: _____
         d.   Date opened: _____
         e.   Source of funds: _____
         f.   Other information: _____
         g.   Balance: _____

<u>Savings</u>
(Individual, joint, Totten trusts, CDs, treasury notes)

3.1   a.   Financial Institution: _____
         b.   Account number: _____
         c.   Title holder: _____
         d.   Date opened: _____
         e.   Source of funds: _____
         f.   Other information: _____
         g.   Balance: _____

3.2   a. Financial Institution: _____
        b. Account number: _____
        c. Title holder: _____
        d. Date opened: _____
        e. Source of funds: _____
        f. Other information: _____
        g. Balance: _____

3.3   a. Financial Institution: _____
        b. Account number: _____
        c. Title holder: _____
        d. Date opened: _____
        e. Source of funds: _____
        f. Other information: _____
        g. Balance: _____

Security deposits (earnest money, etc.)

4.1   a. Location: _____
        b. Title owner: _____
        c. Type of Deposit: _____
        d. Source of funds: _____
        f. Other information: _____
        g. Amount: _____

Other

5.1   a. Location: _____
        b. Title owner: _____
        c. Type of Deposit: _____
        d. Source of funds: _____
        e. Date of deposit: _____
        f. Other information: _____
        g. Amount: _____

B.   Securities

Bonds, notes, mortgages

1.1   a. Description of Security: _____
        b. Title holder: _____
        c. Location: _____
        d. Date of acquisition: _____
        e. Original price or value: _____
        f. Source of funds to acquire: _____
        g. Other information: _____
        h. Current value: _____

Stocks, options, etc.

2.1   a Description of Security: _____
        b. Title owner: _____
        c. Location: _____
        d. Date of acquisition: _____
        e. Original price or value: _____
        f. Source of funds to acquire: _____
        g. Other information: _____
        h. Current value: _____

2.2   a. Description of Security: _____
        b. Title owner: _____
        c. Location: _____
        d. Date of acquisition: _____
        e. Original price or value: _____
        f. Source of funds to acquire: _____
        g. Other information: _____
        h. Current value: _____

2.3   a. Description of Security: _____
        b. Title owner: _____
        c. Location: _____
        d. Date of acquisition: _____
        e. Original price or value: _____
        f. Source of funds to acquire: _____
        g. Other information: _____
        h. Current value: _____

2.4   a. Description of Security: _____
        b. Title owner: _____
        c. Location: _____
        d. Date of acquisition: _____
        e. Original price or value: _____
        f. Source of funds to acquire: _____
        g. Other information: _____
        h. Current value: _____

Broker Margin Accounts

3.1   a. Name and address of Broker: _____
                                          _____
        b. Title holder: _____
        c. Date account opened: _____
        d. Original value of account: _____
        e. Source of funds: _____
        f. Other information: _____
        g. Current value: _____

C. **Loans & Accts Receivable**

1.1 a. Debtor's name and address _____

   _____

  b. Original amount of loan or debt: _____

  c. Source of funds from which
   loan made or origin of debt: _____

  d. Date payment(s) due: _____

  e. Other information: _____

  f. Current amount due:

1.2 a. Debtor's name and address: _____

   _____

  b. Original amount of loan or debt: _____

  c. Source of funds from which
   loan made or origin of debt: _____

  d. Date payment(s) due: _____

  e. Other information: _____

  f. Current amount due: _____

D. **Business Interests**

1.1 a. Business name and address: _____

   _____

  b. Type of business (corporate,
   partnership, sole
   proprietorship, or other): _____

  c. Your capital contribution: _____

  d. Your percentage of interest: _____

  e. Date of acquisition: _____

  f. Original price or value: _____

  g. Source of funds to acquire: _____

  h. Method of valuation: _____

  i. Other relevant information: _____

  j. Current net worth of business: _____

1.2 a. Business name and address: _____

   _____

  b. Type of business (corporate,
   partnership, sole
   proprietorship, or other): _____

  c. Your capital contribution: _____

  d. Your percentage of interest: _____

  e. Date of acquisition: _____

  f. Original price or value: _____

  g. Source of funds to acquire: _____

  h. Method of valuation: _____

  i. Other relevant information: _____

  j. Current net worth of business: _____

E. Life Insurance Cash Value

1.1 a. Insurer's name and address: _____
      _____
   b. Name of insured: _____
   c. Policy Number: _____
   d. Face amount of policy: _____
   e. Policy owner: _____
   f. Date of acquisition: _____
   g. Source of funds to acquire: _____
   h. Other information: _____
   i. Current cash surrender value: _____

1.2 a. Insurer's name and address: _____
      _____
   b. Name of insured: _____
   c. Policy Number: _____
   d. Face amount of policy: _____
   e. Policy owner: _____
   f. Date of acquisition: _____
   g. Source of funds to acquire: _____
   h. Other information: _____
   i. Current cash surrender value: _____

F. Vehicles (automobile, boat, plane, truck, camper, etc.)

1.1 a. Description: _____
   b. Title owner: _____
   c. Date of acquisition: _____
   d. Original price: _____
   e. Source of funds to acquire: _____
   f. Amount current lien unpaid: _____
   g. Other information: _____
   h. Current fair market value: _____

1.2 a. Description: _____
   b. Title owner: _____
   c. Date of acquisition: _____
   d. Original price: _____
   e. Source of funds to acquire: _____
   f. Amount current lien unpaid: _____
   g. Other information: _____
   h. Current fair market value: _____

1.3 a. Description: _____
   b. Title owner: _____
   c. Date of acquisition: _____
   d. Original price: _____
   e. Source of funds to acquire: _____
   f. Amount current lien unpaid: _____
   g. Other information: _____
   h. Current fair market value: _____

G. Real Estate

(including real property, leaseholds, life estates, etc.
at market value—do not deduct any mortgage)

1.1 a. Description: _____
   b. Title owner: _____
   c. Date of acquisition: _____
   d. Original price: _____
   e. Source of funds to acquire: _____
   f. Amount current lien unpaid: _____
   g. Other information: _____
   h. Estimated Current market value: _____

1.2 a. Description: _____
   b. Title owner: _____
   c. Date of acquisition: _____
   d. Original price: _____
   e. Source of funds to acquire: _____
   f. Amount current lien unpaid: _____
   g. Other information: _____
   h. Estimated Current market value: _____

1.3 a. Description: _____
   b. Title owner: _____
   c. Date of acquisition: _____
   d. Original price: _____
   e. Source of funds to acquire: _____
   f. Amount current lien unpaid: _____
   g. Other information: _____
   h. Estimated Current market value: _____

1.4 a. Description: _____
   b. Title owner: _____
   c. Date of acquisition: _____
   d. Original price: _____
   e. Source of funds to acquire: _____
   f. Amount current lien unpaid: _____
   g. Other information: _____
   h. Estimated Current market value: _____

H. Pensions & Trusts
(pension, profit sharing, legacies, deferred compensation, etc.)

1.1 a. Description of trust: _____
b. Location of assets: _____
c. Title owner: _____
d. Date of acquisition: _____
e. Original investment: _____
f. Source of funds: _____
g. Amount of unpaid liens: _____
h. Other information: _____
i. Current value: _____

1.2 a. Description of trust: _____
b. Location of assets: _____
c. Title owner: _____
d. Date of acquisition: _____
e. Original investment: _____
f. Source of funds: _____
g. Amount of unpaid liens: _____
h. Other information: _____
i. Current value: _____

I. Contingent Interests
(stock options, interests subject to
life estates, prospective inheritances, etc.)
1.1 a. Description: _____
b. Location: _____
c. Date of vesting: _____
d. Title owner: _____
e. Date of acquisition: _____
f. Original price or value: _____
g. Source of funds to acquire: _____
h. Method of valuation: _____
i. Other information: _____
j. Current value: _____

J. Household Furnishings
1.1 a. Description: _____
b. Location: _____
c. Title owner: _____
d. Original price: _____
e. Source of funds to acquire: _____
f. Amount of lien unpaid: _____
g. Other information: _____
h. Current value: _____

K. **Jewelry/Art/Antiques**
(only if valued at more than $500.00)

1.1   a. Description: _____
                b. Title owner: _____
                c. Location: _____
                d. Original price or value: _____
                e. Source of funds to acquire: _____
                f. Amount of lien unpaid: _____
                g. Other information: _____
                h. Current value: _____

1.2   a. Description: _____
                b. Title owner: _____
                c. Location: _____
                d. Original price: _____
                e. Source of funds to acquire: _____
                f. Amount of lien unpaid: _____
                g. Other information: _____
                h. Current value: _____

1.3   a. Description: _____
                b. Title owner: _____
                c. Location: _____
                d. Original price: _____
                e. Source of funds to acquire: _____
                f. Amount of lien unpaid: _____
                g. Other information: _____
                h. Current value: _____

1.4   a. Description: _____
                b. Title owner: _____
                c. Location: _____
                d. Original price: _____
                e. Source of funds to acquire: _____
                f. Amount of lien unpaid: _____
                g. Other information: _____
                h. Current value: _____

L. Other Assets
(tax shelter investments, collections, judgments, causes of action, patents, trademarks, copyrights, and any other asset not hereinabove itemized)

1.1   a. Description: _____
    b. Title owner: _____
    c. Location: _____
    d. Original price of value: _____
    e. Source of funds to acquire: _____
    f. Amount of lien unpaid: _____
    g. Other information: _____
    h. Current value: _____

1.2   a. Description: _____
    b. Title owner: _____
    c. Location: _____
    d. Original price of value: _____
    e. Source of funds to acquire: _____
    f. Amount of lien unpaid: _____
    g. Other information: _____
    h. Current value: _____

V. LIABILITIES

A. Accounts Payable

1.1   a. Name and address of Creditor: _____
_____
    b. Debtor: _____
    c. Amount of original Debt: _____
    d. Date of incurring Debt: _____
    e. Purpose: _____
    f. Monthly/other periodic pmt: _____
    g. Other information: _____
    h. Amount of current Debt: _____

1.2   a. Name and address of Creditor: _____
_____
    b. Debtor: _____
    c. Amount of original Debt: _____
    d. Date of incurring Debt: _____
    e. Purpose: _____
    f. Monthly/other periodic pmt: _____
    g. Other information: _____
    h. Amount of current Debt: _____

1.3   a. Name and address of Creditor: _____
       b. Debtor: _____
       c. Amount of original Debt: _____
       d. Date of incurring Debt: _____
       e. Purpose: _____
       f. Monthly/other periodic pmt: _____
       g. Other information: _____
       h. Amount of current Debt: _____

1.4   a. Name and address of Creditor: _____
       b. Debtor: _____
       c. Amount of original Debt: _____
       d. Date of incurring Debt: _____
       e. Purpose: _____
       f. Monthly/other periodic pmt: _____
       g. Other information: _____
       h. Amount of current Debt: _____

1.5   a. Name and address of Creditor: _____
       b. Debtor: _____
       c. Amount of original Debt: _____
       d. Date of incurring Debt: _____
       e. Purpose: _____
       f. Monthly/other periodic pmt: _____
       g. Other information: _____
       h. Amount of current Debt: _____

1.6   a. Name and address of Creditor: _____
       b. Debtor: _____
       c. Amount of original Debt: _____
       d. Date of incurring Debt: _____
       e. Purpose: _____
       f. Monthly/other periodic pmt: _____
       g. Other information: _____
       h. Amount of current Debt: _____

1.7   a. Name and address of Creditor: _____
                               _____
       b. Debtor: _____
       c. Amount of original Debt: _____
       d. Date of incurring Debt: _____
       e. Purpose: _____
       f. Monthly/other periodic pmt: _____
       g. Other information: _____
       h. Amount of current Debt: _____

1.8   a. Name and address of Creditor: _____

                                                         _____

        b. Debtor: _____

        c. Amount of original Debt: _____

        d. Date of incurring Debt: _____

        e. Purpose: _____

        f. Monthly/other periodic pmt: _____

        g. Other information: _____

        h. Amount of current Debt: _____

B.   **Notes Payable**

1.1   a. Name and address
        of note holder: _____

                                        _____

        b. Debtor: _____

        c. Amount of original Debt: _____

        d. Date of incurring Debt: _____

        e. Purpose: _____

        f. Monthly/other periodic pmt: _____

        g. Other information: _____

        h. Amount of current Debt: _____

1.2   a. Name and address
        of note holder: _____

        b. Debtor: _____

        c. Amount of original Debt: _____

        d. Date of incurring Debt: _____

        e. Purpose: _____

        f. Monthly/other periodic pmt: _____

        g. Other information: _____

        h. Amount of current Debt: _____

C.   **Installment Acct. Payable** (security agreements, chattel mortgages)

1.1   a. Name and address of creditor: _____

                                                         _____

        b. Debtor: _____

        c. Amount of original Debt: _____

        d. Date of incurring Debt: _____

        e. Purpose: _____

        f. Monthly/other periodic pmt: _____

        g. Other information: _____

        h. Amount of current Debt: _____

1.2   a. Name and address of creditor: _____

_____

b. Debtor: _____

c. Amount of original Debt: _____

d. Date of incurring Debt: _____

e. Purpose: _____

f. Monthly/other periodic pmt: _____

g. Other information: _____

h. Amount of current Debt: _____

D.   **Brokers Margin Accounts**

1.1   a. Name and address of broker: _____

_____

b. Debtor: _____

c. Amount of original Debt: _____

d. Date of incurring Debt: _____

e. Purpose: _____

f. Monthly/other periodic pmt: _____

g. Other information: _____

h. Amount of current Debt: _____

E.   **Mortgages on Real Estate**

1.1   a. Name and address of mortgagee: _____

_____

b. Address of property mortgaged: _____

_____

c. Mortgagor: _____

d. Original Debt: _____

e. Date of incurring Debt: _____

f. Monthly/other periodic pmt: _____

g. Maturity Date: _____

h. Other information: _____

i. Amount of current Debt: _____

1.2   a. Name and address of mortgagee: _____

_____

b. Address of property mortgaged: _____

_____

c. Mortgagor: _____

d. Original Debt: _____

e. Date of incurring Debt: _____

f. Monthly/other periodic pmt: _____

g. Maturity Date: _____

h. Other information: _____

i. Amount of current Debt: _____

1.3   a. Name and address of mortgagee: _____

_____

b. Address of property mortgaged: _____

_____

c. Mortgagor: _____
d. Original Debt: _____
e. Date of incurring Debt: _____
f. Monthly/other periodic pmt: _____
g. Maturity Date: _____
h. Other information: _____
i. Amount of current Debt: _____

F. Taxes Payable

1.1   a. Description of tax: _____
b. Amount of tax: _____
c. Date Due: _____
d. Other information: _____

G. Loans on Life Insurance

1.1   a. Name and address of insurer: _____

_____

b. Amount of Loan: _____
c. Date incurred: _____
d. Purpose: _____
e. Borrower: _____
f. Monthly/other periodic pmt: _____
g. Other information: _____
h. Amount of current Debt: _____

H. Other Liabilities

1.1   a. Description: _____
b. Name and Address of Creditor: _____

_____

c. Debtor: _____
d. Amount of original Debt: _____
e. Date incurred: _____
f. Purpose: _____
g. Monthly/other periodic pmt: _____
h. Other information: _____
i. Amount of current Debt: _____

1.2   a. Description: _____
      b. Name and Address of Creditor: _____
      _____
      _____
      c. Debtor: _____
      d. Amount of original Debt: _____
      e. Date incurred: _____
      f. Purpose: _____
      g. Monthly/other periodic pmt: _____
      h. Other information: _____
      i. Amount of current Debt: _____

NET WORTH

TOTAL ASSETS: _____

TOTAL LIABILITIES: (minus)   _____

NET WORTH: _____

VI.   ASSETS TRANSFERRED:

List all assets transferred in any manner during the preceding three years, or length of the marriage, whichever is shorter (transfers in the routine course of business which resulted in an exchange of assets of substantially equivalent value need not be specifically disclosed where such assets are identified in the statement of net worth).

DESCRIPTION OF PROPERTY TRANSFERRED	TO WHOM TRANSFERRED & RELATIONSHIP	DATE OF TRANSFER	VALUE
_____	_____	_____	_____
_____	_____	_____	_____
_____	_____	_____	_____
_____	_____	_____	_____
_____	_____	_____	_____
_____	_____	_____	_____
_____	_____	_____	_____
_____	_____	_____	_____
_____	_____	_____	_____
_____	_____	_____	_____

VII.   SUPPORT REQUIREMENTS

[ ]   At this time, deponent is not paying or receiving support.

[ ]   Deponent is at present (paying/receiving) _____ (per week/month) _____, and prior to separation (paid/received) _____ per (week/month) _____ to cover expenses for household necessities, utilities, mortgage.

These payments are being made [ ] (voluntarily) [ ] (pursuant to court order or judgment, and there are) [ ] (no) arrears outstanding [ ] (in the sum of $_____ to date).

[ ]   Deponent requests support of each child in accordance with CSSA and half of all school expenses.

[ ]   Deponent requests for self $_____ per (week/month) _____.

[ ]   The day of the (week/month) _____ on which payments should be made is _____.

VIII. COUNSEL FEE REQUIREMENTS

[ ]   Deponent requests no counsel fees or disbursements a this time.

[ ]   Deponent requests for counsel fees and disbursements the sum of $_____.

[ ]   Deponent has paid counsel the sum _____ and has agreed with counsel concerning fees as follows: _____

_____

[ ]   There is a retainer agreement or written agreement relating to payment of legal fees. (A copy of any such agreement must be annexed).

IX. ACCOUNT AND APPRAISAL FEE REQUIREMENTS

[ ]   Deponent requests no expert fees at this time.

[ ]   Deponent requests for accountant's fees and disbursements the sum of $_____ based on a(n) [ ] (hourly) [ ] (flat rate) fee.

[ ]   Deponent requests for appraisal fees and disbursements the sum of $_____ based on a(n) [ ] (hourly) [ ] (flat rate) fee.

[ ]   Deponent requires the services of an accountant for the following reasons:

_____

_____

[ ]   Deponent requires the services of an appraiser for the following reasons:

_____

_____

X. OTHER DATA

Other Data Regarding the Financial Circumstances of the Parties that Should be Brought to the Attention of the Court:

_____

_____

_____

The foregoing statements [ ] and a rider of __ page(s) annexed hereto and made part hereof, have been carefully read by the undersigned who states that they are true and correct.

_____
Plaintiff

Sworn to before me on

_____, _____.

_____
Notary Public

CLIENT CERTIFICATION

I, _____, HEREBY CERTIFY, under penalty of perjury, that I have carefully read and reviewed the annexed document and that all information contained in that document is true and accurate in all respects to the best of my knowledge and understanding.

I, FURTHER CERTIFY, under penalty of perjury, that neither my attorney, nor anyone acting on my attorney's behalf, was the source of any of the information contained in the annexed document; that I provided all of the information contained in the annexed document to my attorney; and that I understand that my attorney, in executing the Attorney Certification required by 22 NYCRR Section 202.16 (e), is relying entirely upon the information provided by me and upon my certification that all such information is true and accurate.

I, FURTHER CERTIFY, that the annexed document includes all information which I provided to my attorney which is relevant to such document and that my attorney has not deleted, omitted or excluded any such information.

Dated: _____

_____
Plaintiff

REQUEST FOR JUDICIAL INTERVENTION

SUPREME COURT, _____ COUNTY

INDEX #: _____   DATE PURCHASED _____

_____

PLAINTIFF(S):   IAS ENTRY DATE

_____

                                           JUDGE ASSIGNED

DEFENDANTS(S):

_____

_____   R J I DATE

Date issue joined: _____   Bill of particulars served (Y/N): _____

NATURE OF JUDICIAL INTERVENTION   (check <u>ONE</u> box only <u>and</u> enter information)

[ ]   Request for preliminary conference

[ ]   Note of issue and/or certificate of readiness

[ ]   Notice of motion (return date _____) Relief sought _____

[ ]   Order to show cause (clerk enter return date _____)

                Relief sought _____

[ ]   Other ex parte application (specify_____)

[ ]   Notice of petition (return date _____) Relief sought _____

[ ]   Notice of medical or dental malpractice action (specify _____)

[ ]   Statement of net worth

[ ]   Writ of habeas corpus

[ ]   Other (specify _____)

NATURE OF ACTION OR PROCEEDING   (check <u>ONE</u> box only)

MATRIMONIAL   TORTS
[ ]   Contested   — CM   Malpractice
[ ]   Uncontested   — UM   [ ]   Medical/Pediatric   — MM
                                                  [ ]   Dental   — DM
COMMERCIAL   [ ]   *Other Professional — OPM
[ ]   Contract   — CONT   _____
[ ]   Corporate   — CORP   [ ]   Motor Vehicle   — MV
[ ]   Insurance (where insurer is a   [ ]   *Products Liability — PL
        party, except arbitration) — INS
[ ]   UCC (including sales, negotiable   _____
            instruments) — UCC   [ ]   Environmental   — EN
[ ]   *Other Commercial — OC   [ ]   Asbestos   — ASB
        _____   [ ]   Breast Implant   — BI
                                               [ ]   *Other Negligence   — OTN

REAL PROPERTY   _____
[ ]   Tax Certiorari   — TAX   [ ]   *Other Tort (including
[ ]   Foreclosure   — FOR   intentional)   — OT
[ ]   Condemnation — COND
[ ]   Landlord/Tenant — LT   _____
[ ]   *Other Real Property — ORP   SPECIAL PROCEEDINGS
        _____   [ ]   Art. 75 (Arbitration) — ART 75
                                               [ ]   Art. 77 (Trusts) — ART 77
OTHER MATTERS   [ ]   Article 78   — ART 78
[ ]   *_____ — OTH   [ ]   Election Law   — ELEC
                                               [ ]   Guardianship   —
                                                     (MHL Art 81)   — GUARD 81
                                               [ ]   *Other Mental Hygiene — MHYG

        *If asterisk used, please specify further   _____
                                               [ ]   *Other Special Proceedings —OSP

                                                     _____

Check "YES" or "NO" for each of the following questions.

Is this action/proceeding against a

YES   NO   YES   NO

[ ]   [ ]   Municipality: [ ]   [ ]   Public Authority:

(specify _____)   (specify _____)

YES   NO

[ ]   [ ]   Does this action/proceeding seek equitable relief?
[ ]   [ ]   Does this action/proceeding seek recovery for personal injury?
[ ]   [ ]   Does this action/proceeding seek recovery for property damage?

ATTORNEY(S) FOR PLAINTIFF(S):   (NAME(S), ADDRESS(ES), PHONE NO.)

ATTORNEY(S) FOR DEFENDANT (S):   (NAME(S), ADDRESS(ES), PHONE NO.)

Parties appearing pro se (without attorney) should enter information in space provided above for attorneys.

INSURANCE CARRIERS:

RELATED CASES: (IF NONE, write "NONE" below)

Title   Index #   Court   Nature of Relationship

I AFFIRM UNDER PENALTY OF PERJURY THAT, TO MY KNOWLEDGE, OTHER THAN AS NOTED ABOVE, THERE ARE AND HAVE BEEN NO RELATED ACTIONS OR PROCEEDINGS, NOR HAS A REQUEST FOR JUDICIAL INTERVENTION PREVIOUSLY BEEN FILED IN THIS ACTION OR PROCEEDING.

Dated:

_____
                                        (SIGNATURE)

_____
                                        (PRINT OR TYPE NAME)

_____
                                        ATTORNEY FOR

Attach rider sheets if necessary to provide required information

NOTE OF ISSUE (Type or Print)

Calendar No. (if any)...

Index No . . . .

. . . . .Court . . . . .County, N.Y.

Name of assigned judge . . . .

NOTICE OF TRIAL

❑ Trial by jury demanded

❑ of all issues

❑ of issues specified below
    or attached hereto

❑ Trial without jury

Filed by attorney for . . . .
. . . .

Date summons served . . . .

Date service completed . . . .

Date issues joined . . . .

NATURE OF ACTION OR SPECIAL PROCEEDING

Tort:

❑   Motor Vehicle Negligence

❑   Medical Malpractice

❑   Other Tort

❑ Contract

❑ Contested Matrimonial

❑ Uncontested Matrimonial

❑ Tax Certiorari

❑ Condemnation

❑ Other (not itemized above)

   (specify) . . . .

❑ Indicate if this action is brought as a class action. If a medical malpractice action, indicate if panel procedures prescribed by court rules pursuant to section 14B-a of the Judiciary Law have been completed

Amount demanded $. . . . .
Other relief. . . . .
Insurance Carrier(s), if known: . . . .
. . . .

Special preference claimed under. . . . .
on the ground that. . . . .
. . . .

Attorney(s) for Plaintiff(s), Office, P.O. Address, Telephone:

Attorney(s) for Defendant(s), Office, P.O. Address, Telephone

AFFIDAVIT OF SERVICE

State of New York, County of   ss:

being duly sworn, deposes and says that deponent is not a party to the action, is over 18 years of age and resides at

That on the   day of   ,
deponent served the within note of issues and statement of readiness on

attorney(s) for
herein at his/her/their office(s) at

during his/her/their absence from said office
strike out either (a) or (b)
(a) by then and there leaving a true copy of the same with

his/her/their clerk, partner, partner having charge of said office
or
(b) and said office being closed, by depositing the same, enclosed in a sealed wrapper directed to said attorney(s), in the office letter drop or box.

Sworn to before me this
day of   ,

_____ _____

State of New York, County of   ss:

being duly sworn, deposes and says that deponent is not a party to the action, is over 18 years of age and resides at

That on the   day of   ,
deponent served the within note of issue and statement of readiness on

attorney(s) for
the address designated by said attorney(s) for that purpose by depositing same enclosed in a postpaid properly addressed wrapper, in a post office official depository under the exclusive care and custody of the United States post office department within New York State.

Sworn to before me, this
day of   ,

ADMISSION OF SERVICE

Due service of a note of issues and statement of readiness of which the within is a copy admitted

this . . . .

day of . . . ., ...

. . . .

(Items 1-7 must be checked)

	Completed	Waived	Required
1. All pleadings served			
2. Bill of particulars served			
3. Physical examination completed			
4. Medical reports exchanged			
5. Appraisal reports exchanged			
6. Compliance with section 202.16 of the Rules of the Chief Administrator (22 NYCRR 202 16) in matrimonial actions			
7. Discovery proceedings now known to be necessary completed			

	YES	NO
8. There are no outstanding requests for discovery		
9. There has been a reasonable opportunity to complete the foregoing proceedings		
10. There has been compliance with any order issued pursuant to section 202.12 of the Rules of the Cruel Administrator (22 NYCRR 202.12)		
11. If a medical malpractice action, there has been compliance with any order issued pursuant to section 202.56 of the Rules of the Chief Administrator (22 NYCRR 202.56)		
12. The case is ready for trial		

Dated . . . .

(Signature) . . . .

Attorney(s) for: . . . .

Office and P.O. Address . . . .

. . . .

. . . .

Phone No.: . . . .

STIPULATION OF READINESS

Stipulated that the above enumerated proceedings have been completed waived.

Date . . . .

. . . .
Attorney(s) for Plaintiff(s)

. . . .
Attorney(s) for Defendant(s)

SUPREME COURT OF THE STATE OF NEW YORK
COUNTY OF_____
---X

                                    Plaintiff,   Index No.:

-vs-   **NOTICE OF MOTION
                                                        FOR SUBPOENA DUCES
                                                        TECUM**

                                    Defendant.
---X

Please take notice that the undersigned Plaintiff will move this court at a term to be held on
_____, _____, at _____a.m/p.m. upon the attached affidavit for signature
by the Court of the attached Subpoenas Duces Tecum and granting such other and further relief as this
Court may deem just and proper.

Please take further notice that pursuant to CPLR 2214(b) all answering affidavits must be served
upon the undersigned not later than seven days (twelve if by mail) before the return date of this motion
as hereinabove set forth.

DATED: _____

                                            _____

                                            _____

                                            _____

To:_____

SUPREME COURT OF THE STATE OF NEW YORK
COUNTY OF_____
---X

                              Plaintiff,   Index No.:

                                                  AFFIDAVIT IN SUPPORT
-vs-   **OF MOTION**

                              Defendant.
---X

_____, being duly sworn, deposes and says:

1.   I am the Plaintiff in the above entitled action for a divorce, am personally and fully familiar with all of the facts and circumstances hereof, and make this affidavit in support of my application for signature by the Court of Subpoenas Duces Tecum for the following persons or businesses to provide me with the following records or information: _____

_____

_____

_____.

2.   It is necessary that I be provided with this information so that I may fully and competently prosecute this action for divorce.

Dated: _____

                                        _____

Sworn to before me on

_____, _____

_____
Notary Public

SUPREME COURT OF THE STATE OF NEW YORK
COUNTY OF_____

---X

                                    Plaintiff,

-vs-

                                    Defendant.

---X

Index No.:

SUBPOENA DUCES TECUM

IN THE NAME OF THE PEOPLE OF THE STATE OF NEW YORK:

TO:

WE COMMAND YOU, that all business and excuses being laid aside to appear and attend before_____ of this court, to be held at _____, at _____ a.m./p.m., and at any recessed or adjourned dates, to give testimony in this action on the part of the plaintiff and that you bring with you, and produce at the time and place aforesaid, all of those items set forth on the rider annexed hereto, now in your custody and control and all other deeds, evidences and writings, which you have in your possession or power, concerning the annexed items.

Please take notice that compliance with this Subpoena Duces Tecum may be made by production of the item or items required to be produced certified as complete and accurate by the person in charge of said records and no personal appearance to certify such item or items shall be required unless the Court shall order otherwise.

For failure to comply, you will be deemed guilty of a contempt of Court and liable to pay all losses or damages sustained thereby by the party aggrieved, and forfeit FIFTY DOLLARS in addition thereto.

DATED: _____

BY ORDER OF:

_____

J.S.C.

SUPREME COURT OF THE STATE OF NEW YORK
COUNTY OF_____
--X

                              Plaintiff,   Index No.:

                                                  NOTICE OF MOTION
-vs-   **FOR SUBPOENA FOR**
                                                  APPEARANCE

                              Defendant.
--X

Please take notice that the undersigned Plaintiff will move this court at a term to be held on _____ , _____, at _____a.m/p.m. upon the attached affidavit for signature by the Court of the attached Subpoenas for Appearance and granting such other and further relief as this Court may deem just and proper.

Please take further notice that pursuant to CPLR 2214(b) all answering affidavits must be served upon the undersigned not later than seven days (twelve if by mail) before the return date of this motion as hereinabove set forth.

DATED: _____

                              _____

                              _____

                              _____

To:_____

SUPREME COURT OF THE STATE OF NEW YORK
COUNTY OF_____
--X

                                          Index No.:
                              Plaintiff,
                                          AFFIDAVIT IN SUPPORT
-vs-   **OF MOTION**

                              Defendant.
--X

_____, being duly sworn, deposes and says:

1.   I am the Plaintiff in the above entitled action for a divorce, am personally and fully familiar with all of the facts and circumstances hereof and make this affidavit in support of my application for signature by the Court of Subpoenas for Appearance for the following persons to present testimony regarding:

_____
_____
_____
_____.

2.   It is necessary that I be provided with this information so that I may fully and competently prosecute this action for divorce.

Dated: _____

                                          _____

Sworn to before me on

_____, _____

_____
Notary Public

SUPREME COURT OF THE STATE OF NEW YORK
COUNTY OF_____

---X

                                        Plaintiff,   Index No.:

                                                                  **SUBPOENA FOR
                                                                  APPEARANCE**

-vs-

                                        Defendant.
--------------------- --X

        IN THE NAME OF THE PEOPLE OF THE STATE OF NEW YORK:

        TO:

        WE COMMAND YOU, that all business and excuses being laid aside to appear and attend

before _____ _____ of this court, to be held on

_____, _____, at _____ a.m./p.m., and at any recessed or adjourned

dates, to give testimony in this action on the part of the plaintiff.

        For failure to comply, you will be deemed guilty of a contempt of Court and liable to pay all

losses or damages sustained thereby by the party aggrieved, and forfeit FIFTY DOLLARS in addition

thereto.

        DATED: _____

                                        BY ORDER OF:

                                        _____
                                                    J.S.C.

SUPREME COURT OF THE STATE OF NEW YORK
COUNTY OF_____
--X

                                                    Index No.:

                                    Plaintiff,
                                                    NOTICE OF APPEAL

-vs-

                                    Defendant.
--X

      PLEASE TAKE NOTICE that _____ hereby appeals to the
Supreme Court, Appellate Division, _____Department, from a Judgment of the
Supreme Court of the County of _____, (Hon. J._____) entered in
the _____County Clerk's office on _____, from each and
every part thereof and from each and every intermediate order therein entered.

      Dated: _____

                                        _____

                                        _____

                                        _____

    To:

SUPREME COURT OF THE STATE OF NEW YORK
COUNTY OF_____
--X

                                    Plaintiff,   Index No.:

-vs-   **NOTICE OF
APPEARANCE:
MATRIMONIAL ACTION**

                                  Defendant.
--X

Please take notice, that the defendant hereby appears in the above entitled action and is represented by the undersigned/appears pro se. Defendant demands that a copy of the complaint and all papers in this action be served upon the undersigned at the address listed below.

Dated:_____

_____ (Name)

_____ (Address)

_____ (Address)

                                              _____

                                              _____

                                              _____

To:

SUPREME COURT OF THE STATE OF NEW YORK
COUNTY OF_____
--X

                         Plaintiff,   Index No.:

-vs-   **VERIFIED ANSWER**

                       Defendant.
--X

Defendant, answering the complaint, alleges the following:

1. Defendant denies the allegations in paragraphs ___ of the complaint.

2. Defendant denies knowledge or information sufficient to form a belief with respect to the allegations contained in paragraphs ___ of the complaint.

Affirmative Defenses:

_____

Counterclaims:

_____
_____
_____

Dated: _____

_____
_____
_____

To:

SUPREME COURT OF THE STATE OF NEW YORK
COUNTY OF_____
--X

Plaintiff,

-vs-

**Affidavit Pursuant
to Domestic Relations
Law Section 75-j**
INDEX No.:

Defendant.
--X

_____ _____, being duly sworn deposes and states:

1. That I am the Plaintiff in the above-entitled action, and as such, am fully familiar with the facts and circumstances of this matter.

2. That there are _____ children of the marriage, to wit:

    <u>Name</u>   <u>Date of Birth</u>

3. That the present address of the children is _____ _____,
    _____, New York _____ _____.

4. That the residences of the children within the last _____ years are _____
    _____
    _____

5. That during the past _____ years, the children have lived with both parents.

6. That I have not participated as a party, witness, or in any other capacity in any other litigation concerning the custody of the same children in this or any other state.

7. That there are no presently pending, nor have there been any custody proceedings concerning the children in this State, or any State, Territory, or Country.

8. That there is no person who is not a party to the proceedings, who has physical custody of the children or claims to have custody or visitation rights with respect to the children.

9. That I have submitted this Affidavit in support of my application for a Default Judgment in the above-captioned matter.

Sworn to before me on
_____ _____, _____.

_____   _____
Notary Public   Plaintiff

SUPREME COURT OF THE STATE OF NEW YORK
COUNTY OF_____
--X

Plaintiff,   Index No.:

-vs-   **NOTICE OF MOTION**
                              FOR ALTERNATE
                              SERVICE

Defendant.
--X

Please take notice that the undersigned Plaintiff will move this court at a term to be held on
_____, _____, at _____a.m/p.m. upon the attached affidavits for an order

❑   allowing Plaintiff to have Defendant served with the Summons in this matter pursuant to
     CPLR §308(2), by serving a person of suitable age and discretion at Defendant's residence
     or place of business

❑   allowing Plaintiff to have Defendant served with the Summons in this matter pursuant to
     CPLR §308(4), by affixing a copy of the Summons to the door of Defendant's residence
     or place of business

❑   allowing Plaintiff to have Defendant served with the Summons in this matter pursuant to
     CPLR §316, by publication in _____ once in three
     successive weeks

_____

_____

_____

To: _____

SUPREME COURT OF THE STATE OF NEW YORK

COUNTY OF__ _____

--X

Plaintiff,

Index No.:

-vs-

AFFIDAVIT IN SUPPORT OF MOTION

Defendant.

--X

_____, being duly sworn, deposes and says:

1. I have attempted to personally serve the Defendant on _____ occasions as follows:

_____

_____.

2. I have been unable to serve the Defendant because _____ _

_____.

3. I believe that further attempts to personally serve the Defendant will be unsuccessful.

Dated: _____

_____

Sworn to before me on

_____, _____

_____

Notary Public

SUPREME COURT OF THE STATE OF NEW YORK
COUNTY OF_____

--X

Plaintiff,

Index No.:

-vs-

ORDER DIRECTING

SERVICE

Defendant.

--X

Upon reading the affidavit of _____ sworn to on _____, and

of _____ sworn to on _____, and the Summons with

Notice / Summons and Verified Complaint in this action for divorce, and

❑ it appearing that the present whereabouts of the Defendant cannot be ascertained;

❑ it appearing that _____ attempts have been made to serve the Defendant personally;

it is hereby

❑ ORDERED, that the summons herein be served upon the Defendant by publication in accordance
with the requirements of CPLR §316 by setting forth a copy of the summons with notice bearing
the legend "Action for Divorce" and the relief sought herein and that said publication shall be made
in the English language in one newspaper, namely _____,
published at _____, New York, once each week on the same day for
three consecutive weeks, which newspaper is most likely to give notice to the Defendant; first publication of the summons shall be made within twenty days after the granting of this order; the
requirement of mailing a copy of the summons to the Defendant is dispensed with, it appearing that
there is no place that can be ascertained with due diligence where Defendant would receive mail and
that service as herein provided will be sufficient.

❑ ORDERED, that the summons herein be served upon the Defendant by service upon a person of
suitable age and discretion at the Defendant's residence or place of business and mailing a copy to
said person, pursuant to CPLR §308(2).

❑ ORDERED, that the summons herein be served by affixing a copy of it to Defendant's residence or
place of business and mailing a copy to the Defendant, pursuant to CPLR §308(4).

Dated: _____   _____
J.S.C.

SUPREME COURT OF THE STATE OF NEW YORK
COUNTY OF_____

--X

Plaintiff,

Index No.:

-vs-

**ORDER TO SHOW
CAUSE**

Defendant.

--X

Upon the affidavit of _____sworn to

on _____ and upon all of the papers and proceedings herein,

Let the Defendant show cause before this court on _____. at

___ ____ am/pm to be held in the county of _____, in

_____ _____ or as soon thereafter as the

parties can be heard why an order should not be made

Granting _____

_____

_____

And such other and further relief as this Court may deem appropriate and it is further

ORDERED that pending hearing of this motion and further order of this court, the defendant, his agents, employees, attorneys and representatives be restrained and enjoined form concealing, dissipating, utilizing, transferring or in any way disposing of or encumbering the assets held by the Defendant as marital property and any income, accretions, additions, accumulations and emoluments thereof including without limitations the following assets: _____

_____

_____

Sufficient reason therefore appearing, let personal service of this order and a copy of the papers upon which it is granted, together with the summons and complaint herein upon the Defendant personally or upon the attorney for the Defendant pursuant to CPLR 2103 (b) on or before _____, be deemed sufficient and that answering affidavits if any be served at least two days before the return date of this motion.

ENTER

_____
J.S.C.

COUNTY CLERK, _____ COUNTY

CREDIT CARD COLLECTION
AUTHORIZATION FORM
[Electronic Filing]

_____
Name

hereby authorizes the County Clerk of _____ County to charge the following credit card number(s) for payment of filing fees and other court-related expenses. (N.B. The Monroe County Clerk only accepts Master Card and Visa Cards.)

PLEASE PRINT:

Master Card No.: _____   Exp. Date: _____

Visa Card No.: _____   Exp. Date: _____

Discover Card No.: _____   Exp. Date: _____

American Express No.: _____   Exp. Date: _____

Diner's Club No.: _____   Exp. Date: _____

Name as it appears on card: _____

Cardholder's mailing address: _____

City: _____   State: _____   Zip Code: _____

Business Phone No.: _____   Fax No.: _____

*In the event the charge against this account is denied, you will be notified immediately to make payment in cash, money order or certified check.

This form will be kept on file in the County Clerk's office and shall remain in effect until specifically revoked in writing. It will be maintained in a separate file from the court papers and will not be available to the public. It is the responsibility of the individual/firm/company named herein to notify the County Clerk's office of the new expiration date when a credit card has been renewed, or if a card has been canceled or revoked.

Signature: _____   Date: _____

For official use only

Identification No.: _____   Date Received: _____

SUPREME COURT, _____ COUNTY, STATE OF NEW YORK

FACSIMILE TRANSMISSION COVER SHEET

TO: _____

FROM: _____
      Name of Filing Party or Attorney

_____

Address of Filing Party or Attorney

_____

Telephone No. of Filing Party or Attorney

_____

Facsimile No. of Filing Party or Attorney

DATE OF TRANSMISSION: _____

NUMBER OF PAGES TRANSMITTED (including cover sheet): _____

CASE NAME: _____

INDEX NUMBER: _____

NATURE OF PAPER (*e.g.*, answer, affidavit, etc.): _____

COMMENTS: _____
_____
_____

PLEASE NOTE

Papers may be transmitted at any time of the day or night and will be deemed filed upon receipt of the facsimile transmission; provided, however, that when payment of a fee is required, the papers will not be deemed filed unless accompanied by a completed credit card authorization sheet. Papers that require the payment of a fee must be filed with the County Clerk, not the Supreme Court.

Submissions in excess of 50 pages will not be accepted.

Fax Filing Form #1(a): Cover Sheet for Fax Transmission - Supreme Court

SUPREME COURT _____ COUNTY, STATE OF NEW YORK

Confirmation of Receipt of Facsimile Transmission

Date: ___/___/___

To: _____

Address: _____

Fax number: _____

Case caption: _____ _____

	Index #: _____ _____
-vs-	Assigned justice: _____
	_____
	(if applicable)

_____

Date filed: ___/___/___

Number of pages received: _____

Additional notice to sender [applicable if checked]:

____   Index # and/or caption incorrect. Please send corrected information.

____   Pages missing or illegible. Please resend pages ____ through ____.

____   Document/exhibit pages are not numbered. Please number and resubmit.

____   Please contact _____ at ____ - ____ - ____

        Re: _____

SUPREME COURT OF THE STATE OF NEW YORK
COUNTY OF_____
---X

                              Plaintiff,   Index No.:

-vs-   **AFFIDAVIT IN SUPPORT
OF MOTION FOR
TEMPORARY RELIEF**

                            Defendant.
---X

_____, being duly sworn, deposes and says:

1. I am the plaintiff in the above entitled action for divorce, am personally and fully familiar with all of the facts and circumstances hereof and make this affidavit in support of my application for _____ _____

2. Because this application is based primarily upon the financial circumstances of the parties and the needs of the family, I shall not set forth any facts relating to the merits of this action except as they may pertain specifically to the relief herein sought.

3. The parties were married on _____, _____. I am _____ years old and my spouse is _____ years old. We have _____ children of the marriage, named _____. We separated on _____, _____, and the children currently reside with _____.

4. I am requesting temporary custody of the children because of the following, and visitation as follows: _____ _____.

5. I am in urgent need of child support because: _____ _____.

6. My spouse has the following income and assets: _____ _____ _____.

7. I have the following income and assets: _____
_____
_____.

8. I am requesting spousal support because: _____
_____.

9. I am requesting exclusive use of _____ vehicle because:
_____
_____.

10. I am requesting exclusive occupancy of the marital residence because: _____
_____.

11. I am requesting payment of the household bills because: _____
_____.

12. I am requesting _____
because: _____
_____.

No other application for the relief herein has been made to the Court, Family Court, or any other judge.

Dated: _____   _____

Sworn to before me on

_____, _____

_____
Notary Public

Index

C

capital gains, 44

cars, 45, 57, 71, 72, 90, 119, 125

case law, 10, 11, 36

cash, 44, 55

Certificate of Dissolution, 103, 106

Certification, 65, 80, 85, 86, 89

changing the locks, 130

changing your name, 131

child abuse, 18, 30, 122

child care, 50, 51, 59, 81, 91, 101

child support, 2, 10, 11, 43, 44, 45, 46, 47, 48, 49, 50, 51, 52, 55, 57, 62, 68, 69, 70, 71, 73, 75, 76, 81, 83, 85, 86, 88, 89, 90, 91, 92, 96, 97, 99, 100, 101, 102, 104, 105, 106, 107, 115, 116, 129, 136

standard reserve amount, 49

Child Support Standards Act (CSSA), 43, 48, 49, 50, 51, 68, 85, 104, 105

Child Support Summary Form (UCS-111), 104

Child Support Worksheet, 90, 99, 105

child's age, 41

children, 1, 4, 8, 11, 13, 27, 33, 34, 35, 37, 38, 40, 41, 43, 46, 47, 49, 51, 54, 57, 58, 63, 64, 68, 69, 70, 71, 73, 84, 85, 87, 91, 92, 95, 97, 99, 101, 104, 105, 116, 121, 130, 133, 134, 135

adopted, 43, 84

emancipated, 43

citation, 10, 11

clergy, 3, 84, 132

closing statement, 68

Code of Professional Responsibility, 23

cohabitation, 7, 15

collaborative law, 6, 13, 14

combined parental income, 46

Commissioner of Social Services on Behalf of L.W. v. R.D.W., 49

common law marriage, 129

community property, 55, 129

compromise, 4, 8, 13, 29, 62, 110, 115

Confirmation of Receipt of Facsimile Transmission, 66

consent, 6, 7, 15, 89, 104

Consolidated Laws of New York, 10

consultation, 19, 28

contested divorce, 13, 42, 82, 105, 109, 110, 111, 113, 115, 117, 119

conversion divorce, 75, 78, 85, 129

costs, 6, 19, 20, 21, 30, 50, 82, 88, 124

counseling, 2, 3, 132, 134

court clerks, 61, 66, 68, 77, 120

Court of Appeals, 9, 10

court order, 11, 16, 22, 35, 88, 99, 121, 126, 130

court personnel, 18, 61, 63, 94

court reporter, 38, 62, 117

court system, 9, 23, 61, 62, 63, 65, 67, 69

courtroom, 14, 17, 18, 62, 63, 64, 96

credit card, 58, 66

Credit Card Collection Authorization Form, 66

cross-examination, 67, 119

cruel and inhuman treatment, 9, 14, 15, 129

custody, 2, 10, 18, 33, 34, 35, 36, 37, 38, 39, 40, 41, 42, 49, 50, 57, 68, 69, 70, 71, 73, 75, 81, 82, 89, 91, 92, 95, 97, 99, 101, 115, 116, 117, 119, 122, 129, 134, 136

joint, 34, 35, 37, 49, 70, 87

sole, 34, 82

D

debts, 1, 8, 11, 18, 27, 45, 56, 57, 58, 59, 70, 76, 81, 82, 85, 86, 87, 113, 115

deeds, 58

default, 93

defendant, 5, 15, 16, 63, 65, 67, 80, 83, 86, 89, 90, 93, 98, 99, 100, 101, 102, 104, 105, 109, 116, 117, 119

degree, 17, 56

Department of Motor Vehicles, 125, 132

depositions, 115

Dintruff v. McGreevy, 37

disability, 44, 97

discovery, 112, 113, 115, 119

divorce decree, 1, 8

doctor, 3

Domestic Relations Law (DRL), 6, 7, 8, 10, 12, 43, 57, 97, 103, 106, 126, 130

domestic violence, 10, 17, 26, 27, 30, 36, 121, 122

drugs, 34, 35, 37, 39

due diligence, 125, 126

duress, 7, 130

legal aid, 21, 49, 121, 123
legal custody, 34
legal divorce, 1, 2, 8, 129
legal separation, 2, 8, 9, 26, 76
life insurance, 45, 50, 55, 58
Linda R. v. Richard E., 37
living separate and apart, 78
loans, 57, 58, 87

M

maintenance, 2, 45, 53, 54, 55, 57, 68, 69, 71, 72,
    73, 75, 76, 81, 82, 85, 86, 88, 92, 96, 99, 101,
    116
marital assets, 54, 59, 69
    freezing, 69
marital property, 54, 55, 56, 57, 82, 115, 119,
    129
matrimonial and family law, 20
matrimonial referee, 18, 62, 67, 96
mediation, 6, 13, 14, 20, 25, 26, 27, 28, 29, 30,
    33, 38, 41, 110
    shuttle, 26
Medicare, 45
Memorandum, 26, 29, 77, 78
memorandum of agreement, 29
Memorandum of Understanding, 26
mental health professional, 2, 3
mental illness, 7
military, 18, 44, 98
moral fitness, 36
mortgage, 57, 58

N

nail and mail, 126
negotiation, 40
neutral, 14, 25, 28, 30
New York Reports, 10, 11
New York State Bar Association, 19
New York State Case Registry Filing Form, 97,
    103
New York Supplement, 10
no-fault divorce, 14, 129
non-custodial parent, 41, 49, 50, 51, 92
nonlegal separation, 2
nonmonetary contributions, 49
notary, 65, 72, 78, 83, 85, 86, 89, 90, 91, 95, 97,
    113, 119, 124, 127, 129

Note of Issue, 93, 106, 112, 113
Notice of Appeal, 120
Notice of Appearance, 84, 104, 117, 118
Notice of Appearance: Matrimonial Action, 117,
    118
Notice of Entry, 104, 107
Notice of Motion for Alternate Service with
    Affidavit in Support of Motion, 127
Notice of Motion for Permission to Proceed as a
    Poor Person with Affidavit in Support of
    Application to Proceed as a Poor Person, 123
Notice of Motion for Subpoena Duces Tecum,
    113
Notice of Motion for Subpoena for Appearance,
    114, 120
Notice of Publication, 126
Notice of Settlement, 97, 103

O

opening statement, 67
Order Directing Service, 127, 128
Order of Protection, 121, 122
Order to Show Cause, 70, 72, 111

P

paralegal, 20
parental kidnapping, 122
parenting time, 34, 41, 75
parents, 13, 34, 35, 37, 40, 42, 43, 44, 46, 49, 50,
    51, 69, 115, 133, 134, 136
parties, 5, 7, 13, 14, 15, 16, 25, 26, 27, 28, 30,
    31, 53, 54, 57, 62, 69, 70, 77, 109, 116
payment plan, 21
pensions, 44, 58, 102
personal and confidential, 125, 126
personal service, 98, 125
photos, 39
physical divorce, 2
physical incapacity, 7
plaintiff, 5, 15, 16, 63, 65, 67, 80, 81, 82, 85, 86,
    89, 90, 93, 94, 95, 100, 101, 103, 105, 109,
    116, 117, 119, 124
Poor Person Order, 123, 124
Postcard, 93
preliminary order, 40
prenuptial agreements, 130
privacy, 28